A THEOLOGY OF THE SPIRIT IN THE FORMER PROPHETS
A PENTECOSTAL PERSPECTIVE

A Theology of the Spirit in the Former Prophets

A Pentecostal Perspective

Rick Wadholm Jr.

CPT

CPT Press
Cleveland, Tennessee

A Theology of the Spirit in the Former Prophets
A Pentecostal Perspective

Published by CPT Press
900 Walker ST NE
Cleveland, TN 37311
USA
email: cptpress@pentecostaltheology.org
website: www.cptpress.com

Library of Congress Control Number: 2018939262

ISBN-13: 978-1-935931-72-0

Dedication
This, as my first monograph, is dedicated to my wife, Jenn, and
children: Bryce, Abbigail, Cambria, and Zoë.

CONTENTS

Chapter 9
Conclusion: Contributions and Suggestions for

ACKNOWLEDGEMENTS

This book essentially follows my PhD thesis, which has demanded much time and energy (as one might expect) over the last five plus years. First, and foremost, I would like to acknowledge the great many sacrifices of my wife (Jenn) and children (Bryce, Abbigail, Cambria, and Zoë) who have borne the brunt of my absence with grace and encouragement while I spent many days and nights working on this project. I love them dearly for the commitments and sacrifices they have made with grace. Over our twenty years of marriage, Jenn has been a consummate inspiration to me personally to seek the deeper life of the Spirit and be a faithful man of God in everything (not least in the work of writing). She has lovingly encouraged me to persist in the calling that she shared with me from the beginning for the pursuit of a PhD (resulting in this book) and demonstrates to me the life of a woman of the Spirit after the likes of Deborah the wise judge and prophetess.

When I began this journey, I was the pastor of a small rural Assembly of God congregation in Karlstad, Minnesota. I am grateful for the many ways in which this project was birthed and commenced while sharing life with this Pentecostal fellowship and my numerous pastor friends of the upper Midwest. In the midst of this journey my family moved from the pastorate to an academic (and administrative) role at Trinity Bible College and Graduate School in Ellendale, North Dakota. I have been encouraged to pursue this project in fresh ways by this Pentecostal community. The administration (particularly President Dr Paul Alexander), faculty, staff, and students (thinking particularly of the two classes I taught on the Former Prophets) have been my sounding board and offered immeasurable support. At Trinity, I have had the distinct privilege of presenting multiple chapters and parts of chapters and receiving invaluable feedback particularly from professors Bob Wadholm and Justin Gibson with whose fellowship my life is enriched beyond measure.

My dear *Doktorvater*, John Christopher Thomas, has been an inspiration to me as a Pentecostal scholar with the heart of a pastor and the insight of a prophet. The times with Dr Thomas, Dr Lee Roy

Martin (always the insightful Pentecostal Old Testament scholar and preacher), and my fellow PhD students that met twice a year at the Centre for Pentecostal Theology in Cleveland, TN, are yet another reminder to me of the many joys of the fellowship of the Spirit. Our table fellowship (at the Centre and numerous Cleveland restaurants) was always stimulating and I would return from those times with fresh energy for this work as the work of the ministry. Among those students, I wish particularly to acknowledge the friendship and insights of Randall Ackland, Johnathan Alvarado, Daniel Isgrigg, Jared Runck, Steffen Schumacher, Lisa Ward, and Ben Wiles. While not a part of this cohort, I wish to thank Daniel Morrison for those regular brief chats mutually to encourage each other toward the finish line. I would also like to thank my two PhD examiners for their valuable insights to make this project better and for their gracious comments toward its publication: Drs. Jacqueline Grey and William Kay. Finally, I am grateful to John Christopher Thomas and Lee Roy Martin for their careful readings of this manuscript and for considering this project worthy to be published by CPT Press as a part of that growing constructive contribution to Pentecostal scholarship globally of which they continue to labor so faithfully.

This has proven a far more difficult and enjoyable journey then when I first set out to write it. Along the way I have taken several turns (Lord willing for the better) and discovered more of my voice in the academy and for the Church. While the many people named above are deserving of even more credit than I have here given them (and others who have not been specifically named), any remaining errors or faults are certainly my own to bear.

Rick Wadholm, Jr
https://www.rick.wadholm.com/

PREFACE

This book represents essentially the work of my PhD thesis for Bangor University, Wales (UK) with only minor modifications. As such, it represents the academic language and structure necessary toward a successful completion of a PhD. While it is written for an academic readership it is hoped that the ideas and manner of reading Scripture (proposed and followed) might prove to bear fruit in the Church. As an academic volume within the field of Biblical studies it follows a (thesis/dissertation) structure of history of interpretation, methodology (in this case primarily a literary and theological hermeneutic that entails a *Wirkungsgeschichte*), and exegesis of specific texts. As a theological contribution, it offers a chapter of overtures toward Pentecostal theological constructions in light of the foregoing reading/hearing of the text of Scripture following the methodology proposed.

This work bears the imprints of Pentecostal passion to see greater outpourings of the Spirit in these last days as a declaration of Jesus' soon coming with the kingdom of God. This flows from an understanding of these Old Testament texts as still relevant to contemporary experiences of the Spirit (though decidedly in the light of Jesus as God's self-revealing one to pour out his Spirit). For too long the church has regarded these Spirit texts as 'primitive' or belonging to another age. There are numerous ways in which listening alongside the early Pentecostals (in the *Wirkungsgeschichte*) recaptures stronger senses of continuity between the periods of the Testaments than often prevails. Such a read of continuity recognizes that the Spirit has always been present and working toward God's kingdom. It also attempts to hear how the abounding nature of the Spirit is centered in the person and work of Jesus.

I have intentionally written as a Pentecostal preacher and teacher with the aim of both hearing and presenting the text from and for that Pentecostal vantage point. This is not to suggest that there are no other ways and contexts for an appropriate reading of these texts, but only to attempt critical faithfulness to (and from) my own context. The voice of this volume is intended to add to the chorus of voices on the Spirit in the Former Prophets as the first of its specific kind. It is also intended to be heard alongside the growing number of book length volumes being produced through the work of the Centre for Pentecostal Theology – CPT Press and the Journal for Pentecostal Theology Supplement Series – which are expanding the critical and necessary conversations among, by, and for Pentecostalism and Pentecostal studies worldwide.

It is my prayer that this study will provoke further reflection as Pentecostals upon the Scriptures and the function of the Spirit to accomplish God's plans for ultimate redemption. This can only be done through a careful attentive en-Spirited praxis of God's Word lived in the midst of Christ's body.

ABBREVIATIONS

Early Pentecostal Periodicals

AF   *The Apostolic Faith*
BC   *Bridal Call*
CE   *The Christian Evangel*
CGE   *The Church of God Evangel*
LRE   *The Latter Rain Evangel*
PE   *The Pentecostal Evangel*
PHA   *The Pentecostal Holiness Advocate*
TBM   *The Bridegroom's Messenger*
TP   *The Pentecost*
WE   *The Weekly Evangel*
WW   *Word and Witness*

Other

AB   Anchor Bible Series
ABD   Freedman, D.N. (ed.), *Anchor Bible Dictionary* (6 vols; Garden City, Doubleday, 1992)
ACOT   Apollos Commentary on the Old Testament Series
AGH   *Assemblies of God Heritage*
ANE   Ancient Near East/ern
AT   Altes Testament ('Old Testament')
BASOR   *Bulletin of the American Schools of Oriental Research*
BCE   Before the Common Era
BHS   *Biblia Hebraica Stuttgartensia* (Stuttgart: Deutsche Bibelgesellschaft, 1990)
BSac   *Bibliotheca Sacra*
CBC   Cambridge Bible Commentary
CBQ   *The Catholic Biblical Quarterly*
CEB   Common English Bible
CEV   Contemporary English Version

DOT:HB	Arnold, B.T. and H.G.M. Williamson (eds.), *Dictionary of the Old Testament: Historical Books* (Grand Rapids, MI: InterVarsity, 2005)
EBC	Expositor's Bible Commentary Series
ESV	English Standard Version
ETT	English Translations
EvQ	*Evangelical Quarterly*
EvT	*Evangelische Theologie*
ExpTim	*Expository Times*
HTR	*Harvard Theological Review*
ICC	International Critical Commentary Series
JBL	*Journal of Biblical Literature*
JBQ	*Jewish Biblical Quarterly*
JEPTA	*Journal of the European Pentecostal Theological Association*
JPT	*Journal of Pentecostal Theology*
JPTSup	JPTSup Series
JRT	*Journal of Religious Thought*
JSOT	*Journal for the Study of the Old Testament*
JSOTSup	Journal for the Study of the Old Testament Supplement Series
KTU	Keilschrift Texte aus Ugarit
LXX	Septuagint (sometimes distinguishing manuscripts between LXX^A [Codex Alexandrinus] and LXX^B [Codex Sinaiticus])
MT	Masoretic Text
NAB	New American Bible
NAC	New American Commentary Series
NAS	New American Standard Bible (1995)
NET	New English Translation
NIBC	New International Biblical Commentary
NICOT	New International Commentary on the Old Testament
NIDOTTE	VanGemeren, W.A. (gen. ed.), *New International Dictionary of Old Testament Theology and Exegesis* (5 vols; Grand Rapids, MI: Zondervan, 1997)
NIVAC	New International Version Application Commentary Series
NJB	New Jerusalem Bible
NLT	New Living Translation (second edition)
NRSV	New Revised Standard Version

OTL	Old Testament Library Series
RB	*Revue Biblique*
RQ	*Restoration Quarterly*
RSPT	*Revue des sciences philosophiques et théologiques*
RSR	*Revue de science religieuse*
RSV	Revised Standard Version
SBLDS	Society of Biblical Literature Dissertation Series
SBJT	*Southern Baptist Journal of Theology*
TDNT	Kittel, G., and G. Friedrich (eds.), *Theological Dictionary of the New Testament* (trans. G.W. Bromiley; 10 vols; Grand Rapids, MI: Eerdmans, 1964-1976)
TLOT	Jenni, E., and C., Westermann (eds.), *Theological Lexicon of the Old Testament* (trans. M.E. Biddle; 3 vols; Peabody, MA: Hendrickson, 1997)
TMSJ	*The Master's Seminary Journal*
TrinJ	*Trinity Journal*
TWAT	Botterweck, G.J., G.W. Anderson, and H.Ringgren (eds.), *Theologisches Wörterbuch zum Alten Testament* (3 vols; Stuttgart: W. Kohlhammer, 1973-1977)
TWNT	Kittel, G., and O. Bauernfeind (eds.), *Theologisches Wörterbuch zum Neuen Testament* (10 vols; Stuttgart: W. Kohlhammer, 1949-1979)
VT	*Vetus Testamentum*
VTSup	Vetus Testamentum Supplements
WBC	Word Biblical Commentary Series

INTRODUCTION

The Spirit Begins to Stir

My imagination has been captured by the stories of the Former Prophets – Joshua, Judges, 1-2 Samuel, and 1-2 Kings – since I was a child. My father (a Pentecostal minister) would read to us children through these texts for many of our nightly devotions. As a boy with a sometimes wayward heart, the stories of violence and perversity were enough to spark my love of these stories or at least my continuing inquisitiveness about how such stories made it into our 'Holy Bible'. The stories I encountered were not the sanitized versions of Sunday school with the felt-board visuals. The judges offered me haunting dilemmas in their work as deliverers countered by their seeming penchant for waywardness. These were characters that I wondered at in amazement that they could receive the Spirit like myself. I had imagined myself being anointed a king someday like Saul and David (with hopes of being more like the latter than the former). Their exploits and foibles again always seemed to catch me off-guard. Finally, the likes of the prophets and their sudden appearance in the text (seemingly out of nowhere) made me wonder about their abilities and their life outside the text. Were these figures really so close to God that they could hear him, see his workings, speak and act on his behalf even in the face of recalcitrant royals? Most of the prophets left just as quickly as they had arrived, but always leaving me with more questions than answers. Through this all, I wondered at how the God of Israel could pour out his Spirit upon such individuals and why? Could he really care so much for Israel that he would prove faithful to them though they were ever unfaithful in return? At the least it gave me hope for myself as the often wayward, though Spirit-baptized, boy who still wanted to enjoy the presence of the Lord. It also gave me great fear, because there was nothing in these texts to suggest these individuals were guaranteed in their own personal salvation even if they could work the tangible salvation of so many around them. It was this latter idea that convinced me of the need to stay in step with the Spirit. I had surmised (by the Spirit's leading) that a life of power without purity was no guarantee that the Spirit would remain with me indefinitely.

Then in 2009, as a rural church pastor of an Assemblies of God congregation, I read two articles which set the trajectory for this project. The first one was a very brief article by E.R. Lee in *Enrichment* addressing the Baptism in the Holy Spirit as an Old Testament promise.[1] The article offered a sidebar recommending reading several specific books on the Holy Spirit. I took up the challenge and ordered two of them the next day and read them through multiple times over several months (Wilf Hildebrandt's *An Old Testament Theology of the Spirit of God* and Stanley Horton's *What the Bible Says about the Holy Spirit*).[2] These offered me a purview into the then (for me) unknown riches of a pneumatology in the Old Testament. Within days of reading the first article I happened upon a second article that drew upon my own passion for the texts of the Former Prophets. This piece covered every text referring to the Spirit in the so-called 'Historiographic Writings' that gives considerable attention to the Former Prophets.[3] The combination of the two articles inspired me to take seriously what a Pentecostal theology of the Spirit drawn from the Former Prophets might look like.

I found my research direction set for this study presented here (though I did not formally begin for another three years). This quest was that of a Pentecostal pastor and burgeoning scholar desirous to know the Spirit more intimately and to make the Spirit known to others within the Pentecostal community, and the wider church and world. All of this was taken up in order to bear greater witness to the

---

[1] E.R. Lee, 'Baptism in the Holy Spirit: Old Testament Promise', *Enrichment* 14.4 (2009), pp. 116-19. The sidebar is on page 119.

[2] W. Hildebrandt, *An Old Testament Theology of the Spirit of God* (Peabody, MA: Hendrickson, 1995); and S.M. Horton, *What the Bible Says about the Holy Spirit* (rev. edn; Springfield, MO: GPH, 2005).

[3] D.I. Block, 'Empowered by the Spirit of God: The Holy Spirit in the Historiographic Writings of the Old Testament', *SBJT* 1.1 (1997), pp. 42-61.

person and work of the God (Father, Son, and Spirit) who had been present from the first broodings of the Spirit over the great waters of the deep and never left himself without a witness in the world.

The Flow of the Spirit

The overall flow of this project follows a path now beginning to become well-trodden.[4] Chapter one opens with a history of interpretation. The primary contributors and their monographs that might frame a study of the Spirit in the Former Prophets are examined. While the survey is not comprehensive of every work which addresses the Spirit in the Former Prophets, those which provide key examples are examined. This literature survey reveals the lack of detailed treatment of the Former Prophets for developing any pneumatology, let alone constructing a Pentecostal theology. Notable are two broad movements within those offering a theology of the Spirit: an historical and a theological movement through the texts of the Former Prophets in search of the Spirit. Chapter two is concerned with the methodology for engaging the Spirit in the Former Prophets. It moves through a sort of narratological Pentecostal hermeneutic of the Former Prophets that is then laid out for engaging the Spirit in the Former Prophets. This chapter supposes my own church community to be able to offer constructive contributions for hearing the Spirit in the Former Prophets toward a Pentecostal theology of the Spirit in the Former Prophets. Chapter three provides a history of effects (or *Wirkungsgeschichte*) approach by hearing the Spirit texts of the Former Prophets alongside early North American Pentecostals (specifically the journals from 1906-1920) in order to offer a better orientation to how Pentecostal communities have interpreted these texts in their formative years.

Chapters four through seven then apply the hermeneutic of chapter two to the groupings of texts of the Spirit in the Former

---

[4] K.E. Alexander, *Pentecostal Healing: Models in Theology and Practice* (JPTSup 29; Blandford Forum: Deo, 2006); C.E.W. Green, *Toward a Pentecostal Theology of the Lord's Supper: Foretasting the Kingdom* (Cleveland, TN: CPT Press, 2012); H.O. Bryant, *Spirit Christology in the Christian Tradition: From the Patristic Period to the Rise of Pentecostalism in the Twentieth Century* (Cleveland, TN: CPT Press, 2014); and M.L. Archer, *'I Was in the Spirit on the Lord's Day': A Pentecostal Engagement with Worship in the Apocalypse* (Cleveland, TN: CPT Press, 2015).

Prophets. As such, the chapters that follow are larger literary units which include multiple references to the Spirit of Yahweh/God but are grouped together as narratological units for the sake of succinctness and framing. Chapter four addresses the judges who explicitly experience the liberating Spirit of Yahweh. Chapter five addresses Saul and David's musical and prophetic experiences of the Spirit of Yahweh/God both for good and ill. Chapter six addresses the ambiguities of the Spirit in the context of the prophet Micaiah. Chapter seven addresses the passing of the Spirit of true prophetic sonship from Elijah to Elisha. Chapter eight then attempts a constructive Pentecostal theology of the Spirit in light of the study of the Spirit in the Former Prophets laid out in the preceding exegetical chapters and the *Wirkungsgeschichte* of chapter three. Finally, the concluding chapter briefly summarizes the contributions of this study and entertains multiple potential directions for future study brought to light through what has preceded.

Bound by the Spirit

Any study is necessarily limited in scope. This one is bounded by two notable factors worth explaining briefly here at the beginning: (1) the texts of the Former Prophets are one boundary; and (2) the texts of the Former Prophets specific to the Spirit (רוח) of Yahweh/God is another boundary.

The first boundary provides a smaller number of texts than the entirety of the Old Testament. This means that 1-2 Chronicles, which offers another comparative reading of the story of Israel in the land, is not brought into the study despite multiple references to the Spirit therein. Several volumes have previously been written on the Spirit in the Old Testament and are discussed below though none of them follow anything comparable to the Pentecostal methodology, and *Wirkungsgeschichte*, proposed here, nor offer a constructive Pentecostal theology of the Spirit. The Former Prophets offers a narrative that flows sufficiently along as to permit a comparable reading strategy and engagement through the corpus.[5] Further, this limitation seems

---

[5] No contention is made by this study that the various books of the Former Prophets, or parts therein, are crafted by any single or multiple individuals. They are instead grouped following the nomenclature of the Hebrew canon without any claims concerning the priority, or not, of such a canon.

fitting as there appears to be a tendency to neglect the Former Prophets in pneumatological studies overall.

The second boundary is followed to eliminate the broad approaches taken by some in their proposed theologies of the S/spirit.
Thus, it allows for a more focused study of the Spirit in relation to
the *divine* Spirit of the God of Israel instead of discussions of such
ideas as the anthropological and meteorological uses of רוח also
found in the Former Prophets.

1

A History of Interpretation: Finding the Spirit in the Former Prophets with Help from Elijah

Introduction

The need for this project becomes readily apparent in any survey of the literature dealing with the Spirit in the Former Prophets (Former Prophets).[1] One notable example is that of Yves Congar who wrote a three-volume set on the theology of the Holy Spirit. The total number of pages given to discussing the Spirit in the Former Prophets is four.[2] In a volume by Sergius Bulgakov, out of nearly 400 pages only four are given to the Spirit in the Old Testament and there are

---

[1] In the work which follows, the use of capitalization is intentional with regard to the 'Spirit' including in citations of the works of each author. Where these authors have written in all lower case, this has been maintained. In the analysis offered there is a specific choice to offer the capitalized form. This does not inherently suggest that the referent is the confessed third person of the trinity but does suggest some form of proper noun usage.

[2] Y. Congar, *Je crois en l'Esprit Saint* (Paris: Les Editions du Cerf, 1979) English translation: *I Believe in the Holy Spirit* (trans. David Smith; 3 Volumes in One; New York: Crossroad, 2000), pp. 3-6. J. Moltmann, *The Spirit of Life: A Universal Affirmation* (trans. Margaret Kohl; Minneapolis, MN: Fortress, 1994), attributes his own analysis of the Spirit in the Former Prophets largely to Congar's own work, pp. 43-47, esp. p. 43 n. 13 where he specifically cites Congar's influence, along with the *THAT* article cited below in footnote 10. These four pages are not presented as a standalone appropriation of the Former Prophets but include other texts throughout.

absolutely no Biblical references at all to the Spirit in the Former Prophets. The only mention is a generalized comment, in passing, that the Spirit endowed judges, kings, and prophets (among others) as prelude to the 'New Testament Pentecost'.[3] Even Clark Pinnock's well received *Flame of Love: A Theology of the Holy Spirit* has no mention of any kind with regard to the Spirit in the Former Prophets.[4]

It would seem that Leon Wood's comments about the need for and lack of research on the Spirit in the Old Testament is fitting:

> The Holy Spirit not only had an important part in the creation of man, but He had a vital work in respect to man thus created. As noted, most discussions of that work are based on the New Testament. When references are made to the Holy Spirit in the Old Testament, the interest is usually limited to noting that His existence is recognized in certain passages. Little is said relative to the nature of His work as manifested in these passages.[5]

Though he originally penned these words in 1976 little has changed even in the wake of the continuing explosive growth of Pentecostal and Charismatic constituents worldwide. One might have expected such study to be offered with some concomitant relation to the growth of this pneumatic emphasis in the wider Church. However, the lack of actual scholarly interaction with the texts of the Old Testament, let alone the text of the Former Prophets, with regard to the development of a theology of the Spirit remains a lacuna on the theological landscape.[6] All of this despite the numerous more general

---

[3] S. Bulgakov, *The Comforter* (trans. Boris Jakim; Grand Rapids, MI: Eerdmans, 2004), p. 159.

[4] C.H. Pinnock, *Flame of Love: A Theology of the Holy Spirit* (Downers Grove, IL: IVP Academic, 1996).

[5] L. Wood, *The Holy Spirit in the Old Testament* (Grand Rapids, MI: Zondervan, 1978; republished Wipf & Stock, 1998), p. 39. See several explicit examples (notably even in their subtitles) of the use of the Old Testament with this regard in the following: J.K. Heckert, *The Teaching of Paul on the Holy Spirit: In Light of the Old Testament and the Literature of the Intertestamental Period* (ThD thesis; Concordia Seminary, 1971) and the most recent update of R. Stronstad, *The Charismatic Theology of St. Luke: Trajectories from the Old Testament to Luke-Acts* (Grand Rapids, MI: Baker Academic, 2012).

[6] As another poignant example there are no articles on the 'S/spirit' in B.T. Arnold and H.G.M. Williamson (eds.), *Dictionary of the Old Testament: Historical Books*

works on the Spirit which have shaped certain traditions since just before the turn of the twentieth century and which continue to be produced.[7] There have been a number of unpublished theses written on the topic of the Spirit in the Old Testament, with several focused primarily on the issue of the salvific and/or indwelling role of the Spirit in the Old Testament with many lacking any significant interaction with the text of the Former Prophets.[8] The following critical

---

(Downers Grove, IL: IVP, 2005). Not only are there no articles on this topic, but there is nothing on this topic listed in the entire index.

[7] G. Smeaton, *The Doctrine of the Holy Spirit* (Edinburgh: T&T Clark, 1882); A.B. Simpson, *The Holy Spirit or Power from on High? Part I: The Old Testament* (Harrisburg, PA: Christian Publications, 1896); H.G. McIlhany, *The Holy Spirit in the Old Testament. A Thesis* (Staunton, VA: Stoneburner & Prufer, 1900); G.C. Morgan, *The Spirit of God* (New York: Revel, 1900); W.C. Scofield, *The Holy Spirit in Both Testaments* (New York: Fleming H. Revell, 1903); P. Volz, *Der Geist Gottes* (Tübingen: J.C.B Mohr, 1910); W. Barclay, *The Promise of the Spirit* (Philadelphia, PA: Westminster, 1960); W.H. Griffith-Thomas, *The Holy Spirit of God* (Grand Rapids, MI: Eerdmans, 1964); C.C. Ryrie, *The Holy Spirit* (Chicago, IL: Moody Press, 1965); D. Moody, *Spirit of the Living God: What the Bible Says about the Spirit* (Nashville, TN: Broadman, 1968); A.W. Pink, *The Holy Spirit* (Grand Rapids, MI: Baker, 1970); E. Schweizer, *Heiliger Geist* (Stuttgart: Kreuz, 1978); A.I.C. Heron, *The Holy Spirit* (Philadelphia, PA: Westminster, 1983); J.F. Walvoord, *The Holy Spirit: A Comprehensive Study of the Person and Work of the Holy Spirit* (Grand Rapids, MI: Zondervan, 1991); S. Ferguson, *The Holy Spirit* (Leicester, England: Inter-Varsity, 1996); D.G. Bloesch, *The Holy Spirit: Works & Gifts* (Downers Grove, IL: IVP Academic, 2000); M. Dreytza, *Der Theologische Gebrauch von Ruah im Alten Testament: Eine Wort-und Satzsemantische Studie* (Basel; Giessen: Brunnen Verlag, 1990); V.-M. Kärkäinnen, *Pneumatology: The Holy Spirit in Ecumenical, International, and Contextual Perspective* (Grand Rapids, MI: Baker Academic, 2002); M. Green, *I Believe in the Holy Spirit* (rev. edn; Grand Rapids, MI: Eerdmans, 2004); C.J.H. Wright, *Knowing the Holy Spirit Through the Old Testament* (Downers Grove, IL: IVP Academic, 2006); J.M. Hamilton, Jr., *God's Indwelling Presence: The Holy Spirit in the Old & New Testaments* (Nashville, TN: B&H Publishing, 2006); G.A. Cole, *He Who Gives Life* (Wheaton, IL: Crossway Books, 2007); I. Satyavrata, *The Holy Spirit: Lord and Life-Giver* (Christian Doctrine in Global Perspective; Downers Grove, IL: IVP Academic, 2009); D.G. Firth and P.D. Wegner (eds.), *Presence, Power, and Promise: The Role of the Spirit of God in the Old Testament* (Downers Grove, IL: IVP Academic, 2011); A.C. Thiselton, *The Holy Spirit in Biblical Teaching, Through the Centuries, and Today* (Grand Rapids, MI: Eerdmans, 2013); T.J. Burke and K. Warrington (eds.), *A Biblical Theology of the Holy Spirit* (London: SPCK, 2014). Notably D. Firth has contributed chapters in *Presence, Power and Promise*, pp. 259-80, and *A Biblical Theology of the Holy Spirit* that deal with the Spirit in the Former Prophets, pp. 12-23.

[8] N.L. Poling, 'A Study of the Idea of the Holy Spirit in the Old Testament and Extra-Canonical Literature' (MA; Bethany Biblical Seminary, 1941); A. Benson, *The*

survey of the major works over the last nearly one and a quarter centuries suggests the need to remedy this lacuna. Therefore, this chapter will offer an overview of the history of interpretation (*Auslegungsgeschichte*) of the Spirit in the Former Prophets and will present a survey of the scholarly literature[9] with an orientation toward delineating distinctions of emphasis for organizing and describing the Spirit in the Former Prophets among these various readings. The approach is both historical and theological in order better to frame the current state of scholarship pertaining to the Spirit in the Former Prophets with an eye toward looking elsewhere for a constructive Pentecostal theology of the Spirit as found in the Former Prophets. The flow of this chapter will take the Elijah/Elisha narrative of 2

Spirit of God in the Didactic Books of the Old Testament (Washington: Catholic University of America Press, 1949); W.M. Stanley, 'An Investigation of the Divine Spirit in the Old Testament' (MA; Butler University, 1960); J.K. Heckert, 'The Teaching of Paul on the Holy Spirit'; K. Zuber, 'Indwelling of the Holy Spirit in the Old Testament' (MA; Grace Theological Seminary, 1981); J.M. King, 'An Exegetical Case for Spirit Indwelling in the Old Testament' (MA; Grace Theological Seminary, 1988); N.M. Pulaski, '*Rûah Haqqodesh*: The Holy Spirit in the Old Testament' (MA; CBN University, 1988); J.M. Ragsdale, '*Ruah YHWH, Ruah 'Elohim*: A Case for Literary and Theological Distinction in the Deuteronomistic History' (PhD; Marquette University, 2007). This last thesis would be a notable exception to discussion of the Former Prophets, although Ragsdale has chosen to frame his analysis along more historical critical avenues notably demonstrated by his choice of 'the Deuteronomistic History' for the title of his thesis. T.J. Sugimura, 'The Role of the Holy Spirit in Old Testament Salvation' (MA; The Master's Seminary, 2009).

[9] The following are a number of journal articles and dictionary entries which are not discussed within the broader work of this chapter: A.B. Davidson, 'The Spirit of God in the Old Testament', *ExpTim* 11 (1899/1900), pp. 21-24; C.A. Briggs, 'The Use of *rûah* in the OT', *JBL* 19 (1900), pp. 132-45; J. Hehn, 'Zum Problem des Geistes im Alten Orient und im AT', *ZAW* 43 (1925), pp. 210-25; P. van Imschoot, 'L' action de l'esprit de Jahvé dans l' AT', *RSPT* 23 (1934), pp. 553-87; 'L' esprit de Jahvé, source de vie dans l' AT', *RB* 44 (1935), pp. 481-501; C. Amerding, 'The Holy Spirit in the Old Testament', *BSac* 92 (1935), pp. 277-91, 433-41; J. Walvoord, 'The Work of the Holy Spirit in the Old Testament', *BSac* 97 (1940), pp. 289-317, 410-34; R. Albertz and C. Westermann, '*rûah* Geist", *TWAT* 2 (1976), pp. 726-53; English translation by M.E. Biddle, '*rûah* Spirit', *TLOT* 3 (1997), pp. 1202-20; F. Baumgartel, 'Geist im AT', *TWNT* 6 (1976), pp. 357-66; English translation by G.E. Bromiley, 'Spirit in the OT', *TDNT* 6 (1968), pp. 359-68; C. Westermann, 'Geist im AT', *EvT* 41 (1981), pp. 223-30; D.I. Block, 'Empowered by the Spirit: The Holy Spirit in the Historiographic Writings of the Old Testament', *SBJT* 1 (1997), pp. 42-61; M.V. van Pelt, W.C. Kaiser, Jr., and D.I. Block, 'רוח', *NIDOTTE* 3 (1997), pp. 1073-78.

Kgs 2.13-18 as a guiding backdrop for this quest for the Spirit. This framework is suggestive of the narratological tendencies of Pentecostal theologizing which is described in the following chapter.

Where is the Spirit of Elijah?

Elijah has selected Elisha (by word of Yahweh) to carry out his role in bringing judgment to Israel and the house of Ahab. Elisha follows him through the cities of the sons of the prophets down to the Jordan and east where he is taken into heaven in a whirlwind while some of the sons of the prophets wait on the western bank. With the taking of Elijah, Elisha tore his own clothing in two and took up the prophetic hairy cloak of Elijah, which had fallen to the ground upon the catching up of Elijah (v. 13).

With the cloak in hand he returned to the Jordan River in full sight of the sons of the prophets and hit the water with the cloak. At this, the waters of the Jordan divided as they had when Elijah had done likewise at the first crossing, with the sons of the prophets on-looking. The sons of the prophets had watched Elijah divide the waters with his hairy cloak and now watch Elisha do the same with the cloak of Elijah. That Elisha should receive and use the cloak of Elijah would serve as a testimony of his filling the role of Elijah to Israel as one endowed with the רוח of Elijah.

The sons of the prophets near Jericho who await Elijah and Elisha's return across the Jordan both confess that the Spirit that had been on Elijah is on Elisha and refuse to believe that Elijah has truly been taken away *permanently* and *replaced* by Elisha (2 Kgs 2.15-18).[10] They stood and watched the same miraculous crossing by Elisha, see him with Elijah's all-too-familiar cloak, and yet seem to fail to discern the presence of the רוח that had been on Elijah that is now on Elisha (despite their words indicating otherwise). In their refusal to accept Elisha as the proper heir to Elijah, the sons of the prophets propose to go on a search for Elijah (2 Kgs 2.16), whom they wrongly believe has been taken and set down somewhere else by the רוח of Yahweh.

---

[10] P.H. House, *1, 2 Kings* (NAC 8; Nashville, TN: B&H, 1995), however, believes that 'Elisha's repetition of the act [of using the cloak to separate the waters of the Jordan and cross over] ... confirm in their minds that Elisha is truly Elijah's successor', p. 258.

Though Elisha initially dismisses their proposal, he eventually relents. They return after three days without finding him. In line with Deut. 21.17 (concerning the passing of the double portion) one might surmise that this instruction in Deuteronomy is fulfilled by Yahweh as true because the one with the רוח of Elijah (and thus Elijah himself) is among them. They should have no need to look elsewhere. And though they initially recognize the Spirit of Elijah upon Elisha they just as quickly seem to reject it as conclusive as indicated by their oppositional request. Their search should have led them to conclude otherwise. It did not. Yet even in their seeming rejection of Elisha in the place of Elijah as 'father' they still defer to his authority for their errant quest.[11]

While their quest pertains specifically to the person of Elijah, it is fitting that they seek for the רוח associated with Elijah. They refuse to believe that the one standing before them (Elisha) now bears that same רוח. For three days they search, but all in vain. The רוח was always before them and even permitted their quest elsewhere. It is this point which seems functionally to provide a helpful analogy for the various quests for the Spirit in the Former Prophets.

Two 'Quests' for the Spirit

Over the last one and a quarter centuries, there have been several broad movements (if they may be labeled as such) or, as they will be broadly labeled here, 'quests' for the Spirit in the Former Prophets: an historical quest and a theological quest. These two quests are not to be regarded as any sort of intentional development of a quest as such (as one finds with the quests for the historical Jesus), but share certain guiding trajectories which seem to have dictated the direction for locating and describing the Spirit in the Former Prophets.

The historical quest has been taken up primarily with such matters as the history of religions with regard to ancient Israelite religion and the development of Israel's texts. This quest for the Spirit found particular impetus from the ground-breaking work of Hermann Gunkel in Germany and just over a decade later by the less widely received work of Irving Wood in the United States. Another resurgence of

---

[11] W.J. Bergen, *Elisha and the End of Prophetism* (JSOTSup 286; Sheffield Academic, 1999), pp. 60-61.

this quest began in the 1950s proceeding into the 1970s. This quest might best be defined by its attempt to locate the Spirit in the Former Prophets within a given reconstructed historical setting in the development of Israelite religion and/or texts.

The second major trend in the quest for the Spirit in the Former Prophets might be referred to broadly as the theological quest for the Spirit given its several streams which have primarily utilized biblical-theological categories and creedal/confessional categories when reading the text of the Former Prophets. This theological quest for the Spirit found primary impetus in the 1970s and has continued to the present and is more broadly represented by several Pentecostal/charismatic scholars. Perhaps a significant contribution to the development of this quest might have been due to the influence of the continuing embrace of Pentecostals by Evangelicalism at large and the charismatic outpourings of the early part of this quest. Many of the monographs written on this topic take as a discussion point some appraisal and/or reorientation with respect to the Pentecostal/charismatic movement at large and thus many of the works of this quest seem to be guided at least in part as a response or reaction to Pentecostal/charismatic claims.[12] This theological quest has taken several turns: one attempting to develop a Biblical theology of the Spirit and the other a more confessional/creedal theology of the Spirit. This quest is thus characterized primarily by application of literary-theological tools as well as dogmas and confessions to the text.

The Historical Quest for the Spirit in the Former Prophets

There are at least two broad subcategories of note in the historical approach to interpreting the Spirit in the Former Prophets which in

---

[12] For several examples, see Green, *I Believe*, p. 8, where he notes that he has specifically taken account of the 'remarkable happenings in Toronto and Pensacola' for the revision to his earlier work in order better to respond to discussions about the baptism in the Holy Spirit and the *charismata*; Bloesch, *The Holy Spirit*, pp. 179-221, who spends an entire chapter specifically addressing Pentecostal concerns while having just spent a chapter discussing eleven other movement's perspectives. While remaining within the Protestant Reformation tradition, Bloesch argues for a deeper appreciation of the Pentecostal contributions to the life and work of the Spirit, pp. 14-17; and Heron, *The Holy Spirit*, who refers to 'The Pentecostal Challenge' to contemporary and historical theologies of the Spirit, pp. 130-36.

this book is labeled (1) history of religions and (2) historical reconstruction. However, each of them takes as their starting point an attempt at historical reconstruction either of the periods of ancient Israel and/or of the texts of ancient Israel.

The first of these approaches shows a preference for locating the Spirit in the Former Prophets in terms of a *history of religions* (*Religionsgeschichtliche*) as this thought was developed particularly among those associated with the University of Göttingen in Germany in the latter 19th century. This approach surmises the development of the Jewish faith along an essentially evolutionary line moving from the more primitive to the more sophisticated. It is based upon the presupposition that Israel's theology expressed in the Biblical accounts was a development of the local beliefs and practices of the given context Israel found itself in at the time of composition. It locates much of the writing of the Former Prophets (and specifically the texts pertaining to the charismatic Spirit in the Former Prophets) to a period early in Israel's theological development and thus being overly simple or 'primitive'. Only in later reflection did Israel conceive of the Spirit in terms not of violence, force, energy, but of wisdom, insight, creativity, and skill. H. Gunkel and I. Wood are two figures who have proposed such an approach to the Spirit in the Former Prophets.

Another development in the historical quest for the Spirit in the Former Prophets involved a turn from overly emphasizing a history of religions approach to a greater emphasis upon the historical reconstruction of the texts of the Old Testament while not ignoring the earlier forms of the history of religions approach. This form of the historical quest is markedly apparent in the works of D. Lys, J.H. Scheepers, L. Neve, and R. Koch.

Hermann Gunkel (1888)[13]

H. Gunkel (1862-1932) was a German Biblical scholar raised in a family traditioned as Lutheran ministers. He initially began his studies at the University of Göttingen in New Testament (1888) where he

---

[13] H. Gunkel, *Die Wirkungen des heiligen Geistes nach der popularen Anshauungen der apostolischen Zeit und der Lehre des Apostels Paulus* (Gottingen: Vandenhoeck & Ruprecht, 1888); in English as *The Influence of the Holy Spirit: The Popular View of the Apostolic Age and the Teaching of the Apostle Paul* (trans. Roy A. Harrisville and Philip A. Quanbeck II; Minneapolis: Fortress Press, 1979, 2008). The English translation and pagination will be cited in the analysis that follows.

published his work on the Holy Spirit, but soon moved to Halle (1889-1894) where he switched to focus on the Old Testament as both a student and professor. He would later teach at Berlin (1894-1907) where he produced several volumes on Genesis. While teaching at several other German universities (Giessen and later Halle-Wittenburg), he completed a third edition of his famous commentary on Genesis (1910), wrote a commentary on the Prophets (1917), and Psalms (1926), among numerous other writings. In his extensive work as a scholar he is noted to have developed *Formgeschichte* (or form criticism) as a methodology and was among the most prominent figures representing the so-called *Religionsgeschichtliche Schule*.

Overall, Gunkel's ground-breaking work on the Spirit is committed to a history of religions approach to the text of Scripture wherein the Old Testament belonged to a less sophisticated and more mystic era that attributed what was not explainable through natural means to 'the Spirit'. While his project is focused upon the Apostolic age and particularly the Pauline contributions to understanding the Spirit, he still offers some significant comments regarding the work of the Spirit in the Old Testament and particularly the Former Prophets, albeit rather brief comments.

Gunkel distinguishes between pneumatic experience and a theology of the Spirit 'where complex religious-historical constructs may be involved'.[14] In this regard, he sets out to demonstrate the sense in which one might regard the pneumatic perspective of the Biblical era as interpreted from a pneumatic perspective particularly in Paul's writings. This work of Gunkel's broke from the traditional historical-critical readings of the S/spirit and acted to provide a new direction in pneumatological studies.[15]

According to Gunkel, 'Almost without exception, only those events that impinge on human existence are described as activities of the Spirit'.[16] His argument is essentially that Paul was a thorough-going pneumatic, not to be confused as inferring that the Spirit was simply some inward ethical conscience or propulsion. In fact, he

---

[14] Gunkel, *The Influence of the Holy Spirit*, p. 8.

[15] A contemporary example of which is most evident in the interweaving of the story of Gunkel with a proposed theological perspective of pneumatic life in J.R. Levison, *Filled with the Spirit* (Grand Rapids, MI: Eerdmans, 2009).

[16] Gunkel, *The Influence of the Holy Spirit*, p. 15.

argues that there must be a distinction maintained between theologizing about the Spirit for doctrinal formulations and pneumatic experiences as such.[17] The pneumatic experience of life is regarded as central (particularly to Pauline practice and congregations).

It was the pneumatic experiences of the Early Church which offered the evidence of God's Spirit. Such evidence (particularly *glossolalia*, according to Gunkel) functioned to testify to possession and indwelling by God's Spirit. Ethical behavior was the manifested proper use of such gifts of the Spirit. But Paul never made a move to a simply ethical/moral S/spirit as so many others of the Jewish writers of the Second Temple period (e.g. Wisdom of Solomon, Philo, etc.). Paul could not conceive of the Spirit as less than enabling powerful manifestations, but that the ethical belonged still to the supernatural working of God's Spirit and Gunkel affirms this throughout.

While he admits (even requires) that the Old Testament understanding of the Spirit of God was powerfully demonstrative, he likens such activities of the Spirit to insanity.[18] And his understanding of Paul does not seem to reach much further. Gunkel almost seems to regard Paul as someone who has sadly embraced the pneumatic, when he seems so reasonable elsewhere in discerning other matters of faith. Thus for Gunkel (and I.F. Wood) what is attributed to the Spirit is simply what has been unexplainable in an earlier time.

Irving F. Wood (1904)[19]

I.F. Wood (1861-1934) was an American Biblical scholar with degrees from Hamilton College (BA – 1885; DD – 1915), Yale (BD – 1892) and the University of Chicago (PhD – 1903). He taught for several years at Jaffna College in what is now known as Sri Lanka and later taught in both China and Japan. He was a professor at the University of Chicago but finished his career by teaching for many years at Smith College. Most of his published works were devoted to the instruction of Christians (adults and children) in reading the Bible with greater clarity and benefit.

---

[17] Gunkel, *The Influence of the Holy Spirit*, p. 8.
[18] Gunkel, *The Influence of the Holy Spirit*, p. 5.
[19] I.F. Wood, *The Spirit of God in Biblical Literature: A Study in the History of Religion* (New York: A.C. Armstrong, 1904).

Wood wrote his PhD dissertation for the University of Chicago on 'The Spirit of God in Biblical Literature'. As the subtitle to his volume states, Irving Francis Wood's book offers a specific 'study in the history of religion'. It therefore belongs to those works viewing the development and even maturation of 'religion' as a move toward a more psychologizing and socializing reading of ancient texts. The working of the Spirit is thus regarded as a primitive, even 'naïve' or 'crude' conception as found in the Old Testament books and most particularly as expounded in the Former Prophets.[20] Wood argues that whatever was regarded by ancient Israel as 'psychically' and 'physically' unexplainable was attributed to the 'Spirit'.[21]

Johannes Hendrik Scheepers (1960)[22]

J.H. Scheepers was born in Fouriesburg, South Africa and grew up to serve the Dutch Reformed Church. Scheepers attended the University of Pretoria and later defended his Doctor of Divinity at the Free University of Amsterdam in 1960 where his dissertation was written on the Spirit of God and the human Spirit in the Old Testament.

His doctoral project is formulated along grammatical and syntactical relations within the Old Testament where he investigates every one of the 389 variegated uses of רוח in the Old Testament. Scheepers is less concerned about historical reconstruction for the texts of the Old Testament and instead primarily gives emphasis to the categories of function as he discerns them.[23] His examination begins with those uses pointing more clearly to 'wind' where he locates a number of passages in the Former Prophets (2 Sam. 22.11, 16; 1 Kgs 10.5; 18.12, 45; 19.11; and 2 Kgs 3.17).[24] From here he turns to working through the texts he believes refer to the human spirit with specific mention of the idea of 'breath' in comparison or in sense (Josh. 2.11;

---

[20] Wood, *The Spirit of God*, pp. 9, 18.

[21] Wood, *The Spirit of God*, pp. 8, 9, 25.

[22] J.H. Scheepers, *Die Gees van God en die Gees van die mens in die Oud Testamentische Studien* (Kampen: J.H. Kok, 1960).

[23] Scheepers, *Die Gees van God*, p. 1; only those references which Scheepers indicates within the Former Prophets will be provided in parentheses in what follows, though he proposes numerous other passages as examples of his various categories.

[24] Scheepers, *Die Gees van God*, pp. 11-30.

Judg. 8.3; 15.19; 1 Sam. 16.23; 30.12; 1 Kgs 10.5; 17.17, 22).[25] He carries along his examination by discussion of רוח as 'extranatural spirit' (Judg. 19.23; 1 Sam. 16.14b-23; 1 Kgs 22.21-24; 2 Kgs 19.7), which he regards as in some manner distinguishable from the Spirit of Yahweh despite the same use of prepositions and verbs in relation to both.[26] This 'spirit' is understood by Scheepers to lack any evidence as having 'a personal being'.[27] The judges are ascribed the רוח to indicate their role in redemptive history as an ascription of only those deeds deemed of the 'most exceptional character' (Judg. 3.10; 6.34; 11.29; 13.25; 14.6, 19; 15.14).[28] The first two kings of Israel were endowed with the רוח in what is concluded to be a permanent endowment and moral alteration (1 Sam. 6.6; 10.5; 16.13, 14).

His final (and lengthiest) chapter discusses the spirit of Yahweh proper.[29] Scheepers regards 2 Kgs 2.9, 15 as sufficiently ambiguous that he includes them in the categories of extranatural (human) spirit and the Spirit of Yahweh.[30] He further contends that the 'spirit of the LORD' in 1 Kgs 18.12 and 2 Kgs 2.16 was intended only to convey an 'original' meaning of divine or powerful wind.[31] He also proposes that רוח in 1 Kgs 22.21 should not be regarded as the Spirit of Yahweh despite the definite article's presence.[32]

Daniel Lys (1962)[33]

D. Lys was a graduate of the Reformed Protestant Seminary in Montpellier, France, and later served as professor there. Lys had earlier written on the subject of נפש in the Old Testament as it pertained to anthropology which heavily informed his later work on רוח.[34] His

---

[25] Scheepers, *Die Gees van God*, pp. 34-92.

[26] The spirit as ''n buite-natuurlike gees', Scheepers, *Die Gees van God*, pp. 96-119.

[27] Scheepers, *Die Gees van God*, p. 311.

[28] Scheepers, *Die Gees van God*, p. 313.

[29] Scheepers, *Die Gees van God*, pp. 120-239.

[30] Scheepers, *Die Gees van God*, p. 310.

[31] Scheepers, *Die Gees van God*, pp. 130-31, wrongly cites the latter reference as 1 Kgs 2.16 on p. 312.

[32] Scheepers, *Die Gees van God*, p. 319.

[33] D. Lys, *Rûach: Le Souffle Dans l'Ancien Testament: Enquête Anthropologique à Travers l'Histoire Théologique d'Israël* (Etudes d'Histoire et de Philosophie Religieuses 56; Paris: Presses Universitaires de France, 1962).

[34] D. Lys, *Nèphèsh: Histoire de l'âme dans la révélation d'Israël au sein des religions proche-orientales* (Etudes d'Histoire et de Philosophie Religieuses 50; Paris: Presses

work on the רוח of the Old Testament offers three variant uses: wind, anthropological רוח, and divine רוח; which he divides along lines of historical and literary periods within the process of the development of the Hebrew Bible: the earliest Hebrew texts (which he labels certain portions of J and E), the early prophetic texts (latter portions of J and E as well as the early writing prophets), the Deuteronomic texts (the Former Prophets and several of the writing prophets), ancient Judaism (the rest of the writing prophets and the historical writings of the Chroniclers), concluding with chapters on the poetic literature and wisdom literature. His work is decidedly anthropological, even as it discusses the divine רוח which is regarded as offering an anthropocentric conception to describe the divine.

It is in his chapter on the Deuteronomic texts that he briefly discusses the רוח in the Former Prophets. Lys' contention is that the Deuteronomic writers were 'rewriting history'[35] and as such were utilizing anthropomorphisms to describe the 'breath' of Yahweh.[36] As such, Lys only discusses a few of the occurrences of רוח in the Former Prophets and even so does this only cursorily: Judg. 3.10; 11.29 (Othniel and then Jephthah and the 'Spirit of the LORD'); 1 Sam. 16.14, 16 (Saul and the 'Spirit of the LORD' being replaced by the 'troubling spirit'); and 1 Kings 22 (Micaiah's message of the 'lying spirit' sent from the heavenly court). His categories in this chapter are limited to the divine and the human and the several pages discussing the divine seem oriented only to discuss the issues of the human 'spirit' or 'heart'.[37]

Lloyd Neve (1972)[38]

L.R. Neve earned a ThD at Union Theological Seminary (in New York) and served as a Lutheran missionary in Japan forty years, writing several volumes on missionary work in Japan. His published work

---

Universitaires de France, 1959) and the work consulted on רוח, Lys, *Rûach*). Note pp. 1-7 of the latter work where Lys discusses the interconnection of these two projects.

[35] Lys, *Rûach*, p. 98, '*réécrivant l'histoire*', all translations are my own.

[36] Lys, *Rûach*, pp. 99-102.

[37] Lys, *Rûach*, pp. 99-102.

[38] L.R. Neve, *The Spirit of God in the Old Testament* (Centre for Pentecostal Theology Classics Series; Cleveland, TN: CPT Press, 2011). This is a reprint (with corrections) of the original version published by Seibunsha in Tokyo, Japan (1972).

on the Spirit in the Old Testament (which was developed from his doctoral dissertation at Union) was groundbreaking, per his own claim, in that it appeared to him to have been the first one written on that specific topic in English with only two other works preceding his own, all the while having their own directions for research (Scheepers in Afrikaans and Dutch; Lys in French).[39] This lacuna was sufficiently felt by Neve for him to note it in his Preface.[40]

Neve's approach to studying the Spirit in the Old Testament is based upon historical critical reconstruction of the *Sitz im Leben* of the various texts. His whole project depends on such reconstructive analysis by locating the texts within a setting to attempt to frame with greater historical precision the development of the concept of the רוח of God within the story of Israel. This requires a relocation of the texts of Scripture in order to ascertain the setting of proposed composition and is argued for by Neve as a method more capable of discerning the emerging notions of רוח as part of the projected questions about the antiquity and development of such notions.[41]

In Neve's reconstruction of the earliest strata of Israelite texts (where he locates the ascriptions of the Spirit for the book of Judges-Samuel), he makes a case for the Spirit concept emerging as a 'revolutionary innovation' along with early Yahwism which suggests to him 'early untamed stages' in Israelite theological reflection tending towards the 'rough and violent' wherein the 'edges [had] not yet [been] rounded off'.[42] It is in this early stage, he argues, where the Spirit of God concept first emerges and has yet to mature into its more nuanced form and beyond this earlier violent, 'frenzied, explosive' expression.[43] Neve believes the 'spirit of God displays the marks characteristic of this early period when it overwhelms and dominates its subject, when its appearance is rough and violent, or when the effects of its coming are only external or temporary'.[44] In this period,

---

[39] Neve does not appear to be aware of the work of I.F. Wood previously noted in this chapter.

[40] Neve, *The Spirit of God*, p. x. In the preface, he notes only the work of Lys and apparently was not aware of Scheepers who does not bear mention in the book or bibliography.

[41] Neve, *The Spirit of God*, pp. 1-4.

[42] Neve, *The Spirit of God*, p. 19.

[43] Neve, *The Spirit of God*, p. 19.

[44] Neve, *The Spirit of God*, p. 13.

he proposes the prophets function as ecstatics (citing 1 Sam. 10.6, 10; 19.20, 23) and 'without apparent warning, the spirit comes on or possesses the human of Yahweh's choice' (citing Judg. 3.10; 6.34; 11.29; 13.25; 14.6, 19; 15.14; 1 Sam. 11.6; 16.13).[45] Neve proposes that 2 Sam. 23.2 and the 'spirit' which David proclaims to speak by is a 'transitional text' from this violent depersonalized era of the Spirit to the prophetic era of the Spirit. His argument is that this text, while transitional, is better equated with 'poetic inspiration' than with David making any claim of 'prophetic inspiration'.[46] This is surmised because Neve believes David's 'oracle' lacks the normal marks of the later prophetic period and because the Spirit is a permanent endowment on David rather than temporal as it is in this earlier historical period.

In his second temporal setting (of four) proposed for the development of Israel's Spirit of God conception, Neve locates the age of the prophets (including the books of Kings) as the age of the men and women of the Spirit. It is in the first portion (during the Omride dynasty in Israel; 1 Kgs 18.12, 22.24; 2 Kgs 2.16) of this extended period that Neve declares that the 'spirit is always closely related to the covenant events, and its reappearance here can mean the reaffirmation of the Sinaitic covenant by the prophets and the reassertion of Yahweh as the sole Lord and sovereign of his people'.[47] He notes the near total absence of the 'ecstatic condition or bizarre conduct associated with the spirit in the earlier period (1 Sam. 10.10, 19.20)'.[48] In this period, Neve proposes the 'prophet' is an ecstatic and thus Elijah and Elisha are never said to 'prophesy' (יתנבא the Hithpael form) in order better to distinguish them from the ravings of the prophets of Baal.[49]

To make his point, Neve suggests the 'hand of the LORD' on Elisha (2 Kgs 3.15) is significant for distinguishing from those whom the 'Spirit' overpowered. Further, when Elijah experiences the theophanic revelations at Horeb, the voice of Yahweh is not to be found

---

[45] Neve, *The Spirit of God*, p. 15.

[46] Neve, *The Spirit of God*, pp. 27-29.

[47] Neve, *The Spirit of God*, p. 31.

[48] Neve, *The Spirit of God*, p. 33.

[49] Neve, *The Spirit of God*, p. 34, and particularly see the discussion on this on p. 34 n. 5.

in the 'wind' (רוח; see 1 Kgs 19.9-12).[50] Finally, Neve describes the contrast between the raving, lying prophets who are '*ruach* prophets' (1 Kgs 22.10, 12, 24) from the 'spirit of God which inspires the true prophets of Yahweh'.[51] Thus, his argument follows that the 'popular image of the *ruach* prophets' was that of 'a fellow with rather wild and bizarre behavior, given to strong drink, laying claim to inspiration by the spirit, and constantly reciting (for a price) cheerful oracles' explaining the believed lack of reference to the Spirit of God by the true prophets of Yahweh.[52] Even so, he admits that there is not a total absence of reference to the Spirit of God in this period, but only a tendency in a number of occasions intentionally to avoid such language.

However, Neve still posits the role of the Spirit of God in this time period as indicating, empowering, and directing prophets and designating charismatic leaders. By this, he means to state that the Spirit inspires the words of the prophets, fills them with power, and places them under the total control of Yahweh.[53] Thus the account of Elijah's translation in the whirlwind is paradigmatic for the total control of the prophet by the Spirit (רוח) of God rather than as a referent to the 'wind' of God. It is providing a poignant theological commentary on the sovereignty of Yahweh over his true prophets.

Finally, Neve argues that the

> Spirit departed from the monarchy from the time of Solomon and moved to the prophetic movement. This is entirely in keeping with the nature of the spirit which is spontaneous, free, and charismatic, characteristics which would make the spirit highly out of place in a monarchical institution bound by hereditary succession.[54]

He further argues that the 'Priestly tradition' could not have given rise to this theology of charismatic endowment following the

---

50 Neve, *The Spirit of God*, pp. 34-35.
51 Neve, *The Spirit of God*, p. 35.
52 Neve, *The Spirit of God*, p. 35.
53 Neve, *The Spirit of God*, pp. 37-41.
54 Neve, *The Spirit of God*, p. 102.

interpretation of Gerhard von Rad.[55] Neve also rejects any origin for
the charismatic Spirit in the 'Wisdom tradition' (this final stage of
development) and instead locates this pneumatic expression within
the 'Prophetic tradition' as having influenced all such texts which
have been previously regarded as within the provenance of the other
writing traditions.[56] Neve concludes his critical analysis by ultimately
defining the spirit of God as 'power, anger, life, mind, will, presence'
that was 'manifested' in the story of YHWH and Israel.[57] For Neve,
it seems, the Spirit is orientation, direction, and enablement in the
texts of the Old Testament where the movement is from uncon-
trolled, overwhelming power (in the earlier stages) to more philo-
sophically and psychologically conceived enablement (in the latter
stages).

Robert Koch (1991)[58]

R. Koch follows the historical critical approach to working toward
the earliest strand of references to the Spirit in the Old Testament as
found in the ecstatic expressions located in many of the references
to the Spirit in the Former Prophets.[59] Born in 1905 in Switzerland,
he studied at the Papal Bible Institute and was a Catholic professor
of Old Testament Exegesis in Hennef, Milan, and Rome. For his
study, Koch relied heavily upon the article by Albertz and Westermann in *THAT* as well as the monograph on the Spirit by D. Lys by
following similar trajectories in his historical reconstruction which
deals specifically with the Former Prophets.[60]

Koch proposes that the רוח is being referred to via suggested syn-
onyms for wind/whirlwind in several texts of the Former Prophets
(2 Sam. 5.24; 1 Kgs 19.11; 2 Kgs 3.17; breath: Josh. 10.40; 2 Sam.
22.16; 1 Kgs 15.29; 17.17).[61] In an excursus, he argues that the 'evil

[55] Neve, *The Spirit of God*, pp. 103-104; citing G. von Rad, *Old Testament Theology* (2 vols.; London: Oliver & Boyd, 1962), I, p. 99.

[56] Neve, *The Spirit of God*, pp. 104-106.

[57] Neve, *The Spirit of God*, pp. 124-25.

[58] R. Koch, *Der Geist Gottes Im Alten Testament* (Frankfurt am Main; New York: P. Lang, 1991), all translations which follow are my own.

[59] Koch, *Der Geist Gottes*, pp. 35-58.

[60] Within this section of Koch's work, *Der Geist Gottes*, pp. 35-58, he cites both the article by Albertz and Westermann and the monograph by Lys thirteen times each.

[61] Koch, *Der Geist Gottes*, pp. 15-17.

spirit' (1 Sam. 16.14-16; 16.23; 18.10) in the Former Prophets is not to be connected directly to Yahweh and proposes this notion arises because Israel had an underdeveloped demonology at that time which would only later become such things as 'Satan' in the Latter Prophets, Job, and the Chronicler.[62]

Koch offers numerous relevant categories for the works of the רוח in the Former Prophets including the enablement of charismatic leaders (Judg. 3.7-11; 6.34; 11.29; 13.24, 25; 14.6, 19; 15.14),[63] ecstatic prophets (1 Sam. 10.6, 10; 11.6; 19.20, 23),[64] and rapture (2 Kgs 2.16).[65] The Spirit is regarded as 'a free gift of the LORD' of 'divine origin', a 'temporary' impartation, and representing the 'mysterious, supernatural and miraculous power' that was unexplainable.[66] This is developed in relation to what Koch believes was 'the oldest time' when the kings were ascribed as ruling with 'charismatic authority'.[67] He further proposes that Elijah marks another key 'turning point in salvation-history' for Israel.[68]

A Summary of the Historical Quest for the Spirit in the Former Prophets

Concluding the discussion of the historical quest for the Spirit in the Former Prophets indicates the following several notions. First, in this quest, historical reconstruction of Israel and the production of literature of the Hebrew Bible is essential for understanding the use of רוח in the Former Prophets. Second, having reconstructed the history of ancient Israel and its literature, the development of a maturing pneumatology emerges. Third, the earliest reconstructed strata of Israel's history and literature uses רוח to refer to things which were unexplainable by natural means at the time of the writing but would later be explained (and supplanted) by notions of wisdom, ability, and skill. This trajectory within the historical quest remains influential for

---

[62] Koch, *Der Geist Gottes*, pp. 35-38.

[63] Koch, *Der Geist Gottes*, pp. 40-41, 'Das charismatische Führertum'.

[64] Koch, *Der Geist Gottes*, pp. 42-43, 'Die ekstatische Prophetie'.

[65] Koch, *Der Geist Gottes*, pp. 44-46, 'Verzückung'.

[66] Koch, *Der Geist Gottes*, p. 50, '*ein* freies Gnadengeschenk *Jahwehs*', 'göttlichen Ursprungs', 'vorübergehend', and 'geheimnisvollenm, übernatürlichen *und* wunderbaren Kraft', original emphasis.

[67] Koch, *Der Geist Gottes*, p. 54, 'In der ältesten Zeit … charismatische Herrschaft'.

[68] Koch, *Der Geist Gottes*, p. 54, 'großen Wendepunkt … Heilsgeschichte'.

many of those of the theological quest noted below even as they each in turn consider it less relevant to the more significant theological reading of the Former Prophets in canonical form.

The Theological Quest for the Spirit in the Former Prophets

While there seem to be primarily two categories of the theological quest for the Spirit (confessional/creedal and biblical-theological), only one of these has shown a decidedly different approach than the former historical quest concerning the Spirit in the Former Prophets: the biblical-theological. While the confessional-creedal approach has focused on later developments of the theology of the Spirit (with only scant attention to the text of the Old Testament),[69] the biblical-theological approach has opened fresh avenues of exploration within the text of the Former Prophets by attempting more careful attention to the contours of the text of Scripture itself in its final form(s) and at times offering essentially theological commentaries of the Biblical texts. It is thus only the biblical theological works which are discussed in detail for their contributions to a theology of the Spirit in the Former Prophets. The writers which best represent this approach include the likes of G.T. Montague, S.M. Horton, L. Wood, M. Welker, W. Hildebrandt, and J. Rea.[70]

George T. Montague (1976)[71]

G.T. Montague (1929-) was born in Texas, entered the Marianist order in 1945 and was ordained a priest in 1948. He studied at the University of Dayton, Ohio, and later at Marianist International Seminary at the University of Fribourg (Switzerland) where he received

---

[69] Barclay, *The Promise of the Spirit*; Griffith-Thomas, *The Holy Spirit of God*; Ryrie, *The Holy Spirit*; Pink, *The Holy Spirit*; Schweizer, *Heiliger Geist*; Congar, *Je crois en l'Esprit Saint*; Heron, *The Holy Spirit*; Walvoord, *The Holy Spirit*; Moltmann, *The Spirit of Life*; Ferguson, *The Holy Spirit*; Pinnock, *Flame of Love*; Bloesch, *The Holy Spirit*; Kärkäinnen, *Pneumatology*; M. Green, *I Believe in the Holy Spirit*; Bulgakov, *The Comforter*; Cole, *He Who Gives Life*; Satyavrata, *The Holy Spirit*; C.R.J. Holmes, *The Holy Spirit* (Grand Rapids, MI: Zondervan, 2015).

[70] Firth and Wegner (eds.), *Presence, Power, and Promise*, is an edited volume which offers several chapter length contributions which represent the proposed biblical-theological approach.

[71] G.T. Montague, *The Holy Spirit: Growth of a Biblical Tradition* (New York: Paulist Press, 1976).

his doctorate of Sacred Theology in 1960. He has served in faculty and administrative positions at St. Mary's University (San Antonio, 1961-1972), Marianist American Seminary (St. Louis, 1972-1974), and University of St. Michael's College in the Toronto School of Theology (1975-1979). He has continued as a lecturer and visiting professor at numerous schools and has served as a major contributor to the Catholic charismatic renewal movement in multiple formal and informal capacities.

Montague offers a project which, similar to L. Neve, proposes a historical reconstruction of the order of the texts of Scripture. However, his overall project is oriented toward a full Biblical survey (Old and New Testaments) as a guiding rubric rather than simply a critical examination of the Old Testament text in order to develop his theology of the Spirit. He rearranges some of his material according to the historical reconstructionist notions mentioned above but works to allow the literary contours of the text to drive his theological conclusions.

In Montague's estimation much of the material of the Former Prophets belongs among the earliest strata of traditions in Israel concerning the concept of the Spirit.[72] He admits it is somewhat arbitrary that his work places the Deuteronomist's theology prior to the Pre-exilic prophet's, because he regards the work of the Deuteronomist as being completed by the 5th century BCE. However, he also regards the work of the Deuteronomist to include far earlier traditions from the monarchical period.[73] Even here he begins with the Former Prophets (in canonical order) and follows with where Deuteronomy might drive the theology of the Former Prophets (thus resulting in the so-called Deuteronomic/Deuteronomistic History).

'The major contribution of the book of Judges to the understanding of the spirit lies in its very graphic interpretation of the charismatic leadership of this period as the work of the *ruah Yahweh*, the spirit of the Lord.'[74] Montague lists those endowed with the Spirit of Yahweh as Othniel (3.10), Jephthah (11.29), Gideon (6.34; 7.2), Samson (13.25; 14.6, 19; 15.15), and even includes (as implicit through

---

[72] Montague, *The Holy Spirit*, pp. 17-32.

[73] Montague, *The Holy Spirit*, p. 17.

[74] Montague, *The Holy Spirit*, p. 17.

being named a prophetess) Deborah (4.4). He regards these Spirit endowments in Judges each to be for national deliverance and not to pertain in the slightest to 'ethical holiness of individual or people' and never being 'tied to any institution or rite'.[75] From these texts he surmises that the Spirit endowment is usually granted with regard to requests for help.[76]

In Montague's extended discussion of the Spirit material in 1 Samuel, he describes the connection made between the prophetic and the monarchic and the endowment connected on several occasions to the rite of anointing (e.g. 1 Sam. 9.26-10.13). He describes the event of endowment as associated with the likelihood of 'ecstatic' or 'religious fervor' brought about by the use of musical instrumentation. In this regard, he notes the link to Elisha's call for 'a minstrel to dispose him to prophesy' (2 Kgs 3.15) and David's use of his harping 'to chase the evil spirit from Saul' (1 Sam. 16.14-23).[77] Saul's Spirit endowment and prophesying lead to the people of Israel asking rhetorically after Saul's status in contrast to the prophets who, Montague proposes, 'appeared and functioned in a purely charismatic, non-structural way' without being able to indicate their 'particular lineage to give them status in Israelite society'.[78] Montague describes the Spirit of God which rushes upon Saul when he hears the report of Israel harangued by Nahash the Ammonite (1 Sam. 11.6) as 'not one which encourages passivity but on the contrary one that inspires a holy aggressivity to establish the justice and the kingdom of God' in much the same manner as Jesus was 'flush with anger' at the plight of humanity bound and suffering (citing Mk 3.5; 10.14; and 11.15-17).[79]

On David's Spirit endowment, Montague notes a distinction between Saul's delayed endowment in relation to his kingly anointing by Samuel and David's immediate endowment (1 Sam. 16.13). He

---

[75] Montague, *The Holy Spirit*, p. 18.

[76] Notably Montague, *The Holy Spirit*, p. 18, cites three passages to prove his point: 3.10; 4.3; and 16.28. However, the last of these nowhere refers to a Spirit endowment, but only to Samson praying for avenging vindication and his accomplishing such. While the Spirit is noted in several other places in the life of Samson, the Spirit is not mentioned explicitly in this text.

[77] Montague, *The Holy Spirit*, p. 20.

[78] Montague, *The Holy Spirit*, p. 20.

[79] Montague, *The Holy Spirit*, pp. 20-21. He improperly cites the passage as 1 Sam. 11.5 instead of 1 Sam. 11.6 in his subheading on p. 20.

further notes, however, that unlike in the case of Saul, David's enthronement is delayed until after numerous victories though the Spirit had already come upon him. Montague likens this to the messianic anointing with the Spirit upon Jesus with a distinct distance of time until Jesus was proven victorious over enemies finally to be enthroned (pointing to Acts 2.36).[80]

Montague goes on to describe the absolute graciousness of the gift of the Spirit to be either maintained upon the sinful (as in the case of David) or withdrawn from the sinful (as in the case of Saul). He regards the Spirit as the gift of God to be given or taken as Yahweh sees fit (1 Sam. 16.14-23).[81] Thus, the Spirit is not *ipso facto* imparted with the playing of music, even as the playing of music at the hands of David still brings reprieve to Saul from the 'evil spirit from the LORD'. Montague notes the lack of any mention of the Spirit of God replacing the evil spirit.[82] He does still regard this sending of the evil spirit as an artifact of 'the popular mind in those early days' which he believes was 'not far along in theological sophistication'.[83]

Montague proposes that protection is offered by the Spirit of God in 1 Sam. 19.20, 23 as the Spirit overcomes Saul on his way to David. This overwhelming state leaves Saul powerless in the presence of Samuel and David 'in a prophetic frenzy' in the same manner as the servants sent to fetch David and in the same sense as the prophets who are met along the way.[84]

Not only does the Spirit protect, but the Spirit also transports as in the case of Elijah the prophet (1 Kgs 18.12; 2 Kgs 2.16). This, Montague considers, is not so much a matter of 'miraculous vanishing,' but an 'underlying suggestion … that the messengers of the Lord are endowed with a spiritual subtlety appropriate to their vocation'.[85] This movement by the Spirit is likened to the carrying of Ezekiel to various places (Ezek. 3.14; 8.3; 11.11, 24; 40.2), the taking of Jesus to the pinnacle of the temple and a high mountain (Lk. 4.5),

---

[80] Montague, *The Holy Spirit*, p. 21.
[81] Montague, *The Holy Spirit*, p. 22.
[82] Montague, *The Holy Spirit*, p. 23.
[83] Montague, *The Holy Spirit*, p. 22.
[84] Montague, *The Holy Spirit*, p. 24.
[85] Montague, *The Holy Spirit*, p. 25.

and Philip suddenly being snatched away from the wilderness where he baptized the eunuch (Acts 8.39).

The problematic message of Micaiah the prophet to Ahab is described as belonging to 'a very primitive stage in the development of the relationship of the spirit-world to the world of man'.[86] Montague proposes the solution to the 'lying spirit from the LORD' in Micaiah's vision is not to be conceived as being *of* Yahweh (and thus guarding the goodness of Yahweh) and instead 'more akin to "the breath of the Lord"' rather than another being more distinct from Yahweh. He draws three points from this account: (1) there is no guarantee that one claiming the Spirit is actually speaking the truth, (2) discernment is necessary for all prophecies, but particularly those that offer direction instead of simply speaking to morality which might more readily be discerned via study of the text of the Scriptures, and (3) majority approval does not guarantee trustworthiness.[87] Claims to the direction of the Spirit are thus claims that lie beyond the purview of the community apart from the passage of time and the fulfillment or lack thereof.

Finally, Montague describes the function of the Spirit upon Elisha's request at the passing of Elijah and receives both the Spirit of Yahweh and the spirit of Elijah (2 Kgs 2.9, 15). He notes numerous comparisons of this endowment and its ramifications particularly in relation to Jesus and his disciples suggesting a theological link between the accounts. This serves as a paradigm (along with the anointing of Saul and David by Samuel) of the role of the prophet and those receiving the endowment of the Spirit were thus committed to 'remain faithful to this spirit of which they are not the autonomous lords but humble recipients'.[88] Montague ties the giving of the Spirit to the rites of laying on hands (Joshua in Deuteronomy) and by other means of visible endowment (like the mantle of Elijah and the anointing of Saul and David). This charismatic Spirit protects from danger, guards movements, signifies authority, and empowers for victory.[89]

---

[86] Montague, *The Holy Spirit*, p. 26.
[87] Montague, *The Holy Spirit*, pp. 26, 27.
[88] Montague, *The Holy Spirit*, p. 32.
[89] Montague, *The Holy Spirit*, p. 32.

Stanley M. Horton (1976, 2005)[90]

S.M. Horton (1916-2014) was educated at Gordon College (MDiv) in 1944, Harvard University (STM) in 1945, and Central Baptist Theological Seminary (ThD) in 1959. He has been regarded a 'premier theologian' among Pentecostals.[91] Horton was ordained with the Assemblies of God (USA) in 1942 and served at several institutions including Central Bible College in Springfield, MO, from 1948-1978, then from 1978-1991 at the Assemblies of God Theological Seminary. He also was an itinerant professor globally and served as the president of the Society for Pentecostal Studies from 1979-1980. Horton wrote prolifically for the Pentecostal fellowship to which he belonged.

His contribution to the study of the Spirit in the Former Prophets occurs in the form of his monograph, *What the Bible Says about the Holy Spirit*, which was originally published in 1976, then updated and republished in 2005. In 2008, this volume was described as 'the definitive text on that topic in universities and seminaries around the world'.[92] This volume attempts to discuss every passage in the Bible that speaks of the Spirit. Horton dedicates an entire chapter to 'The Spirit in the History of Israel' (pp. 33-54) where he discusses the passages of the Former Prophets almost exclusively.

Horton proposes that Judges is intentionally shaped by the passages concerned with the Spirit and the Spirit-endowed judges.[93] When he writes that the Spirit 'came upon' Othniel he mentions that some read the Hebrew as 'was upon', but he rejects this reading. However, after discussing only briefly the Spirit upon Othniel, he then commences to discuss the Spirit with Deborah despite the lack of explicit texts referring to the Spirit in the Deborah story. He draws this out by indicating her wisdom via a prophetic and judging function and surmises that she was Spirit-endowed as well, but without any specific explanation beyond this. He gives space to discussing the

---

[90] Horton, *What the Bible Says about the Holy Spirit*.

[91] As cited by L.E. Olena, 'Stanley M. Horton: A Pentecostal Journey', *AGH* 29 (Spring 2009), pp. 4-14 (5). This was the title of a program specifically dedicated to Horton at Evangel University, April 3-4, 2008, p. 14 n. 1.

[92] Olena, 'Stanley M. Horton', p. 12, citing again the 2008 event at Evangel University.

[93] Horton, *What the Bible Says about the Holy Spirit*, p. 36.

'clothing' of the Spirit and Gideon as to how best to translate the verb לבש. He concludes that the best reading of this text is that Gideon was filled with the Spirit and that 'the Spirit put on Gideon'.[94] He notes Jephthah's foolish vow and admits that the Spirit still enabled him to lead Israel to victory despite this failure.[95] Samson is regarded as having been afforded a godly upbringing (contrary to Jephthah), and also failed. This failure is believed by Horton to indicate the grace of the God of Israel.[96] While Samson was 'stirred' by the Spirit to take action against the Philistines, yet he remained always in control under the power of the Spirit.[97] Horton concludes that Judges portrays the Spirit of Yahweh never as 'a mere influence coming from a God who is far away. [Instead,] God Himself is always present personally and in power in His Spirit.'[98]

Horton's discussion of the books of Samuel attempt again to include one not explicitly stated to be Spirit endowed: Samuel.[99] He goes on to address the singing prophets that are connected to Samuel (and Saul) and the nature of prophecy in these texts as not predictive, but as worshipful 'singing and playing for God under the inspiration of the Spirit'.[100] With regard to David's endowment with the Spirit, Horton notes that it was continuance contrasted with 'Samson and Saul' whose 'experiences were temporary and intermittent' even though Saul had the Spirit 'available to him' he did not take advantage of this opportunity and instead continued into further disobedience.[101] This continuing experience of the Spirit is described as 'a rising experience, a growing experience'.[102] This endowment enabled David to become the great prophetic psalmist of Israel.[103] When the Spirit of Yahweh departed from Saul, he received 'a spirit of judgment' from Yahweh that Horton contends was neither 'an evil spirit

---

[94] Horton, *What the Bible Says about the Holy Spirit*, pp. 38-39.

[95] Horton, *What the Bible Says about the Holy Spirit*, p. 39.

[96] Horton, *What the Bible Says about the Holy Spirit*, p. 40.

[97] Horton, *What the Bible Says about the Holy Spirit*, p. 41.

[98] Horton, *What the Bible Says about the Holy Spirit*, p. 42.

[99] Horton, *What the Bible Says about the Holy Spirit*, pp. 42-44.

[100] Horton, *What the Bible Says about the Holy Spirit*, pp. 44-45.

[101] Horton, *What the Bible Says about the Holy Spirit*, pp. 46-47.

[102] Horton, *What the Bible Says about the Holy Spirit*, p. 46.

[103] Horton, *What the Bible Says about the Holy Spirit*, p. 46.

or demon in the New Testament sense'.[104] However, he further clarifies that this spirit is 'not in the same class with the Spirit of the
Lord'.[105] He believes the Holy Spirit who is God Himself is not like
this spirit, because this spirit is subject to the will of the Spirit (particularly in David's Spirit-ed instrumentation).[106] This troubling spirit
and the prophetic acts of Saul by it and reacting to the minstreling
prophets in 1 Samuel 19 are regarded as 'not normal prophesying,'
but 'more like ravings that came from his resisting the Spirit'.[107]

Finally, Horton takes up the texts of the Spirit in the books of
Kings. He argues that Elijah was so characterized by the Spirit of
Yahweh that when Elisha asks for a double portion of the S/spirit
of Elijah, 'he did not mean Elijah's human spirit or enthusiasm, but
the Spirit of God'.[108] This double portion of the Spirit was the portion of the heir to Elijah's prophetic endowment and thus marked
Elisha as 'successor' to Elijah and leader of the prophetic sons.[109] At
the very end of his chapter, Horton moves briefly to discuss Micaiah,
but only uses this account to contend for prophecy being regarded
as necessarily inspired by Yahweh.[110]

Leon Wood (1978, 1998)[111]

L. Wood (1918-1977) received his education at Calvin Theological
Seminary, New York University, The Oriental Institute at Chicago,
and completed his PhD at Michigan State University. He lectured in
Old Testament studies at Cornerstone University located at Grand
Rapids Theological Seminary for most of his career (1946-1975) and
worked as a translator and editor for the original NIV.

Wood regards all of the occurrences of *Spirit* in the book of
Judges to have 'involved empowerment for physical activity,' even deliverance from enemies and feats of greatness in battle and not having anything to do 'with salvation from sin in any sense'.[112] This latter

---

[104] Horton, *What the Bible Says about the Holy Spirit*, p. 48.
[105] Horton, *What the Bible Says about the Holy Spirit*, p. 48.
[106] Horton, *What the Bible Says about the Holy Spirit*, p. 48.
[107] Horton, *What the Bible Says about the Holy Spirit*, pp. 48-49.
[108] Horton, *What the Bible Says about the Holy Spirit*, pp. 52-53.
[109] Horton, *What the Bible Says about the Holy Spirit*, p. 53.
[110] Horton, *What the Bible Says about the Holy Spirit*, p. 54.
[111] Wood, *The Holy Spirit*.
[112] Wood, *The Holy Spirit*, p. 41.

issue is pertinent to his wider discussion of continuity/discontinuity of the work of the Spirit in the two testaments.

Wood regards Hiram in 1 Kgs 7.13, 14 as being 'filled' (Heb. מלא) with the Spirit even though the text itself only states he was 'filled with wisdom and understanding, and cunning to work all works of brass'. Wood draws the connection between Hiram and Bezalel, Oholiab, and the other craftsmen who were likewise 'filled' with the 'spirit of wisdom' to craft the materials of the tabernacle in Exod. 28.3. He notes the phrase 'spirit of wisdom' is used of Joshua (Deut. 34.9) and predictively of the Christ (Isa. 11.2) where, the latter of which, he concludes 'surely the Holy Spirit is in view'.[113] He places this occurrence of the 'Spirit' under the rubric of enablement for craftsmanship. Again, he notes that there is no connection to 'salvation from sin' in this passage and the several others concerned with craftsmanship (Exod. 31.3, 6; 1 Chron. 28.11, 12).

Wood argues that both Elijah and Elisha 'were continuously Spirit-empowered' according to the account of Elijah's translation to heaven in 2 Kings 2. This is extrapolated by means of Elisha's request for the 'double portion' of the 'spirit' which had been upon Elijah (apparently considered to reside with Elijah) and therefore a remaining upon Elisha to carry out the mantled prophetic task of Elijah. In the manner Elisha believed Elijah to be Spirit-endowed, so Elisha desired for himself.[114] Both Elijah and Elisha were conceivably 'in constant need of special help. They were full-time prophets, occupied daily with divinely assigned tasks. Therefore, they had a continuous need for Spirit-empowerment and God met them in that need.'[115]

In discussing the spirit-endowment of King Saul, Wood ascribes a continuous empowerment at least from the second endowment in 1 Sam. 11.6 until the removal of the 'spirit' in 1 Sam. 16.14. He believes the endowment was only temporarily given at the initial endowment in 1 Sam. 10.6, 10.[116] God had given Saul 'a new heart' according to 1 Sam. 10.9 and thereby effected some great change to Saul's

---

[113] Wood, *The Holy Spirit*, pp. 42 n. 4, 50.
[114] Wood, *The Holy Spirit*, pp. 45, 46.
[115] Wood, *The Holy Spirit*, p. 48.
[116] Wood, *The Holy Spirit*, p. 50.

'personality' by giving him 'confidence', yet following Wood's argument this change was only 'temporary'.[117]

Wood describes David's Spirit endowment as a 'continuous empowerment' from the day of his anointing to be king at the hands of Samuel, until the end of his days. This is judged to be continuous by the use of the phrase 'from that day forward' with regard to the Spirit of YHWH coming upon David (1 Sam. 16.13). This endowment would be persistent to uphold and enable David to do whatever would be necessary till the day of his kingship and then to enable him to rule as 'the finest ruler possible'.[118] Even here, Wood regards the spirit endowment of David to pertain only to equipping for service and not salvific for dealing with sin.

Wood believes that both David and Saul (though also the others endowed in Judges) needed special endowment of the Spirit due to the lack of appropriate background for the work required of them, the need for courage in the face of overwhelming obstacles, and naturally timid personalities.[119] Spirit endowment in these passages is thus concluded by Wood to be task oriented even while potentially personality altering. However, he only speaks to some of the cases he has listed (Moses, Joshua, Saul, and David) and fails to answer why others are not said to receive such endowment particularly those regarded as the less nationally necessary endowments: Othniel, Gideon, Jephthah, and Samson.[120] Instead he contrasts these national figures with the likes of Samuel and Solomon, the former of which was not truly 'national' and the latter of which had been raised in the courts of a king and therefore had a 'much less demanding' need for Spirit endowment.

John Rea (1990)[121]

J. Rea (1925-2012) held a ThD (Grace Theological Seminary) with further degrees from Wheaton College and Princeton University. He was a surveyor of the Dothan excavations in Israel (1953), contributed to the New American Standard Bible (1971), and was the

---

[117] Wood, *The Holy Spirit*, pp. 60, 105, 106, 114.

[118] Wood, *The Holy Spirit*, p. 51.

[119] Wood, *The Holy Spirit*, pp. 53-63.

[120] Wood, *The Holy Spirit*, pp. 62, 63.

[121] J. Rea, *The Holy Spirit in the Bible: All the Major Passages about the Spirit* (Lake Mary, FL: Creation House, 1990).

managing editor of the *Wycliffe Bible Encyclopedia* (1975), among numerous other publications and projects including serving as Emeritus Professor of Old Testament at Regent University in Virginia Beach, VA, where he retired.

Rea edited a small volume on the Holy Spirit in 1972.[122] This was followed in 1990 by his major work entitled: *The Holy Spirit in the Bible: All the Major Passages about the Holy Spirit.* This was then later followed by *Charisma's Bible Handbook on the Holy Spirit*[123] which was a re-publication under a new formatting of his *The Holy Spirit in the Bible.* Because of the significance of his contribution in his 1990 publication, that is the volume which is drawn on for this survey. He notably discusses the Spirit in the Former Prophets intermittently between pp. 48-83.

Rea contends for the testimonial value of the endowment of the Spirit of Yahweh marking men and women[124] (meaning Deborah) as leaders of Israel up to David's time.[125] He first discusses David's early function as Spirit-endowed leader of Israel who was victorious over Israel's enemies and prophetically sang and inquired of Yahweh.[126] He contends, citing 2 Sam. 23.1-3a, that David equates 'the Spirit of Yahweh with the God of Israel' resulting in his prophetic singing.[127]

Rea then briefly discusses the four individuals stated explicitly to have been Spirit endowed giving particular focus to the Hebrew terms used. Concerning Othniel as 'pattern for those who follow' he indicates that the Hebrew means the Spirit was 'actively present upon'

---

[122] J. Rea (ed.), *The Layman's Commentary on the Holy Spirit* (Plainfield, NJ: Logos International, 1972).

[123] J. Rea, *Charisma's Bible Handbook on the Holy Spirit* (Lake Mary, FL: Creation House, 1998).

[124] Rea refers to the evidence on 'him or her' and includes her in the list of the previous paragraph along with the four judges named with the Spirit explicitly on them, *The Holy Spirit in the Bible*, p. 49. Later, p. 54, he notes the four explicit mentions and parenthetically claims, 'This is not to suggest that the other judges operated only in their natural wisdom and strength'.

[125] Rea, *The Holy Spirit in the Bible*, p. 49.

[126] Rea, *The Holy Spirit in the Bible*, pp. 50-51.

[127] Rea, *The Holy Spirit in the Bible*, p. 51. However, the poetic structure of 2 Sam. 23.1-3a suggests that the first bicolon רוּחַ יְהוָה דִּבֶּר־בִּי // וּמִלָּתוֹ עַל־לְשׁוֹנִי is properly indicating that the Spirit of Yahweh is compared to 'his word' where the next bicolon אָמַר אֱלֹהֵי יִשְׂרָאֵל // לִי דִבֶּר צוּר יִשְׂרָאֵל picks up that it is the God of Israel//the Rock of Israel who has spoken.

him.[128] He offers both readings of Gideon as ambiguously either 'the Spirit clothed Gideon or that He clothed Himself with Gideon'. In the end he suggests (noting the LXX reading and Lk. 24.29 using the same LXX term) that the Spirit clothed Gideon.[129] For Samson, the Spirit initially 'began to stir' him with the meaning of 'to trouble or agitate'.[130] Afterward, the Spirit rushed upon him as it did Kings Saul and David. He notes, 'Their activity provides valuable insights into the work of the Holy Spirit in the modern renewal movement'.[131]

With regard to Saul, Rea contends that the transformed heart connected with his Spirit endowment should not be read as resulting in any 'lasting transformation or regeneration in Saul'.[132] He argues that the endowment had a twofold purpose: (1) to offer a 'charismatic demonstration' of Yahweh's appointment of Saul as chosen, and (2) to empower and embolden him to respond to the oppression of the enemies and bring about deliverance.[133] The troubling spirit that came upon Saul once the Spirit of Yahweh left him does not seem to Rea to have been 'a morally evil demon'.[134] Finally, when Saul is overcome by the Spirit, as he tries to get to David at Ramah, he prophesies and strips 'naked' to demonstrate the conflict between Saul's spirit and the Holy Spirit with the Holy Spirit proving victorious. 'It was not that Saul became a frenzied ecstatic; rather the supernatural power of the Spirit turned the frustrated ruler into a praising man.'[135]

Rea contends that while David's Spirit empowerment 'was similar to that of his predecessors … it was even more extensive in its scope, its continuance and its significance as a type'.[136] While those previously endowed experienced only 'occasional and temporary' enablement, David maintained a constant presence of the Spirit in power.[137] This is argued for why David becomes the standard by which all later

---

128 Rea, *The Holy Spirit in the Bible*, p. 54.
129 Rea, *The Holy Spirit in the Bible*, p. 54. He appears to only be reading the LXX^A text, not noting the variant within the LXX tradition.
130 Rea, *The Holy Spirit in the Bible*, p. 55.
131 Rea, *The Holy Spirit in the Bible*, p. 55.
132 Rea, *The Holy Spirit in the Bible*, pp. 55-56.
133 Rea, *The Holy Spirit in the Bible*, p. 56.
134 Rea, *The Holy Spirit in the Bible*, p. 57.
135 Rea, *The Holy Spirit in the Bible*, p. 58.
136 Rea, *The Holy Spirit in the Bible*, pp. 59, 64.
137 Rea, *The Holy Spirit in the Bible*, pp. 59-60.

kings of Judah are judged.[138] It is further used to point to the coming Spirit-empowered Messiah who would know the abiding of the Spirit.[139]

Elijah serves as the 'model prophet' after Moses.[140] According to Rea, Elijah (along with Moses and David) experienced the continuous endowment of the Spirit.[141] Elijah's passing of his mantle to Elisha and Elisha receiving the double portion 'in-the-form-of-your-spirit' indicated that Elisha received the portion of the first born son and thus became the 'chosen successor' of Elijah in receiving the Spirit of Yahweh that had been on Elijah. Rea contends that this same ability to be clothed with the Spirit is available as a 'result of Pentecost' to 'all of Christ's followers' in the same manner as for Elisha.[142]

Michael Welker (1994)[143]

M. Welker (1947-) is a German theologian of the Protestant Church in Germany (*Evangelische Kirche in Deutschland*) holding doctorates in systematic theology (Tübingen under the supervision of J. Moltmann) and philosophy (Heidelberg). He served as professor of Systematic Theology (1983-1987) at Tübingen, chair of Reformed Theology (1987-1991) at Munster, and professor of Dogmatics (1991-present) at Heidelberg. Welker has also been a lecturer at the University of Chicago, McMaster University, Princeton Theological Seminary, and Harvard Divinity School. Welker came to write 'God the Spirit' (drawing from numerous lectures he had previously delivered in theology) as a result of working toward a fuller discussion of the

---

138 Rea, *The Holy Spirit in the Bible*, p. 59.

139 Rea, *The Holy Spirit in the Bible*, pp. 60-61

140 Rea, *The Holy Spirit in the Bible*, p. 74.

141 Rea, *The Holy Spirit in the Bible*, p. 75.

142 Rea, *The Holy Spirit in the Bible*, pp. 82-83.

143 M. Welker, *God the Spirit* (trans. John F. Hoffmeyer; Minneapolis, MN: Augsburg Fortress, 1994), p. ix, which is a translation from the original German *Gottes Geist: Theologie des Heiligen Geistes* (Neukirchen-Vluyn, Germany: Neukirchener Verlag, 1992) and all citations are from this English translation. Since his initial work, Welker has edited two volumes pertaining specifically to the Spirit: *The Work of the Spirit: Pneumatology and Pentecostalism* (Grand Rapids, MI: Eerdmans, 2006) and *The Spirit in Creation and New Creation: Science and Theology in Western and Orthodox Realms* (Grand Rapids, MI: Eerdmans, 2012).

contours of a Christian theology when he found himself returning 'again and again' to the Spirit as a sort of *prolegomena* to that work.

Welker argues that the Spirit is not as nebulous and undefinable as many have contended. He states that the Spirit in the Former Prophets came upon 'a specific human being' who would then be successful 'in restoring loyalty, solidarity, and the capacity for communal action'.[144] This endowment was not simply for military engagement, nor to produce super humans, but for the restoration of the community to live more fully.[145] While Welker contends the Spirit gives life, he also notes the inherent danger of Spirit empowerment noting the particular account of Jephthah (Judg. 11.30-37).[146] The account of Samson (who Welker emphatically notes: brawls, lies, cheats, commits arson, and murders) is intended to speak to two realities concerning Israel as a community. They are caught in the dialectical tension of embrace and distancing with Israel's neighbors[147] and they are weak, gullible, and easily defeated, but the Spirit enables with cunning and strength toward victory.[148] In contrast to this, in the Saulide narratives, Welker notes both an empowering and disempowering by the Spirit which are performed 'simultaneously'.[149] This further confusion for the people in their discerning the work of the Spirit is heightened by the account of Micaiah in 1 Kings 22. The 'lying spirit' remains for the hearers ill-defined.[150] Who is lying and who is speaking the truth when it is the Spirit who inspires both? Such distinctions can apparently only be discerned by those enabled by the Spirit to discern just what the Spirit is doing in any given situation. According to Welker, 'The chief difficulty in understanding the Spirit and the Spirit's action lay in mediating, on the one hand, the *undeniable evidence* of the Spirit's action and, on the other hand, the fact that it *cannot be predicted, calculated, or controlled*'.[151]

---

144 Welker, *God the Spirit*, pp. 53, 56-7.
145 Welker, *God the Spirit*, pp. 52, 57-61.
146 Welker, *God the Spirit*, p. 62.
147 Welker, *God the Spirit*, pp. 66-67.
148 Welker, *God the Spirit*, p. 71.
149 Welker, *God the Spirit*, pp. 74-83.
150 Welker, *God the Spirit*, pp. 84-98.
151 Welker, *God the Spirit*, p. 99, original emphasis.

Wilf Hildebrandt (1995)

W. Hildebrandt has a DTh (2004) from the University of South Africa writing his thesis on 'The Cessation of Prophecy in the Old Testament'. He holds ministerial credentials with the Pentecostal Assemblies of Canada and serves as the Dean of Education and Director of Intercultural Studies at Summit Pacific College (Abbotsford, BC) where he has been on faculty since 2004. Hildebrandt's contribution to a pneumatology of the Old Testament is found in his work entitled, 'An Old Testament Theology of the Spirit of God' which was a significant expansion of his ThM thesis at Regent College (1989).[152] He names a number of authors who have written on this topic to whom he is indebted (e.g. G. Montague, L. Wood, P. Volz, and D. Lys), but makes special mention of the work of L. Neve as influential for his own project.[153]

Hildebrandt categorizes the usage of רוח along thematic lines. He notes רוח as referring to the human emotional state (Josh. 2.11; 5.1; Judg. 9.23; 15.19; 1 Sam. 1.10; 30.12; 1 Kgs 10.5; 21.5; 2 Kgs 19.7),[154] 'breath' or 'anger' (Judg. 8.3),[155] representing 'an independent personality' (1 Kgs 22.21, 22),[156] facilitating the preservation of Israel's kings (2 Sam. 22.16),[157] making the judges 'charismatic' leaders in order to preserve Israel (Judg. 3.10; 6.34; 11.29; 13.25; 14.6, 19; 15.14, 19),[158] transporting (1 Kgs 18.12; 2 Kgs 2.16) and inspiring prophets (2 Sam. 23.2; 1 Kgs 22.24),[159] restraint (1 Sam. 19.20, 21),[160] and overcoming and causing Saul to prophesy and to be changed until the רוח departs from him and comes upon David to serve as the leader of Israel (1 Sam. 10.6, 10; 16.13, 14; 19.20, 23).[161] The Spirit can cause otherwise unexplainable ecstatic experiences which may be regarded either

---

152 W. Hildebrandt, *An Old Testament Theology* and his unpublished thesis 'An Investigation of rûah as the Spirit of God in the Hebrew Canon' (MA; Regent College, 1989).

153 Hildebrandt, *An Old Testament Theology*, p. xvi.

154 Hildebrandt, *An Old Testament Theology*, p. 16.

155 Hildebrandt, *An Old Testament Theology*, p. 85.

156 Hildebrandt, *An Old Testament Theology*, p. 90.

157 Hildebrandt, *An Old Testament Theology*, p. 21.

158 Hildebrandt, *An Old Testament Theology*, pp. 23-24.

159 Hildebrandt, *An Old Testament Theology*, pp. 26-27, 175.

160 Hildebrandt, *An Old Testament Theology*, pp. 170-72.

161 Hildebrandt, *An Old Testament Theology*, pp. 24, 26.

positively or negatively (1 Sam. 19.20; 2 Kgs 5.26; 6.12, 17, 32), but which Hildebrandt believes is mostly positive with regard to the true prophets of Israel.[162]

Hildebrandt states that the רוח is present at 'key transition' periods in Israel's history, such as the endowment of Joshua by Moses to lead Israel, the establishment of kingship in Israel, and the turn to the prophets for keeping Israel.[163] His contention is that this is intended to maintain the people of Israel as ruled by a theocracy.[164] The endowment of Spirit-empowered leaders to deliver Israel from oppression particularly militarily is noted in the book of Judges via boldness, ability to muster an army, and military prowess (Judg. 3.7-11; 6.1-8.35; 10.6-18; 13-16). He summarizes that these particularly noted endowments were selectively chosen examples that Israel would understand as typical of all such salvific leaders and thus would not need explication each time a leader was mentioned.[165] While describing the empowerment of Saul as designated king, Hildebrandt emphasizes that 'all leadership [in the Old Testament] must be Spirit empowered'.[166]

A number of the features of Hildebrandt's understanding of particular uses of רוח deserve further discussion. Hildebrandt remains uncertain as to the identity of the רוח רעה which comes upon Saul in place of the רוח of Yahweh. He proposes it might be either 'a demon or a powerful evil influence' (1 Sam. 16.14).[167] He also sees no ultimately distinguishable feature associated with the variant Spirit of Yahweh or God.[168] Concerning the Spirit of Yahweh on David, he contends it is a perpetual endowment citing 1 Sam. 16.13, despite David's later fear of the potential that the Spirit might be removed from him due to his sin involving Bathsheba.[169] He also proposes that the mantle of Elijah placed on Elisha (1 Kgs 13, 19) is 'analogous to the "hand of Yahweh" that comes on the prophet during prophetic

---

[162] Hildebrandt, *An Old Testament Theology*, pp. 161-62.

[163] Hildebrandt, *An Old Testament Theology*, pp. 23-25, 170.

[164] Hildebrandt, *An Old Testament Theology*, pp. 104, 117, 201.

[165] Hildebrandt, *An Old Testament Theology*, p. 119.

[166] Hildebrandt, *An Old Testament Theology*, p. 121.

[167] Hildebrandt, *An Old Testament Theology*, p. 122.

[168] Hildebrandt, *An Old Testament Theology*, p. 172. Others have contended for a certain distinction but do so only via means of designating certain uses as interpolations into the original text, see Ragsdale, 'Ruah YHWH, Ruah 'Elohim'.

[169] Hildebrandt, *An Old Testament Theology*, p. 126.

functions'.[170] According to Hildebrandt, the double-portioned רוח of Elijah that Elisha requests 'must certainly refer to' the Spirit of Yahweh.[171] He further states that the double portion indicates Elisha as the deuteronomic eldest son who would be a family head, or father, over the sons of the prophets.[172] Finally, he believes the grammatically articulated הרוח in 1 Kgs 22.21-23 (which puts lies into the mouths of the court prophets according to the plan of the council of Yahweh) is none other than the Spirit of Yahweh.[173]

A Summary of the Theological Quest for the Spirit in the Former Prophets

To summarize the foregoing work by what has been regarded as the theological quest for the Spirit in the Former Prophets, several features should be highlighted. First, this quest entails far greater reliance and acceptance of the canonical (final) form of the text in tracing the Spirit in the Old Testament and thus the Former Prophets than the historical quest. While the historical quest seeks to establish timelines and ideas behind the text, the theological quest attempts a closer reading of a canonical form of the text. Second, this does not diminish the contention of theological development proposed by the historical quest even as it nuances it to base it more upon final form of the text rather than a reordering of the development of the text. Any ordering of the text at least attempts to allow for certain preset divisions of the canonical form of the text. Third, while there is greater continuity admitted within this approach between the experience of the Spirit in the New Testament and the Former Prophets it still persists in offering a strong disjunction between how one experienced and experiences the Spirit. Finally, it should be noted as significant that all of the authors discussed in this quest are identified with charismatic and/or Pentecostal movements.

Whence the Spirit?

When the sons of the prophets from Jericho saw Elisha, they said, 'The spirit of Elijah rests upon Elisha'. And they went to meet him

---

170 Hildebrandt, *An Old Testament Theology*, p. 139.
171 Hildebrandt, *An Old Testament Theology*, pp. 140, 176-79.
172 Hildebrandt, *An Old Testament Theology*, p. 177.
173 Hildebrandt, *An Old Testament Theology*, p. 181.

and bowed down to the ground before him. They said, 'See, we who are your servants have fifty capable men. Please let them go and look for your master. Perhaps the Spirit of Yahweh has picked him up and cast him upon some mountain or in some valley'. He replied, 'Don't send them', but they pushed him until he was embarrassed and said, 'Send them'. So they sent fifty men who searched for three days and did not find him (2 Kgs 2.15-17).

Against the initial and plain confessional observation of the sons of the prophets of Jericho, there is a concern that the Spirit of Yahweh is somehow elsewhere. And thus their quests to find where the Spirit of Yahweh has taken Elijah all the while the one with the Spirit of Elijah is the very one relenting to leave them to their quests.

In the quests of the 'capable men' sent by the sons of the prophets of Jericho we find a similar search among the historical and theological quests for the Spirit in the Former Prophets. Some would have searched in further locations, others nearer, but all searched elsewhere than where they first confessed the Spirit. Each offers a contribution to the study of the Spirit in the Former Prophets, but each offers only as through glass darkly and only at last in the final admissions of the Spirit as found (in some fashion) in the text before them.

The historical quest points the hearer toward the development of the revelation and understanding of the Spirit in the redemptive-history of Israel. This quest proposes a strong disjunction between earlier and later Israel's self-understanding and thus of the early claims for 'spirit' when something was unexplainable and later could be understood by other more mature means. From a constructive Pentecostal appraisal, in response to this, all that can and would be known of the Spirit was not yet known and would find its fullness in the one coming to baptize in the Spirit and being himself fully endowed with the Sprit. Yet even in this all that might be known remains yet to be made known. This, however, does not typically follow in the trajectories of the historical quest that seems more prone to abandoning 'spirit' language as Israel developed in favor of ideas of 'wisdom' and the writing prophets.

The theological quest points in the direction of the claims of the final form of the text received by a given community which reflects and lives in relation to the Spirit of the text. This quest regards the form of the text received as indicating not an imagined maturation away from spirit language. Yet it has tended to relegate a strong disjuncture between these texts and the world of contemporary hearers by often contending that the New Testament era brings such a disjunctive notion of the Spirit that had in no genuine fashion been experienced in the Old Testament period, and particularly the Former Prophets. However, once again, the Spirit of the Former Prophets seems far more in line with the Spirit in the Pentecostal experience that empowers, anoints, delivers, transforms, and testifies. All of this may be accurate despite that many within this quest belong to the Pentecostal and charismatic streams of the Church.

Both 'quests' have sought (in their own ways) the Spirit in the Former Prophets as in some sense outside of or behind the Former Prophets as those searching the hills and valleys – some further and some seemingly very near. Each has confessed the Spirit as they study the Former Prophets and yet seem to seek the Spirit at times by other means. Perhaps it is time we stop looking elsewhere for the Spirit in the Former Prophets and return to our first confession of the Spirit within the Pentecostal tradition's reading of the Former Prophets as already before us even as we mutually and reciprocally attend further to these words of the Spirit in our Spirit-filled communities. Such a reading proposal is offered in the following chapter that suggests a Pentecostal hermeneutic of the Former Prophets (chapter 2) before hearing the voices of early Pentecostal interpreters (chapter 3) and a close literary and theological reading of the texts of the Spirit in the Former Prophets (chapters 4-7) as a means of developing a constructive Pentecostal theology of the Spirit in the Former Prophets.

2

TOWARD A PENTECOSTAL HERMENEUTIC OF THE FORMER PROPHETS

Introduction

Much has already been written concerning the characteristics of Pentecostals both historical and contemporary that does not bear repeating but impacts what follows.[1] There is a growing corpus of Pentecostal scholarship working on the topic of Pentecostal hermeneutics in general and applied.[2] What is offered here is simply another voice

---

[1] V. Synan, *The Holiness-Pentecostal Movement in the United States* (Eerdmans: Grand Rapids, MI, 1971); W.J. Hollenweger, *The Pentecostals* (Peabody, MA: Hendrickson, 1988); H. Cox, *Fire From Heaven: The Rise of Pentecostal Spirituality and the Reshaping of Religion in the Twenty-First Century* (Reading, MA: Addison-Wesley, 1995); A. Anderson, *An Introduction to Pentecostalism: Global Charismatic Christianity* (Cambridge: Cambridge University Press, 2004); C.M. Robeck, *The Azusa Street Mission and Revival: The Birth of the Global Pentecostal Movement* (Nashville, TN: Thomas Nelson, 2006).

[2] An excellent edited compilation of fourteen articles previously published by the *Journal of Pentecostal Theology* on the topic of Pentecost hermeneutics which includes an introduction by the editor is L.R. Martin (ed.), *Pentecostal Hermeneutics: A Reader* (Leiden: Brill, 2013). The following indicates numerous monographs which cover this topic in various fashions and to varying degrees. R. Stronstad, *Spirit, Scripture and Theology: A Pentecostal Perspective* (Baguio City, Philippines: Asia Pacific Theological Seminary Press, 1995); L.R. McQueen, *Joel and the Spirit: The Cry of a Prophetic Hermeneutic* (Sheffield: Sheffield Academic Press, 1995; Cleveland, TN: CPT Press, 2009); K.J. Archer, *A Pentecostal Hermeneutic for the Twenty-First Century: Spirit, Scripture and Community* (JPTSup 28; Edinburgh: T & T Clark, 2004); R. Waddell, *The Spirit of the Book of Revelation* (JPTSup 30; Blandford Forum: Deo Pub,

added to the oeuvre of that movement from the earliest 'Bible Reading Method' to the triadic approach of contemporary Pentecostals. This movement is offered as entre to the methodology utilized in the interpretation of the Spirit in the Former Prophets in chapters four through seven following the history of effects offered by the study of the early Pentecostal periodicals in the immediate following chapter. The method utilized for this study functions to create a phenomenological experience[3] intended to call for Pentecostal expressions of a Pentecostal hermeneutic. The methodology is thus not simply presented but serves as an invitation to enter into the experience of Pentecostals as one both interpreting and being interpreted.[4] As such, the terms read(ing) and hear(ing) are used interchangeably throughout this proposal in order to highlight the activities of the community in each given context. They are not meant to be separable as acts as such by those seeking to be faithful interpreters. Reading, in this context, requires hearing what is written as text. Hearing happens both textually and extra-textually and implies faith-filled and faithful obedience as genuine hearing.[5]

Pentecostal Interpretations: The Sound of Many Voices

While there is no singular Pentecostal hermeneutic (nor a singular definition of 'Pentecostal'), and some still persist in questioning

---

2005); A. Yong, *Spirit-Word-Community: Theological Hermeneutics in Trinitarian Perspective* (Eugene, OR: Wipf & Stock, 2006); L.R. Martin, *The Unheard Voice of God: A Pentecostal Hearing of the Book of Judges* (JPTSup 32; Blandford Forum: Deo, 2008); B.T. Noel, *Pentecostal and Postmodern Hermeneutics: Comparisons and Contemporary Impact* (Eugene, OR: Wipf & Stock Pub, 2010); J. Grey, *Three's a Crowd: Pentecostalism, Hermeneutics, and the Old Testament* (Eugene, OR: Pickwick, 2011); C.E.W. Green, *Toward a Pentecostal Theology of the Lord's Supper*; L.W. Oliverio, *Theological Hermeneutics in the Classical Pentecostal Tradition A Typological Account* (Leiden: Brill, 2012); C.E.W. Green, *Sanctifying Interpretation: Vocation, Holiness, and Scripture* (Cleveland, TN: CPT Press, 2015); M.L. Archer, *'I Was in the Spirit on the Lord's Day'*.

   [3] I owe this insight to Chris Rouse (PhD seminar, Nov. 17, 2015).

   [4] Making reference to an uncited comment by G. Fee, Pentecostals are noted to 'exegete their experience' per S.R. Graham, '"Thus Saith the Lord"': Biblical Hermeneutics in the Early Pentecostal Movement', *Ex Auditu* 12 (1996), pp. 121-35 (128).

   [5] The emphasis upon the 'hearing' of the text in this fashion is used to great effect following the textual cues of Judges by L.R. Martin, *The Unheard Voice of God*.

whether there should be any, there are noticeable trends toward more clearly defined Pentecostal hermeneutics while still 'in the making'.[6] Perhaps this 'still in the making' is part and parcel of the Pentecostal's *sanctified/sanctifying* interpretation.[7] Claims to any form of Pentecostal hermeneutics must admit no 'claim to possess a pristine and qualitatively unique methodology'.[8] Instead, every hermeneutical approach (including those which might be called Pentecostal) is distinguished 'by the presuppositions on which they build, the questions that they privilege, the interpretive tools they prefer, and the texts to which they attend'.[9] Such a hermeneutical approach is perhaps properly always in the making as an improvisational performance of the Word by the Spirit within the community.

Several broad streams of historical development within the Pentecostal community's hermeneutics have been outlined elsewhere. V.-M. Kärkäinnen notes four broad movements: an 'Oral pre-reflexive stage', a trending toward a Fundamentalist and dispensational bent along with Evangelicalism, a 'quest for a distinctive pneumatic exegesis', and finally an 'Emerging post-modern' movement.[10]

The earliest stage was known for its 'populist hermeneutic'[11] that gave emphasis as often as possible to a literalizing of the text of Scripture and a Spirit-inspired interpretation. From the side of the early Pentecostals a positive self-claim about their hermeneutics noted they used what was termed the 'Bible Reading Method'.[12] This earliest strand of Pentecostal hermeneutics finds its many voices in the following chapter which is concerned with offering a *Wirkungsgeschichte* toward a Pentecostal reading of the Spirit in the Former Prophets. However, it should be noted that one primary contribution to the methodology proposed herein concerns the close literary

---

[6] V.-M. Kärkäinnen, 'Pentecostal Hermeneutics in the Making: On the Way from Fundamentalism to Postmodernism', *JEPTA* 18 (1998), pp. 76-115 (96).

[7] Green, *Sanctifying Interpretation*.

[8] S.A. Ellington, 'Locating Pentecostals at the Hermeneutical Round Table', *JPT* 22 (2013), pp. 206-25 (207).

[9] Ellington, 'Locating Pentecostals', p. 207.

[10] Kärkäinnen, 'Pentecostal Hermeneutics', p. 77.

[11] Graham, '"Thus Saith the Lord"', pp. 121-35.

[12] Archer, *A Pentecostal Hermeneutic*, pp. 99-127.

reading of the texts of Scripture which was notably also a part of the 'Bible Reading Method' of this early reading of Pentecostals.[13]

In the second and third hermeneutical movements, several proposals for hermeneutical approaches by Pentecostals for Pentecostals have been made that seem to borrow more heavily from traditional Evangelical notions of authorial intent for discerning meaning. G. Fee best represents this second approach as he argues for a Pentecostal hermeneutic which seeks authorial intent (divine and human), is Spirit-centered, and admits the tradition in which one reads the text. This methodology seems to belong within the broader 'Evangelical' tradition of interpretive methodologies.[14] It seems to fail to appreciate the experiential nature of Pentecostal hermeneutics and seems rooted in more consistently modernistic and positivistic ideas of Biblical interpretation.[15] Others have attempted to work out similar methodologies (the third movement), but with greater 'pneumatic' emphases in the interpretive processes that suggest the possibility that the Baptism in the Holy Spirit provides special interpretive insights, yet these do not seem to have been as widely accepted as Fee's.[16]

Of particular note is the triadic approach which seems to have arisen with the final so-called post-modern oriented movement.[17] This triadic approach is proposed as Spirit, Word,[18] and community.

---

[13] Archer, *A Pentecostal Hermeneutic*, pp. 221-23.

[14] G.D. Fee, *Gospel and Spirit: Issues in New Testament Hermeneutics* (Peabody, MA: Hendrickson, 1991); B.T. Noel, 'Gordon Fee and the Challenge to Pentecostal Hermeneutics: Thirty Years Later', *Pneuma* 26.1 (2004), pp. 60-80 (63).

[15] One notable early challenger of this methodological approach is offered by Stronstad, *Spirit, Scripture and Theology*.

[16] H.M. Ervin, 'Hermeneutics: A Pentecostal Option', *Pneuma* 3 (Fall 1981), pp. 11-25; T.B. Cargal, 'Beyond the Fundamentalist-Modernist Controversy: Pentecostals and Hermeneutics in a Postmodern Age', *Pneuma* 15.2 (Fall 1993), pp. 163-87; and F.L. Arrington, 'The Use of the Bible by Pentecostals', *Pneuma* 16.1 (1994), pp. 101-107. Ervin and Arrington are both specifically critiqued for an 'elitist' approach to Pentecostal hermeneutics by H.G. Purdy, *A Distinct Twenty-First Century Pentecostal Hermeneutic* (Eugene, OR: Wipf & Stock, 2015), pp. 111-12.

[17] Archer, *A Pentecostal Hermeneutic*; Noel, *Pentecostal and Postmodern Hermeneutics*; and Yong, *Spirit-Word-Community*.

[18] In place of 'Word' might be 'Scripture' following the language of Archer, *A Pentecostal Hermeneutic*. However, the preference for 'Word' has been chosen due to its greater ambiguity and more open-ended interpretive value.

This movement[19] may be best represented by the works of John Christopher Thomas,[20] Kenneth Archer,[21] and Amos Yong.[22] To call this movement 'post-modern' in orientation is only to recognize it shares numerous affinities with post-modernism over and against modernism. B.T. Noel has succinctly recounted this connection with regard to 'their rejection of the "hegemony of reason", openness to narratives, the role of community, and the essential function of experience in epistemology'.[23] This connection is not a wholesale embrace of post-modernity particularly as concerns the notion of the metanarrative. While post-modernism rejects any notion of a metanarrative, Pentecostals locate themselves within the metanarrative of salvation-history as encounter by the community in the Spirit-breathed Word.

Spirit

The Spirit belongs to the Lord, and the Spirit is Lord. The Spirit creates this community, giving it life and sharing its life. The Spirit speaks in and through the community and enables the community to hear that Word. It is the same Spirit which hovered over the waters of the great deep in the beginning. The same Spirit who empowered the saints of old to craft for, judge, deliver, and lead the community. This is the very Spirit that clothes champions to crush the enemies of tribal Israel and comes upon kings to lead the united people of Israel. This same Spirit sings through the strings of David before Saul and in the voices of the saints, singing with words they have not been

---

[19] The term 'movement' is used because of the numbers of Biblical scholars following suit in this methodology both published and forthcoming: L.R. Martin, *The Unheard Voice of God*; C.E.W. Green, *Sanctifying Interpretation*; M.L. Archer, '*I was in the Spirit on the Lord's Day*'; D. Johnson, *Pneumatic Discernment in the Apocalypse: An Intertextual and Pentecostal Exploration* (Cleveland, TN: CPT Press, 2018); and unpublished: K.R. Holley, J. Holley, and S.G. Schumacher.

[20] J.C. Thomas, 'Women, Pentecostalism, and the Bible: An Experiment in Pentecostal Hermeneutics', *JPT* 5 (1994), pp. 41-56; and J.C. Thomas and K.E. Alexander, '"And the Signs Are Following": Mark 16.9-20 – A Journey Into Pentecostal Hermeneutics', *JPT* 11.2 (2003), pp. 147-70.

[21] K.J. Archer, 'Pentecostal Hermeneutics: Retrospect and Prospect', *JPT* 8 (1996), pp. 63-81; *A Pentecostal Hermeneutic*; and 'Pentecostal Story: The Hermeneutical Filter for the Making of Meaning', *Pneuma* 26.1 (Spring 2004), pp. 36-59.

[22] Yong, *Spirit-Word-Community*.

[23] Noel, *Pentecostal and Postmodern Hermeneutics*, p. 9; Ellington, 'Locating Pentecostals', p. 208, also notes this connection of Noel's.

taught. This is the Spirit of the LORD who carries out the words of the prophets and is apportioned to each as needed. This is the same Spirit who richly indwells the community transforming the members for the work of redemption. This is Spirit that both breathes the Word and en-fleshes the Word for and in the community.

Word

This Word which was with God and is God, belongs also to the act and being of enscripturation where this Word finds testimony in Scripture: the Word of Scriptures and the Word of God. The Word, as Scriptures, offers the possibility of yet undiscovered meaning due to its open-endedness even within the canonical boundaries. It is thus a desirable feature of the written Word that is both functionally meta-narrative to the Community, but also supersedes the existence of any single community within a given socio-historical-cultural context. The Word offers the melody of the Spirit to be sung in the harmonies of the community.

This Word is both heard in Scripture and seen in heaven as the one who came down and is now seated at the right hand of the Father who will come again to judge the living and dead. This Word is both enscripturated and enfleshed. This Word is not simply a word spoken, but the Word speaking and answering.

The use of 'Word' in what occurs throughout this chapter is intentionally multifarious in order to allow for just such open-ended readings offered by such a Pentecostal hermeneutic. It is intentionally not to be conflated only with Scripture, though it could never be considered as independent of the revelation of God in Scripture. It is also not only to be heard with regard to the eternal Son, but to that Word which has been given to the community (Israel and the Church) as the Spirit has inspired and made alive within that community. This Word belongs to this pneumatic community, but more significantly this community belongs to this pneumatic Word.

Community

The call for the community to hear what the Spirit is saying is not simply a call for the extant community or bodily community, but for those who have gone before. It is a call to hear along with the confessions and creeds of the Church. It is a call to hear along with the voices of the fathers and mothers of the Church, and the prophets and scribes of Israel. It is a call to hear along with the majority world

Church. It is a call to hear along with the prophets and apostles, princes and paupers, the empowered and dis-empowered of the Church. And it is a call to hear along with the voices of the immediate congregation to which one belongs. This intentionally shifts 'the emphasis away from the individual hermeneut and her commitment to an acceptable and correctly applied method and place[s] primary emphasis upon the community as the spiritual cultural context in which interpretation takes place'.[24]

A need for the community's communal function in hearing what the Spirit says (Word) has been demonstrated in the early years of the Pentecostal movement. The Oneness Pentecostal's rejection of tradition (e.g. the role of the confessions, creeds, Church Fathers) – in place of a populist interpretative method of me, my Bible, and the Spirit – allowed for a failure to hear with the Church what the Spirit had been saying.[25] Instead, Oneness Pentecostals presupposed a rejection of community hermeneutics critically appreciated. The simplified Bible reading method of the early Pentecostals supposed one only needed the Scriptures and the Spirit experienced in testifying power to vouchsafe an interpretation. While this method can (and should) be appreciated for its emphasis upon the Spirit and the Word, it fails to address the function of the community in a fuller fashion. However, contemporary forms of Pentecostal hermeneutics specifically seek to hear (and share in) the voice of the communion of saints.

A Pentecostal interpretation functions as a part of the guide to the interpretive choices for this reading of the Former Prophets. It bears pointing out that such a Pentecostal interpretation is not 'an imposition of a theological system or confessional grid onto the biblical text', nor 'an imposition of a general hermeneutic or theory of interpretation onto the biblical text', that is, 'a form of merely historical, literary, or sociological criticism preoccupied with (respectively) the world "behind," "of," or "in front of" the biblical text'.[26] 'A viable hermeneutic must deal responsibly with the apostolic witness of

---

[24] Archer, *A Pentecostal Hermeneutic*, p. 213.

[25] Graham, '"Thus Saith the Lord"', pp. 128-33.

[26] K.J. Vanhoozer (ed.), *Theological Interpretation of the New Testament: A Book-by-Book Survey* (Grand Rapids, MI; London: Baker Academic; SPCK, 2008), pp. 14, 15.

Scripture in terms of an apostolic experience, and in continuity with the Church's apostolic traditions'.[27] It is this transformative interplay of reading the Word in the Spirit as the communion of saints that serves the Pentecostal hermeneut.[28] Thus, Scott Ellington proposes five accents which characterize Pentecostal interpretations. They are 'narrative rather than propositional', 'dynamic rather than static', 'experience-based', 'seek encounter more than understanding', and 'are pragmatic, emphasizing transformation and application'.[29] These accents speak to the Pentecostal expressions.

That Pentecostal interpretations are more narratival than propositional means that the reader is invited 'to create meaning' rather than seek for meaning via propositional statements and supposed universalizing principles.[30] The storied nature of the Word draws the community by the Spirit into itself wherein what was *that* is now *this* for the community. This entering into the story is not introduced by Pentecostals but seems to belong to the very stories of Scripture themselves which invite participation and experience and presuppose it (Deut. 5.2-3; 1 Cor. 11.23-28).[31] Indeed, Pentecostals 'prefer to interpret Scripture by encounter more than exegesis' and story aids that end.[32] Pentecostals

> understand there [to] be a continuity between written story (Scripture) and oral story (personal testimony). At the moment of fresh encounter with God, the distance between the two collapses, so that my story becomes part of my community's story, which is in turn part of the biblical story.[33]

---

[27] Ervin, 'Hermeneutics: A Pentecostal Option', p. 23.

[28] Vanhoozer, *Theological Interpretation of the New Testament*, pp. 18-22.

[29] Ellington, 'Locating Pentecostals', p. 209.

[30] Ellington, 'Locating Pentecostals', p. 211; K.J. Archer, *A Pentecostal Hermeneutic*, pp. 202, 205.

[31] Ellington, 'Locating Pentecostals', p. 211; 'History, Story, and Testimony: Locating Truth in a Pentecostal Hermeneutic', *Pneuma* 23.2 (Fall 2001), pp. 245-63; Grey, *Three's a Crowd*.

[32] A. Davies, 'What Does It Mean to Read the Bible as a Pentecostal?' in L.R. Martin, *Pentecostal Hermeneutics*, pp. 249-62 (254). This chapter was originally published in *JPT* 18.2 (2009), pp. 216-29.

[33] Ellington, 'Locating Pentecostals', p. 214.

Such experiences are the encounter with the Word whereby the Spirit transforms the community into ever sanctifying communion toward further experiences leading to consummation. Experience both precedes and follows the Pentecostal hermeneutic.[34]

In a manner perhaps fitting the Pentecostal context, the community sways to the singing and prayers, to the cadences of the preacher in the telling of Scripture, in decadent declarative testimonies in response. The movements seem almost random, but they are not. There is a rhythm, with pauses of silence and exclamations of exultation. The Pentecostal community moves as waves upon the sea carried by the unseen wind. The community interprets Scripture in like Pentecostal fashion. There is interpretive movement, holy burning, answering calls, tongues aflame, and grace abounding to each as the Spirit determines.

Pentecostal Interpreters and a Heart Aflame

One is not free to interpret as one pleases and think by doing so that they have offered anything to the text at hand. This would only be a monologue or a drowning out of the voices of the Word, Spirit, and Community. Instead, a necessary prerequisite has been suggested as the 'virtuous reader' or the 'primed reader'. The virtuous reader is one who is characterized by humility, wisdom, trust, love, and receptivity.[35] The primed reader is 'one who is provisionally aware of the pluri-vocal realm; attentive to formational mission; competent with the emergent language, words and backgrounds; and critically engaged with the history of fruitful and abusive reception'.[36] This makes for a reader who is given to reading the textures of the text

---

[34] The contention that experience both precedes and follows the Pentecostal hermeneutic is proposed by Stronstad, *Spirit, Scripture and Theology*, p. 57; also, Ellington, 'Locating Pentecostals', pp. 206-25 (215-7); Thomas, 'Women, Pentecostals and the Bible', pp. 41-56.

[35] R.S. Briggs, *The Virtuous Reader: Old Testament Narrative and Interpretive Virtue* (Grand Rapids, MI: Baker Academic, 2010).

[36] M.R. Malcom, 'Biblical Hermeneutics and Kerygmatic Responsibility', in S.E. Porter and M.R. Malcolm (eds.), *The Future of Biblical Interpretation: Responsible Plurality in Biblical Hermeneutics* (Downers Grove, IL: IVP Academic, 2013), pp. 71-84 (76).

and engaging them as active participant who is transformed in their reading of the text as a living word.

To these should be added the Pentecostal contribution of the *sanctified/sanctifying reader*.[37] Chris Green, following the trajectory of James K.A. Smith, proposes that interpretation 'is not a necessary evil forced on us by the Fall – nor is it overcome now or in the eschaton. Instead, interpretation belongs to human beingness as such, and so is perfected, not superseded, in Christ'.[38] Thus, the sanctified/sanctifying reader is fulfilling their vocation to be both sanctified and sanctifying. 'Viewing Scripture as an act of God's sanctification allows Christ's incarnation to be unique: the Word became flesh, not a text.'[39]

What of Pentecostal interpreters? Preparatory to a discussion of modes of understanding Pentecostal interpretations is a need to describe the ideal Pentecostal interpreters. As practitioners of a type of reader-response hermeneutic, Pentecostals 'emphasize the power of the text to evoke a particular response in the reader, a response which is encoded in the rhetoric, so that the form of the text itself creates its ideal reader'.[40] Indeed, it is a constant reminder that '[r]eading is a dangerous activity. It can change our perspective, stir our emotions, and provoke us to action.'[41] The act of such a reading is 'co-operative' whereby the reader is not passive, but active in the process of creating meaning by being

> drawn into the adventure not only by what the text spells out but also by what it withholds ... to fill in the gaps, to infer what is not given, at least provisionally, until what is unclear at first is clarified

---

[37] Green, *Sanctifying Interpretation*. Though Green does not actually use this specific term, his overall project is built upon the very notion and seeks to follow the trajectory which he laid in this volume.

[38] Green, *Sanctifying Interpretation*, p. 41. In this passage he is engaging J.K.A. Smith, *The Fall of Interpretation* (2nd edn; Grand Rapids, MI: Baker Academic, 2012).

[39] D.P. Lowenberg, 'Reading the Bible with Help from the African Pentecostals: Allowing Africa to Inform our Western Hermeneutics', *Encounter: Journal for Pentecostal Ministry* 9 (Summer 2012), pp. 1-33 (15) [accessed as a PDF at http://www.agts.edu/encounter/articles/2012summer/Lowenberg1_Aug12.pdf on October 15, 2015].

[40] M. Davies, 'Literary Criticism', in R.J. Coggins and J.L. Houlden (eds.), *A Dictionary of Biblical Interpretation* (London: SCM, 1990), pp. 402-405 (404).

[41] M. Davies, 'Reader-Response Criticism', in R.J. Coggins and J.L. Houlden (eds.), *A Dictionary of Biblical Interpretation* (London: SCM, 1990), pp. 578-80 (578).

by what follows. This creation of meaning may change the reader in the process, because literature in the Bible does not simply tell us about the spirit of the past age or its social conditions, but allows us to experience them.[42]

More than this, the Scriptures (illuminated by the Spirit) invite and even command the readers to experience that of which it speaks. This 'ideal reader',[43] as the ideal Pentecostal reader, is both shaped by, and shaping the reading of the text in the pneumatic community in order to 'bring the text to life'.[44] It may be suggested that such an ideal is best found in the core confession and all-encompassing vision of early Pentecostals: Jesus saves, (sanctifies), baptizes in the Spirit, heals, and is the soon coming king.[45]

Pentecostal interpreters are those in the grip of Jesus' transforming redemptive work. Jesus fills their vision and thus their readings of Scripture. This transforming redemptive work of Jesus extends to the manner in which Scripture is read, or better, experienced. This experience of Jesus in turn is the mode through which Pentecostals interpret the Scriptures. Salvation is experienced in the appropriation and confession of Jesus as Lord. This confession being a Spirit empowered confession aligning with the testimony of Scripture and only experienced by the wooing of the Spirit as the Spirit of the Word.

Pentecostal Interpretations as Call and Response

The Pentecostal community is known to worship, preach, sing, and testify, indeed, to *live*, as in a continuous cycle of call and response.

---

[42] Davies, 'Reader-Response Criticism', pp. 578-80 (578).

[43] Davies, 'Reader-Response Criticism', pp. 578-80 (578).

[44] E.W. Davies, *Biblical Criticism: A Guide for the Perplexed* (London: Bloomsbury, 2013), pp. 4, 14.

[45] While it may be granted that 'sanctifies' belongs specifically to the Wesleyan stream of Pentecostalism and not to the so-called 'Finished Work' stream, it seems such is fitting for the emphasis early in Pentecostal development upon sanctification which still stands as a specific hallmark of Finished Work fellowships such as the Assemblies of God and the Pentecostal Assemblies of Canada. Kärkäinnen has specifically noted that this four/fivefold gospel message about Jesus was central to early Pentecostal interpretations, 'Pentecostal Hermeneutics in the Making', p. 79.

The community responds to the call of the Spirit whereby the community calls upon the Spirit who also responds. The Spirit empowered and enlivened community speaks and answers as those formed and transformed by the Word. The Word breathes; the Spirit speaks; the community lives. This interplay of response and call belongs to the essence of this community. This same conversing is that discourse of Scripture in the minds, mouths, and lives of the Pentecostal community.[46]

The texts of Scripture seem to bear a surplus of meaning which exceed any perceived original human authorial intent. Meaning is not an unbounded communal determination any more than it is simply an authorial determinative boundary. Meaning belongs to the engaging correspondences of the authors, texts, and readers. The notion of a single determinate meaning is simply not feasible given the impossibility of totally recovering the original authorial intent. A multiplicity of meanings or polyphony of readings of these texts is inherent to the textual nature of texts as text. They have been preserved in a fashion by which readers will necessarily differ beyond the original ideal and/or real reader. These voices belong to the call and response of the community: authors, texts, and readers.

There is significant interplay of meaning to be found in this call and response of the Pentecostal community. This dramatic interplay is not about 'a set of rules we must follow' but about learning the pneumatic 'repertoire or roles we enact'.[47] The Spirit is present in both the reader of the text and the hearers, in both the authors and the recipients (to each of these: past, present and future). The dynamic call and response hermeneutic of a Pentecostal gathering offers treasures both old and new: voices from ages past, those responding in the present, and the prophetic orientation of those being made into that future idealized pneumatic community. This orientation does not consider itself free from a close reading of the Word, but instead is highly attentive to the ebb and flow of the text. Words within the Word are given great significance and become new

---

[46] McQueen, *Joel and the Spirit*, p. 6.

[47] A.K.M. Adam, 'Poaching on Zion: Biblical Theology as Signifying Practice', in A.K.M. Adam, Stephen E. Fowl, Kevin J. Vanhoozer, and Francis Watson, *Reading Scripture with the Church: Toward a Hermeneutic for Theological Interpretation* (Grand Rapids, MI: Baker Academic, 2006), pp. 17-34 (33). See also Porter and Malcolm, *The Future of Biblical Interpretation*.

opportunities to respond in fresh ways to the work of the Spirit in the community. This careful reading of the text of Scripture belongs to the Pentecostal experience of the text as Word to be discerned and lived by the Spirit.

Pentecostal Interpretations as Tongue-Speech

A Pentecostal approach suggests that interpretations may not belong only to the construct of the 'plain sense' of a text since the Pentecostal community already shows a penchant for appreciating tongue-speech as holding the potential for self-benefit apart from the clear interpretive act of the community (1 Cor. 14.2-18). Meaning is therefore not tied to individual comprehension and yet may be experienced to great benefit by the speaker/hearer in the absence of public tongue-speech. However, in the public speaking of tongues, interpretation must be practiced as a public event to give benefit to all through clear expression of meaning. This place for tongue-speech (private and public) functions well as a type for Pentecostal interpretations: there is place and time for private expressions and experiences of the Scriptures which may benefit the individual greatly, but need more determinate meanings for communal appropriations. It could be argued that Pentecostal 'interpretation and proclamation of Scripture have little to do with intellectual comprehension and all to do with divine self-revelation'.[48] Interpretation for the community can only, thus, allow for the multiple voices of interpretive meaning that edify the whole and are not permitted only to edify the individual speaker who may well enough benefit from the meaning inherent in their experience of the text.

The Pentecostal approach to interpretation seems inherently to involve polyphony of interpretive possibilities. This does not mean, however, that the polyphony is discordant.[49] Pentecostals might say with Hans Urs von Balthasar, 'Truth is symphonic'.[50] In fact, it can (and should) find its basis in the *cantus firmus* of God's self-revelation where they might function in interdependence. Similarly, D.

---

[48] A. Davies, 'What Does It Mean to Read the Bible as a Pentecostal?', *JPT* 18.2 (2009), pp. 216-29.

[49] Porter and Malcolm, *The Future of Biblical Interpretation*, p. 10.

[50] Hans Urs von Balthasar, *Truth Is Symphonic* (trans. Graham Harrison; San Francisco: Ignatius, 1987).

Bonhoeffer, speaking of this issue of polyphony wrote to his friend E. Bethge to 'let the *cantus firmus* be heard clearly … only then will it sound complete and full, and the counterpoint will always know that it is being carried and can't get out of tune or be cut adrift, while remaining itself and complete in itself. Only this polyphony gives your life wholeness, and you know that no disaster can befall you as long as the *cantus firmus* continues'.[51] For Bonhoeffer the *cantus firmus* was pure love for God (that secondarily was love for humankind).

Bonhoeffer's trajectory is shared by the Pentecostal community's interpretation of the Word by the Spirit as centered in 'holy love'. This *cantus firmus* is functionally the Pentecostal community's sanctifying improvisational love of the Word in and through the Spirit. Wherever the tongues may lead is bounded by the community's love in pneumatic discernment of the Word. A potent (and Pentecostally-fitting) image of this creative and dialectical interplay might be found in the ways in which a Black Gospel choir offers fresh voices to an overall movement in impassioned song.[52] The ebb and flow of their cadences and voices, the spontaneous and the planned, press the boundaries of the *cantus firmus*, but are called back again and again to this guiding voice. Tongues (and their interpretations) may be many, but divine love remains as centering melody.[53]

---

[51] D. Bonhoeffer, *Letters and Papers from Prison* (Dietrich Bonhoeffer Works 8; English ed. J.W. De Gruchy; Minneapolis, MN: Fortress, 2010), p. 394. The musical term *cantus firmus* is not italicized in this translation of Bonhoeffer.

[52] For the image of the Black Gospel choir, see J.C. Thomas, '"What the Spirit Is Saying to the Church" – The Testimony of a Pentecostal in New Testament Studies', in K.L Spawn and A.T. Wright (eds), *Spirit and Scripture: Exploring a Pneumatic Hermeneutic* (London: T & T Clark, 2012), pp. 115-29 [122-28].

[53] A. Yong proposes a renewed emphasis upon 'divine love' may in fact be the key to the renewal of Pentecostalism, 'What's Love Got to Do with It?: The Sociology of Godly Love and the Renewal of Modern Pentecostalism', *JPT* 21 (2012), pp. 113-134. He develops this more thoroughly in *Spirit of Love: A Trinitarian Theology of Grace* (Waco, TX: Baylor University, 2012). For several treatments of the early Pentecostal appreciation of divine or holy love, see also K.E. Alexander, 'Boundless Love Divine: A Re-evaluation of Early Understandings of the Experience of Spirit Baptism', pp. 145-70 in S.J. Land, R.D. Moore, and J.C. Thomas (eds.), *Passover, Pentecost, and Parousia: Studies in Celebration of the Life and Ministry of R. Hollis Gause* (JPTSup 35; Blandford Forum, UK: Deo, 2010); and D.T. Irvin, '"Drawing All Together in One Bond of Love": The Ecumenical Vision of William J Seymour and the Azusa Street Revival', *JPT* 6 (1995), pp. 25-53.

Pentecostal Interpretations as *Charismata*

The exercise of the *charismata* is imperative to the life of the community endowed by the Spirit for just such a hearing and speaking of the Word. The community does not simply regard a historical critical approach as sufficient for hearing what the Spirit is saying. Indeed, this community seems likely to consider such a strictly historical reading (a reading behind the text) as potentially only 'another form of cessationism' because it muted other voices.[54] The historical elements are not disregarded, but neither are they allowed to speak with full authority, because the Pentecostal community seeks to read the text of Scripture in its literary, theological, and canonical fullness.

The richness of interpretive possibilities is offered up as various gifts given by the Spirit for the community's movement toward completion but is not that completion itself. The invitation to 'create meaning'[55] is engendered by such a plethora of diverse gifts as given by the Spirit in a move together toward the *telos* of the Word. This diversity of interpretations is both weakness and strength. Its weakness is the lack of objectivity and thus the necessarily tentative nature of interpretations even when affirmed. However, the strength of this is evident in humility and charity shared within and by the Spirit-ed community. It calls for the community to embrace those given different interpretations, but not to do so without also exercising discernment:[56] does this interpretation encourage, rebuke, and edify in love? Does this interpretation resonate with the voice of the Spirit heard in the Word? The community cannot simply mute such voices but must exercise every gift of discernment and edification … all the while seeking the best … seeking what will endure all things.

---

[54] Lowenberg, 'Reading the Bible', pp. 1-33 (16).

[55] Archer, *A Pentecostal Hermeneutic*, p. 205.

[56] As an example of just such a notion of the interplay of the community, Spirit, and Word, see Thomas, 'Women, Pentecostalism and the Bible', pp. 81-94 in L.R. Martin (ed.), *Pentecostal Hermeneutics: A Reader* (Leiden: Brill, 2013). This was originally published in *JPT* 5 (1994), pp. 41-56.

Moving Together

As a Pentecostal in a Pentecostal community, hermeneutics is practiced together with those pneumatically present. Our mutual edification 'depends on our reading Scripture together, in conjunction with our lives of discipleship and worship. By reading the word together, by responding to the word together, by conversing about the word together, we encounter and embody at least a beginning measure of the richness that arises when different servants of the same word practice together'.[57] This hermeneutic of Spirit, Word, and community guides the following interpretation of the Spirit in the Former Prophets through the experience of holy burning, answering calls, tongues aflame, and grace abounding to each as the Spirit determines.

Setting the Tone: A Narrative Approach to the Former Prophets

Allowing the voices to be heard and to add to them seems to warrant a narrative approach to the Word wherein the Spirit within both Word and community come together in the hermeneutical task. 'A narrative method allows for the dialectic interaction of the text and reader in the negotiation of meaning'.[58] Of particular significance is the narrative nature of the Former Prophets and thus the even more fitting narrative approach of the Pentecostal community to hear and experience this text as the story which enters them and which they find themselves entering.[59]

First, this narrative approach will read the texts of the Former Prophets through the lens of the earliest Pentecostal periodicals as a *Wirkungsgeschichte* in order to discern within the historic Pentecostal community in which these texts of the Former Prophets were read and experienced and thus may also be reread in contemporary Pentecostal settings. This further experience of the Spirit texts in the Former Prophets by the early Pentecostals will contribute to the

---

[57] Adam, 'Poaching on Zion', p. 33.

[58] Archer, *A Pentecostal Hermeneutic*, p. 226. These several key orientations are drawn from the ideas offered by K. Archer as helpful for just such a Pentecostal hermeneutic, pp. 212-60.

[59] Ellington, 'Locating Pentecostals', p. 209.

narrative approach via a critical (though charitable) reading of the many voices of the formative years (up to 1920) of Pentecostalism. It is imperative that the Pentecostal community hear the many voices of our forebears who continue to speak by the Spirit through their own experiential hearing of the Word without simply co-opting their approach to interpretation, yet critically engaging it toward a fuller Pentecostal interpretation leading to formation and transformation of the hearing community.

Regarding the narrative approach there are several key orientations to reading the Former Prophets in light of the foregoing hermeneutical movements: (1) a close literary reading, (2) a surplus of interpretive possibilities, and (3) transformative experience of the text. The chapters concerned with interpretation of the Scriptures will offer a close reading of the text listening to the genre as it presents itself and allowing it to be interpreted and to interpret the hearing community. This reading is intended to invite the reader to participate and engage the text at multiple levels and to indwell and experience the Spirit both in the interpretation and in being interpreted. Arguably these narrative texts invite such a participatory function for the community.[60]

Second, this narrative approach will also give careful attention to overall and specific narrative contours of the Former Prophets.[61] In the midst of many voices there are still voices which guide one to remain faithful to the Word and these are best discerned in a close reading of the text that is attuned to the narratorial markers. The Spirit is intentionally heard with the most clarion voice in the voice of the narrator which will become the primary voice to be heard and enjoined in the community functioning as a sort of melody being joined by the many gifts of Spirit-ed harmony to produce a literary and theological Pentecostal hearing of the texts of the Spirit in the Former Prophets. Careful attention will be paid to hearing the voice

---

[60] P.E. Satterthwaite, '6. Narrative Criticism: The Theological Implications of Narrative Techniques', in W.A. VanGemeren (Gen. Ed.), *NIDOTTE* (5 vol.; Grand Rapids, MI: Zondervan, 1997), I, pp. 125-33 (132).

[61] On the function of the narrator as a reliable voice, see R. Alter, *The Art of Biblical Narrative* (New York: Basic Books, 1981), pp. 155-77; M. Sternberg, *The Poetics of Biblical Narrative: Ideological Literature and the Drama of Reading* (Indiana Studies in Biblical Literature; Bloomington, IN: Indiana University, 1999), pp. 84-99; and Satterthwaite, '6. Narrative Criticism', p. 129.

of the narrator as guiding the reading of the narrative flow for such literary markers as characterizations, repetitions, contrasts, ambiguities, and persuasions. While the narrator's voice offers a primary reading for the Pentecostal community it is intended as something like a melody that permits numerous potential harmonies for the hearing community as interpretive possibilities of creative meaning.

Third, this narrative approach is enjoined as a participatory event via interplay of text and reader. As such, this reading of the Former Prophets flows from and enjoins an experience of the Spirit empowering leaders to gather and stand for the community for victory over all that might destroy that community and creating opportunity for life to flourish according to the word of the Lord (like for the judges). This reading evokes both transformation of the Spirit endowed and the challenge of abiding in that same Spirit as provocative prophetic voices offering overcoming songs to cast out troubles and exalt the anointed king (like for Saul and David). This reading calls for discernment in the prophetic community to hear aright the word of the Spirit (like for Micaiah). This reading endows with the double-portioned Spirit of son-ship that the word might advance in power within the community of God's people as testimony of the abiding presence of the faithful One (like for Elijah and Elisha). Thus, I would echo the words of Lee Roy Martin: 'My goal as a Pentecostal reader is to seek for the theological message of the text, to be confronted by it, and then to be conformed to it'.[62]

The Texts Enjoined

Not every text mentioning רוח offers the same engagement for this study. The guiding element for inclusion is the textual connection to Yahweh (or God) suggesting this as the personal Spirit of Yahweh/God even if a troubling one. This means numerous texts lay outside of this study's scope for various reasons such as a proposed (1) meteorological function (2 Sam. 22.11; 1 Kgs 17.45; 19.11; and 2 Kgs 3.17); (2) anthropological function (Josh. 2.11; 5.1; Judg. 8.3;

---

[62] Martin, *The Unheard Voice of God*, p. 62.

15.19; 1 Sam. 1.15; 15.19; 30.12; and 1 Kgs 10.5); or (3) attitudinal function (Judg. 9.23; and 2 Kgs 19.7).[63]

The texts which are enjoined in this study are: Judg. 3.10 (Othniel); 6.34 (Gideon); 11.29 (Jephthah); 13.25; 14.6, 19; 15.14 (Samson); 1 Sam. 10.6, 10; 11.6; 16.14-16, 23; 18.10; 19.9, 20 (Saul); 16.13; 2 Sam. 23.2 (David); 1 Kgs 22.21-24 (Micaiah); and 2 Kgs 2.9, 15-16 (Elijah and Elisha). The Pentecostal narrative approach above informs the readings offered in chapter four (the judges), five (Saul and David), six (Micaiah), and seven (Elijah and Elisha) respectively. However, this Pentecostal reading is also informed by the voices of the early Pentecostals in chapter three in the ways in which they heard the Spirit in these same texts toward chapter eight's constructive Pentecostal theology of the Spirit in the Former Prophets.

A Constructive Journey

Chapter eight carries forward the hermeneutical approach of Spirit, Word, and community through literary and theological movements of the Spirit texts of the Former Prophets. Functions of the Spirit are drawn from the exegetical chapters (four through seven) and separated by the groupings of these chapters to provide literary-theological functions in order to orient the study toward the Pentecostal theology of the Spirit in the Former Prophets. This facilitates the Pentecostal theological engagement for hearing and responding to these texts of the Former Prophets. Melissa Archer has carried out a similar methodology in her work on a Pentecostal hearing of worship in the Apocalypse.[64]

The narratological approach to the Former Prophets that is offered in chapters four through seven provides the basis for the theological overtures concerning the Spirit in chapter eight. Various categories are offered which are drawn from the narratological readings and following the chapter headings of four through seven: The

---

[63] Block, 'Empowered by the Spirit of God', p. 61. Block provides a helpful chart for the numerous categories and sub-categories he proposes. Judges 9.23 is questionable as to its exclusion from this study given that the spirit is attributed to God. I have chosen to exclude it (against Block's own proposal) as it is best read as an 'attitude' or 'disposition' than the more personal qualities that might be noted in the texts included in this thesis.

[64] Archer, *'I Was in the Spirit on the Lord's Day'*, pp. 61-66.

Liberating Spirit, Strings of the Spirit, Discerning the Spirit, and the Double Portion Spirit. These provide a broad framework of overtures for both allowing the various narrative contexts to frame the functions of the Spirit as well as to intersect from one narrative context to the others since many of the functions of the Spirit are shared across the narratives of the Former Prophets.

These theological overtures of the first part of chapter eight then find resonance in the Pentecostal hearing which is offered via Pentecostal theological categories of construction in relation to the Spirit: abiding, purity, baptism, power, music, anointing, and the Lord Jesus Christ. This second movement of chapter eight offers a further harmony with the narratological readings from chapters four through seven. This functions to provide movement toward how Pentecostals might both hear and respond to the Spirit in the Former Prophets in ways that are mutually constructive.

3

A HISTORY OF EFFECTS OF THE SPIRIT IN THE FORMER PROPHETS IN EARLY PENTECOSTAL PERIODICAL LITERATURE

Introduction

The former chapter concerned with offering a Pentecostal hermeneutic of the Spirit in the Former Prophets draws upon the way in which Pentecostals have tended to understand their interpretation of Scriptures as text and experience intersecting and engaging one another. This hermeneutic is evident in the ways the early Pentecostals themselves experienced the very texts they were interpreting and found insights and affirmations for, along with critiques of, their experiential interpretations. The text was both interpreted by and interpreting these early Pentecostals.

As such, the following history of effects (*Wirkungsgeschichte*) of the early Pentecostal periodical literature (1906-1920) offers insight into early Pentecostal interpretations of the explicit Spirit texts of the Former Prophets (which are engaged in chapters 4-7 that follow). These insights illuminate the many ways that these biblical texts may be brought to bear on Pentecostal pneumatology, even if primarily with regard to function rather than ontology. Taking note of the insight of W.J. Hollenweger, followed shortly thereafter by S. Land, the first ten years of Pentecostalism reflects the 'heart' of Pentecostalism.[1] These early years provide a vision of spirituality that is not offered here simply to be fossilized but to be critically engaged by contemporary Pentecostalism and appropriated as providing a trajectory for a constructive Pentecostal theology of the Spirit in the Former Prophets.

A number of works have followed this insight about the place of early Pentecostalism as central to the development of a Pentecostal identity. Some of these have combined it with the methodological proposal of U. Luz's *Wirkungsgeschichte* that traces the effects which a particular piece of literature has had on certain readers as an avenue for a reading methodology.[2] This combining of the insight of Hollenweger and the methodological contribution of Luz has led a number of writers (particularly those influenced by work of J.C. Thomas)[3] to carry out their own practice of a *Wirkungsgeschichte* of the early Pentecostal literature and its potential for contributing to contemporary theologies within the broad tent of Pentecostalism.[4] The ways in which the early Pentecostals heard the Spirit in the Former Prophets offers a window into influential ways in which the Spirit might still be heard in the Pentecostal practice and experience of these texts. At the very least it offers an orientation toward the ways in which early Pentecostals made use of such texts as part of their overall hermeneutic that drew upon experience through reading and reading through experience.

In order to assess the contributions of the early Pentecostals, the following nine series of periodicals which are represented within this study include *The Apostolic Faith* (AF), *The Bridal Call* (BC), *The Bridegroom's Messenger* (TBM), *The Church of God Evangel* (CGE), *The Latter*

---

[1] Hollenweger, *The Pentecostals*, p. 551; and S.J. Land, *Pentecostal Spirituality: A Passion for the Kingdom* (JPTSup 1; Sheffield: Sheffield Academic Press, 1993; Cleveland, TN: CPT Press, 2010), p. 47. Citations follow the pagination of the Sheffield publication.

[2] U. Luz, *Matthew in History: Interpretation, Influence, and Effects* (Minneapolis: Fortress, 1994).

[3] Thomas and Alexander, "'And the Signs Are Following'", pp. 147-70; and J.C. Thomas, 'Healing in the Atonement: A Johannine Perspective', in *The Spirit of the New Testament* (Blandford Forum: Deo, 2005), pp. 175-89.

[4] Alexander, *Pentecostal Healing*; Green, *Toward a Pentecostal Theology of the Lord's Supper*, pp. 74-181; Bryant, *Spirit Christology in the Christian Tradition*, pp. 464-508; and Archer, *'I Was in the Spirit on the Lord's Day'*, pp. 68-118. All of these monographs were originally PhD theses under the supervision of J.C. Thomas.

Rain Evangel (LRE), *The Pentecostal Holiness Advocate* (PHA), *The Pente-cost* (TP), *The Pentecostal Evangel* (PE; also called *The Christian Evangel* CE* and *The Weekly Evangel* WE), and *Word and Witness* (WW). Sadly, the extant copies of *Pentecostal Testimony* (1909-1912; edited by W.H. Durham), *The Pentecostal Herald* (1915-1920; edited by G.C. Brinkman of Chicago), and *The Whole Truth* (1911; edited by J. Bowe and serving as the periodical of the Church of God in Christ) did not contain references pertinent to the Spirit in the Former Prophets and thus were not included in this study. Also, it should be noted that only those texts which were relevant to the predetermined Spirit texts in the Former Prophets were examined in this study.

The following offers a brief introduction to each of these journals and provides some sense of context for understanding them better. *The Apostolic Faith* was published by the Azusa Street Mission and pri-marily edited by W.J. Seymour between September 1906 and May 1908. *The Bridal Call* was a monthly periodical edited by A. Semple McPherson between the pertinent dates of June 1917 and December 1920. It eventually became the official publication of the Interna-tional Church of the Foursquare Gospel. *The Bridegroom's Messenger* was published between the pertinent dates of October 1907 and No-vember 1920. It was primarily edited by E.A. Sexton. *The Church of God Evangel* entails the earlier *The Evening Light and Church of God Evan-gel*. This weekly serial was published between the pertinent dates of March 1910 and December 1920 with the primary editor being A.J. Tomlinson and functioning as the official publication of the Church of God in Cleveland, TN. *The Latter Rain Evangel* was a monthly pe-riodical published at The Stone Church in Chicago between the per-tinent dates of October 1908 and December 1920. It was edited by the pastor of Stone Church: W.H. Piper. *The Pentecostal Holiness Advo-cate* was published as a weekly between the pertinent dates of May 1917 and December 1920 with the primary editor as G.F. Taylor and being the official publication of the Pentecostal Holiness Church. *The Pentecost* was a monthly publication between the pertinent dates of August 1908 and December 1910. It was primarily edited by J.R. Flower and A.S. Copley. *TP* was initially published in Indianapolis, but quickly moved to Kansas City, MO. The Pentecostal Evangel went through several name changes over its existence. This entails the variant names of this weekly periodical *The Christian Evangel* (*CE*; between the dates of July 1913 and March 6, 1915, and again from

June 1, 1918 until October 4, 1919) and *The Weekly Evangel* (*WE*; between the dates of March 13, 1915 and May 18, 1918). It was named *The Pentecostal Evangel* for the pertinent dates from October 19, 1919 until December 1920. The primary editors over these years were J. Roswell Flower and E.N. Bell. Initially this publication was part of the Gibeah Bible School in Plainfield, IN, under the auspices of Flower until the formation of the Assemblies of God in 1914 at which point E.N. Bell's weekly periodical, *Word and Witness*, and *PE* were both regarded as official periodicals of the Assemblies of God. Being moved to Findlay, OH, the two publications were merged into *The Christian Evangel* beginning in 1916. Finally, *Word and Witness* was a monthly publication whose extant copies range from August 1912 until December 1915 when it was merged with *PE* as the only official periodical of the Assemblies of God. It was primarily edited by E.N. Bell and functioned as a periodical of the Church of God in Christ until the formation of the AG in April 1914.

The years 1906-1920 were selected due to their significance in the founding of Pentecostalism within the U.S. context and also that of numerous Pentecostal fellowships in the U.S., and the concomitant influence upon future generations through their interpretations of Scripture. The choice of an end-date of 1920 offers a more comprehensive exposure to these early periodicals, beyond Hollenweger's first ten years, in order to offer a further engagement with the development of early Pentecostal thought from earlier idealisms through the turbulence of theological debates and the repercussions of their context post-World War One. The intention of this reading methodology is that this might further elucidate a constructive Pentecostal theology of the Spirit in the Former Prophets that critically engages these early Pentecostal readings.

An early influential editor of one of these Pentecostal periodicals, S.H. Frodsham, notes a pertinent reflection utilizing the Former Prophets as a framework of the Pentecostal outpouring with specific regard to the 'New Issue'[5] which confronted the Fourth General Council of the Assemblies of God (1916) meeting in St. Louis:

---

[5] The 'New Issue' pertained to the nature of God and the question of Trinitarian ontology versus Oneness ontology. With regard to the beliefs of Oneness Pentecostals and their history, see D. Reed, *'In the Name of Jesus': The History and Beliefs of Oneness Pentecostals* (JPTSup 31; Blandford Forum: Deo, 2008).

When this Pentecostal Revival commenced it seemed to many of us that we were being led by our Joshua out from the wilderness, over the Jordan, into the promised land. But after a few years there has been a tendency in this movement to come out of the experiences of the book of Joshua into those of the book of Judges where we read, 'Everyone did that which was right in his own eyes.' This new spirit has crept in and brought shipwreck and havoc in many directions. Like Samuel of old, the Council has endeavored to bring a spirit of unity into the ranks of spiritual Israel, and although we are troubled by an occasional Saul, we are fixing our spiritual vision on the coming of our David, yea, the coming of the great David's greater Son, and our one desire is that His will shall be done in all things, and we know it is His will that we shall all be one.[6]

The spiritual journey noted by Frodsham following the books of the Former Prophets picks up the Christocentric nature of the early Pentecostal interpretations that bears connections to the Pentecostal full-gospel message: Jesus saves, sanctifies, baptizes in the Spirit, heals, and is soon coming King. The language of 'spirit' which plays a role in this process is noted in both positive and negative fashion as can be witnessed below in the readings of the early periodicals. What follows in the review of the periodicals is arranged thematically according to the canonical texts that they are engaging which are noted to include accounts of the 'Spirit'.[7] The canonical ordering is developed in the next four chapters of this volume (Ch. 4: 'The Liberating Spirit'; Ch. 5: 'The Strings of the Spirit'; Ch. 6: 'Discerning the Spirit'; and Ch. 7: 'The Double Portion Spirit') where specific literary and theological interpretations are offered in readings of the Spirit texts of the Former Prophets.

---

[6] S.H. Frodsham, 'Notes from an Eyewitness at the General Council', *WE* 161 (Oct. 21, 1916), pp. 4-5 (4).

[7] Micaiah is placed before Elijah/Elisha due to the Spirit text for Elijah/Elisha occurring in 2 Kings 2 and Micaiah in 1 Kings 22.

Judges

The Book of Judges is stated to offer 'an imperative lesson ... for Pentecostal people' to have no leader in times of peace and addresses those who do 'not constantly recognize the presence of God'.[8] This 'lesson' demonstrates the manner in which early Pentecostals learned from the Book of Judges how to maintain the life and power of the Spirit in their lives in order to enjoy the ever abounding blessings of God and His divine love.

Thus, like Acsah who asked her father Caleb for 'a blessing' and 'springs of water' so must those who 'have received the outpouring of the Holy Spirit' not think that they 'have exhausted the divine supply of water' of this 'Latter Rain'.[9] Like the Spirit clothing Gideon in Judg. 6.34, one sister in 1909 testifies to experiencing divine love in the Spirit when the 'Spirit clothed Himself with me that hour!'[10] Another testimony notes that it was by the Spirit that Gideon was 'equipped ... for leadership and conflict'.[11] Z.R. Thomas (citing Judg. 21.21-23) praises God 'that when the Spirit of God gets into our feet to make us dance we can dance with joy and with all our might too, praise his name. And see and behold if the daughter, [sic] of Shiloh come out to dance'.[12]

Samson

The likeness to Samson is present in numerous texts indicative of the experience of overcoming power enabling the early Pentecostal witness to advance. By the Spirit, Samson was 'anointed' with 'supernatural power'.[13] T.B. Barratt, a Methodist minister from Norway, received his baptism in the Holy Spirit after many days of earnest seeking. He described the endless hours of praying and singing in various

---

[8] A.P. Collins, 'Pentecostal Bible Course: Lesson 8, Judges', *WE* 175 (Feb. 3, 1917), p. 13.

[9] A.R. Flower, 'Daily Portion from the King's Bounty', *WE* 147 (July 8, 1916), p. 9.

[10] Miss E. Sisson, 'The Holy Ghost and Fire: Some Inspiring Experiences', *LRE* 1.8 (May 1909), pp. 6-10 (8). She improperly gives the citation as chapter five of Judges.

[11] E.M. Stanton, 'The Holy Spirit', *TBM* 10.190 (Jan. 1, 1917), p. 4.

[12] Z.R. Thomas, 'Operations of the Holy Spirit', *CGE* 5.24 (June 13, 1914), pp. 5, 8 (5).

[13] Stanton, 'The Holy Spirit', p. 4.

tongues and that this made him feel as 'strong as a lion' and that he knew 'now where ... Sampson [sic] got [his] strength from'[14] and this was confirmed for him 'by personal experience'.[15] S.C. Perry contends that trials must await those who follow the Lord 'in the last days' and to 'take new courage and press toward the great glory which seems so near to be revealed,' such as when Samson was empowered to overcome the lion.[16] H.L. Faulkner, a missionary to China testified on November 2, 1913, that when leaders came to throw he and his Pentecostal work out of the city, '[It] seemed supernatural power came upon me and I felt like Sampson [sic]'.[17]

Thus, Samson can serve as a type of Christ Jesus who, by the Spirit, better fulfills the role to deliver the people of God and guarantee the blessings of life. According to one writer, Jesus acts as 'our Samson' to guarantee the fruitfulness of his vineyard when he will 'catch the foxes, tie them up and burn them'.[18] An editorial in *TBM* in 1913 declares that the 'Spirit of Christ in His Church, like Samson in Gaza, "arose at midnight" in the Reformation calling the Church to prepare for the soon coming of the Lord Jesus as King'.[19] F.J. DeBardeleben testified to finding in prayer and holiness 'One with me ... stronger than Sampson [sic]'.[20]

Samson also functions as an example of those who might be used by the Lord and empowered by His Spirit yet give in to temptation and be stripped of that power. A warning is issued to not give in to temptation like Samson and thus 'be shorn of our power and God depart from us'.[21] In a 1915 Sunday School lesson by A.R. Flower, the 'lamentation [of Israel] ... for Samson when shorn of his

---

[14] T.B. Barratt, 'Baptized in New York', *AF* 1.4 (Dec. 1906), p. 3.

[15] E.A. Sexton, 'Who Hath Believed Our Report? And to Whom is the Arm of the Lord Revealed?' *TBM* 1.15 (June 1, 1908), p. 1; and 'Pastor Barrett and the Work in Europe', *WE* 135 (Apr. 15, 1916), pp. 4-5 (4).

[16] S.C. Perry, 'We Must Press Forward if We Win in the End', *CGE* 8.21 (June 2, 1917), p. 3.

[17] H.L. Faulkner, 'Keeping the Door Open in the Face of Danger', *LRE* (Jan. 1914), pp. 6-8 (7).

[18] 'Fruit unto God', *WE* 167 (Dec. 2, 1916), p. 6.

[19] 'Editorial: Our Coming King', *TBM* 6.125 (Jan. 15, 1913), p. 1.

[20] F.J. DeBardeleben, 'Atlanta, Ga', *CGE* 9.27 (July 6, 1918), p. 4.

[21] L. Garr, 'Portion of a Letter from Sister Garr', *TBM* 3.66 (July 15, 1910), p. 3.

strength after playing himself into the hands of the harlot Delilah' is likened to the wailing that should be offered 'for those who after sharing God's favor have left their first love and made affinity with the world and its allurements'.[22] An editorial in *CGE* in 1910 warns that the end of those who would quench the Spirit is like 'poor Samson' who had given in to Delilah, had his hair cut, lost his strength and, finally, his eyes.[23] Samson's hair is the mark of his 'consecration' and its loss exemplifies one's own loss of the Spirit in being 'shorn of … power' and 'Ichabod' being written over one's life.[24]

A number of the editors of these periodicals took care to try to distinguish in their own writing, and that of others, between the Spirit endowment of Samson and the contemporary experience of the Spirit in Pentecostal circles. G.F. Taylor explains the baptism of the Holy Spirit in the fifth paragraph of the 'Basis for Union' confessed by The Pentecostal Holiness Church indicating that the Spirit has always been with humankind and came upon 'numbers of Old Testament saints' with special mention of Samson. He does point out that somehow with Jesus the Spirit is 'without measure' and similarly baptizes in the Spirit 'in a measure never received by man before the day of Pentecost'.[25]

Dealing with a doctrinal question about Spirit baptism, E.N. Bell answers with a question further to answer, 'Can a child of God who has never received the gift of the Holy Ghost possess and exercise any one of the nine gifts of the Spirit as in 1 Cor. 12:8-11?' He contends that while this can happen, using Samson as example, it 'is not God's normal way of bestowing the gifts' on such persons and

---

[22] A.R. Flower, 'Amos the Fearless Prophet', *WE* 116 (Nov. 20, 1915), p. 2.

[23] 'Better Obey God than Listen to Man', *CGE* 1.6 (May 15, 1910), pp. 1-2 (2). Those 'foolish men from the highest ranks of education' who are 'duped and coddled on the lap of that weak devil possessed woman' of Christian Science, 'Mrs. Eddie [sic]' (Mary Baker Eddy) are also likened to Samson under the wiles of Delilah. This functions as an example of the need for women not to govern men even as they are entreated to 'preach … sing, shout and pray': 'A New One Started: Women to Keep Silent in the Churches', *CGE* 5.17 (Apr. 25, 1914), pp. 1-3 (2-3).

[24] W.J. Taylor, 'The Vipers that Come Out of the Fire: "God Left Him to Try Him"', *LRE* 10.3 (Dec. 1917), pp. 5-9 (9).

[25] G.F. Taylor, 'Basis of Union: Chapter XV. The Baptism of the Holy Ghost', *PHA* 1.38 (Jan. 17, 1918), p. 8.

particularly it is not 'God's way of working in this gospel age'.[26] A. Semple McPherson argued that the evidence of Spirit baptism was not as temporary nor such 'poor evidence' which is 'easy to imitate' as 'shaking' like Samson who 'went out and shook *himself*'.[27]

In 1920, Mrs. F. Hodges lists for the readers of *PE* the various enemies of Israel and their spiritual significance in relation to contemporary Pentecostals who have lost the power of the Spirit. She points to the Gibeonites as those with the 'spirit of "elevation"' who use the gifts of the Spirit to make a name for themselves. Like Samson, who did not know the Spirit had left him, such a '"gifted" worker has been shorn of spiritual power through regarding himself as a "reservoir" of power and gifts, instead of a "channel only"'.[28]

A.J. Tomlinson offers an extended message on Samson and notes several features about Samson with regard to the Spirit: the Spirit moved personally upon him in a punctiliar manner disregarding the historical point at which Samson found himself in redemption history.[29] He notes that 'this is not so strange' for those of 'us that have the Holy Ghost and are moved by the same ever Blessed Spirit of God'.[30] He states, 'The Spirit does not move us all the time, but he moves every one "at times" that is baptized with the Holy Ghost'.[31] Tomlinson further notes the mysterious nature of the moving of the Spirit 'delivering people from sin' by the example of the Spirit moving Samson to kill a lion as part of his delivering Israel from the Philistines.[32] Since the Spirit 'does not deceive' it behooves interpreters of what the Spirit is doing to offer right interpretation and not be like Samson's wife who, by deceiving Samson into explaining his riddle, suffered the fate of her 'and her father being burned with fire'.

---

[26] E.N. Bell, 'Questions and Answers', *CE* 292-293 (June 14, 1919), p. 5.

[27] A. Semple McPherson, 'What is the Evidence of the Baptism of the Holy Ghost?' *PE* 312-313 (Nov. 1, 1919), p. 6, original emphasis.

[28] Mrs. F. Hodges, 'The Enemies in the Land', *PE* 328-329 (Feb. 21, 1920), pp. 6-7 (7).

[29] A.J. Tomlinson, 'Samson and His Exploits: The Power of God Will Aid Any One under Certain Conditions: Faith and Obedience Will Work out Wonders', *CGE* 10.39 (Sept. 27, 1919), p. 1.

[30] Tomlinson, 'Samson and His Exploits', p. 1.

[31] Tomlinson, 'Samson and His Exploits', p. 1.

[32] Tomlinson, 'Samson and His Exploits', p. 1.

A similar end is likely for anyone similarly misinterpreting the work of the Spirit.[33]

Tomlinson contends that we must not give in to the 'spirit that is in the world' like the wife of Samson deceiving one moved by the Spirit. The Spirit of God alone can properly interpret what is of the Spirit. Preachers who once knew the power of God but have 'lost their power' through a deceitful self-confidence can be 'shorn of their strength similar to poor pitiful Samson'.[34] Tomlinson concludes,

> Faith and obedience will work wonders, but if you play and sleep around like Samson did first thing you know you will have no faith and it will be largely because you failed to obey in heeding admonitions or advices, or the wooings of the Spirit or the plain written Word of God.

> The people that know their God shall be strong and do exploits in these awful days, and God needs a host of them to fire the world with gospel truth. It is not Samson's kind of exploits that are needed now, but exploits of Christian living and fellowship and love, power and might by the Holy Ghost to herald the gospel message to the ends of the earth.[35]

Thus, Tomlinson's resounding call in 1919 to the readers of *CGE* was for those who would faithfully minister the full gospel and not be dissuaded by any deceiving naysayers of this Pentecostal message.

LRE published a 1919 sermon by H.H. Cox contending just like Samson,

> [there] are thousands of God's people today who are living under this delusion [of still having Pentecostal power]. They were once baptized in the Holy Ghost; the power of God was resting upon

---

[33] Tomlinson, 'Samson and His Exploits', p. 1.

[34] Tomlinson, 'Samson and His Exploits', p. 1.

[35] Tomlinson, 'Samson and His Exploits', p. 1. In 1917, a prayer request offering a similar metaphor as Tomlinson noted in 1919, was sent to E.A. Sexton from Brother J.O. Lehman concerning converts in South Africa who 'are brands from the burnings' that they might 'be like Samson's foxes running among the heathen and burning up all the devil's crops', J.O. Lehman, 'From Brother J.O. Lehman', *TBM* 10.198 (Apr. 1. 1917), p. 3. Tomlinson published a journal called *Samson's Foxes* in 1901-1902.

them, but today they are shorn of their power, and sad to say, they know not the Spirit has departed from them.[36]

Likewise, O.C. Wilkins in a 1920 article in *PHA* argues,

There are many people today who seem like Samson was after he had been shorne of his locks. Delilah represents the world when she got Samson to go to sleep she had his locks cut off. If the world can get us to compromise we will become under a hypnotic influence of the world, then when it is too late we will wake up to the fact that our power is gone and we are left in a blind condition to the glorious light and liberty of our God.[37]

Wilkins further contends that just as Samson's power did not come from 'his fine polished weapon' but from 'the power of God' likewise those Pentecostal preachers who were 'rough material' have 'become mighty instruments in the hand of God'.[38]

The Spirit in the Book of Judges can thus be yielded to for mighty victories over sin and darkness or quenched through abandoning oneself to the lustful voice of the spirit of the age. The baptism in the Spirit is regarded as granting strength and thus giving voice to the greatness and goodness of the Lord. The Spirit of Judges can put joy in the heart and a dance in the foot. Equally important, the sanctified life and the proper interpretation of the workings of the Spirit must be guarded at risk of the pride of the Spirit's blessed presence be shorn from the once Spirit baptized saints.

The engagement with the Spirit in Judges in these early Pentecostal writings offers the following ideas regarding the Spirit. (1) The Spirit flows ceaselessly to give life for those who continue in seeking. (2) The Spirit clothes, like Gideon, with divine love. (3) The Spirit equips for leading the people of God. (4) The Spirit enables such leaders to overcome in conflicts through their empowerment and anointing for power-filled witness. (5) The Spirit gives joy that might be demonstrated in dancing. (6) The Spirit is the Spirit of Christ Jesus who leads into victory. (7) The Spirit can be quenched or lost by unfaithfulness in giving in to temptations even by those once baptized

---

[36] H.H. Cox, 'Perpetual Victory for the Child of God: "Let Thy Head Lack No Ointment"', *LRE* 11.9 (June 1919), pp. 2-4 (3).

[37] O.C. Wilkins, 'Sermon', *PHA* 4.14 (Aug. 5, 1920), pp. 5-6 (5).

[38] Wilkins, 'Sermon', pp. 5-6 (5).

in the Spirit. (8) The Spirit, as the Spirit of Jesus, is more abundantly poured out in these last days than even it was in the days of the judges. (9) The Spirit gives a more abiding witness than the judges received. (10) The Spirit most normally gives charismatic endowments to those receiving the baptism in the Holy Spirit first. (11) The Spirit does not deceive and thus alone is the proper interpreter of what was always the Spirit's revelation.

1-2 Samuel

The Spirit endowed deliverers would give way to Spirit endowed delivering kings whose anointing would signify the authority to deliver and to lead the people of God. It would also speak to the need for the sanctified and Spirit-baptized life. Saul and David, both anointed by the Spirit of the Lord would provide ways of conceiving humility, faithfulness, strength, sanctification, demonization, *charismata*, tarrying, and even dancing.

Saul

The early Pentecostals noted the promise and disappointment of Saul as a Holy Spirit appointed deliverer and king of Israel. Saul had 'at one time been anointed with the Spirit,' but he 'disobeyed God, and instead of repenting in dust and ashes he thought more of honor before the people than of God's favor'.[39] Saul is an example of one who became 'puffed up and wanted to be leader' and thus the 'anointing [of the Spirit] left him'. Therefore one must remain 'little in our own light before God' in order to maintain the 'anointing on us … to reach others'.[40] Saul's sin was being 'unwilling to die to self and self interest [sic]'.[41] Saul serves as an example in *LRE* of the experience that 'even in these days men who are covetous and disobey the

---

[39] K. Klaus, 'He That Overcometh', *BC* 1.12 (May 1918), pp. 12-14 (13). A similar claim is made indicating Saul's anointing, but not using any direct reference to the Spirit in H. Dingee, 'David and the Mulberry Tree', *BC* 2.2 (July 1918), pp. 6-7 (6).

[40] R.B. Hayes, 'Slack Up in Pentecostal Saints', *TBM* 4.87 (June 1, 1911), p. 3.

[41] A. Weaver, 'Why We Have Failed God: "No Flesh Shall Glory in His Presence"', *LRE* 9.6 (Mar. 1917), pp. 16-20 (20).

commands of God' find 'the oil [of anointing] ceases to flow'.[42] Saul functions as a byword of one who 'died for his transgressions' in a short unsigned prophetic message published in *TBM* to encourage persistent faithfulness.[43] G.H. Montgomery contends in *PHA* that salvation can indeed be lost by sharing the account of Saul who failed to remain faithful.[44]

According to one *CE* Sunday School lesson: 'God granted Saul the opportunity of wonderful service; but he failed in spite of all His [sic] good attainment. His life proved that though at times the Spirit of God was *upon* him still he did not have the Spirit of God *in* him.'[45] As Saul did, who had to 'stand still' and listen to the word of God through Samuel, if we do likewise, we 'will know the power, the sweetness of the heavenly anointing without whose unction we can never render effective service to God'.[46]

In a later article of *WE*, Frodsham contrasts Saul of Kish with Saul of Tarsus as examples of those who either listen to the Lord or listen to their own thoughts. He opens with an interpretation of a tongue given in a service he had recently attended: 'Speak not in veiled criticism. Speak not your own thoughts. Satan gives many, many thoughts. Wait on Me for My words and thoughts. Watch your thoughts, your words. Let me speak My own words through you. Do not grieve one another with your words. Do not speak one against another.'[47] Saul of Kish was humble and was thus given 'another heart' and the Spirit of God came upon him. He failed when he listened 'to the reasonings of his own mind' rather than the word of the Lord. Saul of Tarsus met Jesus on the road to Damascus and was soon renamed Paul ('little') and refused to use the 'reasoning of his own mind'.[48]

Offering a direct challenge to an article by a 'Mr. Wheatlake in the Chicago paper' who was challenging the Pentecostal movement, A.J.

---

[42] H.H. Cox, 'Perpetual Victory for the Child of God', *LRE* 11.9 (June 1919), pp. 2-4 (3).

[43] 'The Word of God', *TBM* 10.178 (Jan. 1, 1916), p. 1.

[44] G.H. Montgomery, 'Can We Fall From Grace?' *PHA* 4.21 (Sept. 23, 1920), p. 2.

[45] 'Sunday School', *CE* 79 (Feb. 27, 1915), p. 2, emphasis added.

[46] 'Sunday School', p. 2.

[47] S.H. Frodsham, 'The Renewed Mind', *WE* 158 (Sept. 23, 1916), pp. 6-7 (6).

[48] Frodsham, 'The Renewed Mind', pp. 6-7 (6).

Tomlinson contends that Wheatlake might be 'the Saul' who required his men to abstain from eating anything (1 Sam. 14.24). While the army of Israel obeyed Saul, Saul's son Jonathan was absent from hearing this curse and ate some honey and his 'eyes were enlightened'. Likewise, Tomlinson continues, 'Here is the honey of the Holy Ghost all around this gentleman and still his eyes are not enlightened. Probably some of his superiors have charged him to stay away from the "tongues" people, as he calls them, and their doctrine, or probably he is the Saul that is uttering the charge.'[49]

Several of Saul's specific failures are highlighted in the Pentecostal literature: his failure to kill King Agag of Amalek and seeking the necromancer of Endor. The former failure stands for the 'Saul spirit'[50] of sparing Agag which was dubbed the failure to put 'all carnality and sin to death'[51] as the Spirit of the Lord commands and empowers to do.[52] W.J. Seymour writes,

> We cannot bring Agag among the children of Israel, for God says he must die. Saul saved Agag, which represented saving himself, the carnal nature or old man; but Samuel said Agag must die, and he drew his sword and slew him. Christ's precious word, which is the sword of Samuel, puts all carnality and sin to death.[53]

The following is found in the weekly Sunday School lesson of *WE*: 'Too true I fear it is, that the lack of continued power and unction in many of us comes from the spared Agag – the good flesh of our lives'. The 'Saul spirit' of shifting blame for disobedience all the while claiming personal obedience is the lot of 'many today'.[54] Later, *WE* readers in 1917 are called not to be like Saul who spared Agag, but to have the enemies of God utterly defeated in their lives through

---

[49] A.J. Tomlinson, 'Hold Steady Now: Be Something and Do Something for God and His Great Church: The Rays of Light Still Shine', *CGE* 8.19 (May 19, 1917), p. 1. There is an error in the date of this paper as 'May 19, 191'.

[50] 'Sunday School: April 4, 1915. Saul Rejected by the Lord', *WE* 83 (Mar. 27, 1915), p. 2.

[51] W.J. Seymour, 'Christ's Messages to the Church', *AF* 1.11 (Oct.-Jan. 1908), p. 3.

[52] Seymour, 'Christ's Messages to the Church', p. 3.

[53] Seymour, 'Christ's Messages to the Church', p. 3.

[54] 'Sunday School: April 4, 1915. Saul Rejected by the Lord', *WE* 83 (Mar. 27, 1915), p. 2.

the enthronement of the Christ. 'The natural man wants to spare King Agag and the *best*. Have you not also spared your spiritual enemies through disobedience. Hand over your enemy to your Samuel, who will "slay utterly" with the sword of His mouth'.[55] Finally, J.H. Patterson contends that we must not be like Saul sparing Agag and the good things, but must '"Slay utterly!" everything of the old life'.[56] This failure utterly to mortify the flesh would lead the believer ultimately to abandon the faith.

Saul seeking the necromancing woman of Endor raises sin to another level: the apostasy of spiritism. Thus, Saul is called an 'apostate king' and compared to an 'apostate tribe', Dan, an 'apostate disciple', Judas, and an 'apostate church', Laodicea, in order to point to 'the time of apostasy' which Mrs. A.R. Flower argued pertained to her day in 1914.[57] Saul's summoning of Samuel is accessing the 'devil's mirrors' which are 'lying spirits' bringing judgment on all who supposed to find help in the 'mirror' rather than the glass of Jesus.[58] Similar to Flower, G.F. Taylor, in 1918, refers to the 'days of [Saul's] apostasy [when he] consulted the necromancer' being akin to the present era with the spiritualism of the day.[59] This is regarded by A.P. Collins (1919) as the fulfillment of prophecy (citing 1 Tim. 4.1) concerning the 'sudden impetus given to Spiritism by the war' and exemplified by Saul's 'turning away from God to Spiritism'.[60] Between March and November 1920, A.C. Dixon, S.H. Frodsham, E.N. Bell, E.L. Moore, and H.J. Tomlinson also address the rise in spiritualism in their day (post-World War I) pointing to Saul's transgression as a prime example of the judgment against such practices.[61] F.J. Lee

---

[55] 'Triumphing over the Principalities and Powers of Darkness', *WE* 174 (Jan. 27, 1917), p. 6, original emphasis.

[56] J.H. Patterson, 'A Good Soldier of Jesus Christ: A Timely Talk', *WE* 202 (Aug. 11, 1917), pp. 4-5 (5).

[57] Mrs. A.R. Flower, 'Pentecostal Notes on International Sunday School Lesson', *CE* 63 (Oct.17, 1914), p. 2.

[58] H.E. Wallis, 'The Mirror and the Glass: Jas. 1:23 R.V., and 1 Cor. 13:12', *WE* 176 (Feb. 10, 1917), pp. 2-3 (2).

[59] G.F. Taylor, 'Basis of Union: Chapter XXVI: Spiritualists', *PHA* 1.52 (Apr. 25, 1918), p. 4.

[60] A.P. Collins, 'Outline Bible Studies', *CE* 290-291 (May 31, 1919), p. 7.

[61] A.C. Dixon, 'Spiritualism – Is It of God or of the Devil? An Address', *PE* 330-31 (Mar. 6, 1920), pp. 3, 6-7; *The Bridegroom's Messenger* 13.221 (Mar. 1920), also reprinted this article citing 'Alliance Weekly' as their source and noting a 'number

(1920) covers similar ground and concludes that 'we His [Jesus'] followers have dealings with the one Spirit, the Holy Ghost, but the many spirits we rebuke and shall not be contaminated with them'.[62] Thus the Pentecostal leaders as a whole offered condemning words against the rising specter of spiritualism and those who seek to communicate with the spirits (dead or otherwise). This is contrasted sharply by Pentecostal writers to the 'one God-given Spirit to guide His children'.[63]

Not only did Saul serve as a negative example, but he was also regarded as clearly demonized.[64] Such denunciations and warnings as were listed above were not without counter claims among Pentecostals that despite even the demonization of the likes of Saul one should not attack those who at one time had been numbered among the Pentecostals (following the example of David treatment of Saul). Flower wrote in *TP* in 1910 of those

---

of good articles on Spiritism [which] have been published recently', p. 4; S.H. Frodsham, 'The Menace of Spiritualism: As Seen from the Pentecostal Viewpoint', *PE* 338-339 (May 1, 1920), pp. 6-7; E.N. Bell, 'Questions and Answers', *PE* 342-343 (May 29, 1920), p. 5; E.L. Moore, 'Spiritualism, Science, Witchery, and Future Telling', *CGE* 11.24 (June 12, 1920), p. 4; H.J. Tomlinson, 'Communicating with the Dead', *CGE* 11.46 (Nov. 20, 1920), p. 4. Homer Tomlinson notes in this article that over the 'past year' numerous magazines had highlighted spiritualism and 'devoted large space to discuss the possibilities of communicating with the dead', p. 4. This comment would likely explain the sudden spate of articles addressing this issue. A. Conan Doyle had recently published a work entitled 'The New Revelation' (1918) that was widely read and promoted Spiritism, followed by another book promoting the same, 'The Vital Message' (1919).

[62] F.J. Lee, 'Delving Into the Forbidden', *CGE* 11.35 (Aug. 28, 1920), p. 3.

[63] E.S. Hubbell, 'The Search for Truth', *WE* 211 (Oct. 20, 1917), pp. 8-9 (8).

[64] J.R. Flower declares, 'The evil spirit was a demon – a messenger of Satan, permitted by God for Saul's discipline, with the possibility of effecting his repentance. God can cause evil spirits and the Devil himself to aid in the accomplishing of His purpose', 'Sunday School: May 2, 1915. Saul Tries to Kill David', *WE* 87 (Apr. 24, 1915), p. 2. G.F. Taylor also refers to Saul's state as being 'demon possessed', 'Sunday School Lesson', *PHA* 4.8 (June 24, 1920), pp. 5-6 (6). E.N. Bell interprets the 'evil spirit from God' in 1 Sam. 18.10 and the 'lying spirit' in 1 Kgs 22.22 as 'demon spirits' because he says, 'All evil spirits are demons, and all spirits that tell lies are demons. The Spirit of God never lies'. He further contends that the 'evil spirit' is only 'from God' in that God permits Satan to torment some as a judgment of God for disobedience, 'Questions and Answers', *PE* 322-323 (Jan. 10, 1920), p. 5.

who have put their hands on those who at one time were filled with the Holy Spirit, but now are in a cold condition, and the result has been disastrous. They forget that David would not raise his hand against Saul even though he was possessed of an evil spirit, simply because the king was anointed of God.[65]

Similarly some are regarded as having 'betrayed a murderous spirit in their denouncing of some other possibly innocent brother'.[66] In other words, while denouncing must happen it was to be done with the utmost of concern that one might in fact endanger the Spirit with them if they did not admit the Spirit who had been with others.

It should be noted that Saul is not always used as a negative example, but also occasionally serves as a positive example of humility and hard work. The 'oneness of the Spirit' that can be enjoyed by believers seeking and granting forgiveness leads to greatness just as the smallness of Saul in his own eyes early on led to his being made king of Israel.[67] Saul is an illustration of Pentecostal teaching being true even if those who have 'spoken in tongues during the last ten years, goes wrong ... the baptism in the Holy Spirit remains the same'.[68] According to W.W. Simpson in 1915 in *LRE*, Saul's anointing by Samuel and the 'Holy Spirit' coming on him, was not negated by his failure to obey fully, have the Spirit leave him, and be overcome by a troubling spirit.[69] Such events did not negate the faithfulness of the initial anointing.

A Sunday School lesson in *CE* in 1915 offers extended treatment of the positive role-modeling of Saul. Saul's choice as king of Israel was understood as a 'Divine grace' due to his being from 'the

---

[65] J.R. Flower, 'An Important Warning', *TP* 2.5 (Apr. 1, 1910), p. 6; a similar case is made in 'Sunday School: May 16, 1915', *WE* 89 (May 8, 1915), p. 2, which seems likely to have been written by his wife, A. Reynolds Flower though this lesson is officially unsigned.

[66] 'Sunday School: May 2, 1915. Saul Tries to Kill David', *WE* 87 (Apr. 24, 1915), p. 2.

[67] H.J. Johns, 'Is Your Hand Withered? Blessings in the Path of Humility', *LRE* 11.10 (July 1919), pp. 18-21 (20).

[68] W.W. Simpson, '"At This Time as at First": What the Baptism in the Holy Spirit Meant upon the Life of a Missionary', *LRE* (Nov. 1915), pp. 2-6 (5).

[69] Simpson, '"At This Time as at First"', p. 5.

insignificant tribe of Benjamin'.[70] He is regarded as acting in an 'especially commendable' manner during the time of his initial private and public anointings by Samuel up to his deliverance of the people of Jabesh-Gilead (who are 'professed Christians' that 'compromise with … the world and Satan').[71] Saul's 'interest in the sorrows of his people is the occasion of his being thrust forth into active service. "The spirit of God came upon Saul." v. 6. This led to a most practical expression of sympathy and was all the preparation needed for leading Israel to a mighty victory.' The author cites passages deemed worthy to compare to this as: Judg. 3.10; 6.34; 11.29; Lk. 24.49; Acts 10.38.[72] The victory is thus regarded as a victory 'against sin' and Saul's faith became 'contagious' just 'as the joyful sound of the Gospel is today to souls oppressed and stricken by the adversary'.[73] Further, Saul is regarded as remaining humble and having an 'unusual love and generosity'; rather than developing 'a spirit of intolerance' toward those who had previously rejected his kingship, he extended 'a spirit of forgiveness and divine love' and thus 'God honored him in all their eyes'.[74] In a later issue of *WE*, the lesson is summarized, 'Saul's attitude of waiting, his meekness and quiet dignity under persecution should speak to our hearts' (citing the KJV of Prov. 16.32 '… he that ruleth his spirit [is better] than he that taketh a city').[75]

Humility and hard work are further elaborated elsewhere in *CGE*. One 1915 author uses Saul's returning to farming after being anointed king as an example of remaining 'busy' in order to be used of God. Thus, the author contends, Saul was 'thrust out into prominence by God and the people instead of boasting what he was going to do because the Lord had chosen him to be king'.[76]

Some simply give a positive witness of Saul in comparing Saul's experience of the Spirit and Pentecostal experience. E.M. Stanton, writing for *TBM* in 1917, believes Saul was 'anointed to witness for

---

[70] 'Sunday School: March 14, 1915. Saul Gains His Kingdom', *CE* 80 (Mar. 6, 1915), p. 2.

[71] 'Sunday School: March 14, 1915', p. 2.

[72] 'Sunday School: March 14, 1915', p. 2.

[73] 'Sunday School: March 14, 1915', p. 2.

[74] 'Sunday School: March 14, 1915', p. 2.

[75] 'Sunday School: March 28, 1915. God's Mercies to Disobedient Israel (Review)', *WE* 82 (Mar. 20, 1915), p. 2.

[76] 'God Calls Busy People', *CGE* 6.22 (May 29, 1915), p. 1.

God' by the Spirit and David was anointed 'to rule over Israel'.[77] Stanton further clarifies that while the Spirit 'did dwell in them,' the distinction in the New Testament era and following was that the Spirit was not their 'inner personal possession'.[78] However, he argues, 'Men, in the Old Testament times, were as really convicted of sin, regenerated and sanctified by the Spirit as they are now' including Saul who is immediately professed to prophesy by the Spirit as one of the 'holy men of God' mentioned in 2 Pet. 1.21.[79]

Saul and his three groups of messengers being overcome by the Spirit and prophesying, finding themselves stripped and on the ground, overwhelmed by the prophetic functions to demonstrate the Biblical precedence for 'physical manifestations' of the Spirit like 'violent shakings of the body, persons falling and lying and rolling on the floor as though in the grip of a powerful electric current'.[80]

Like Saul, one is 'turned into another man' when that person becomes 'a child of God'. A.W. Orwig thus argues in a 1916 issue of *WE* that there is a post-conversion experience in which one needs to be 'turned into another man'.[81] He writes, using Saul's transformation and Spirit endowment in 1 Sam. 10.6,

> Someone may perhaps say that referred to Saul's new official relation to God. Possibly it did, in a degree. But unquestionably it included Saul's spiritual relation to God. 'The Spirit of the Lord' coming upon any one can hardly fail to affect him morally and religiously.
>
> Is it not true, then, that in a very important sense, every Christian may be 'turned into another' person subsequent to regeneration and adoption into the divine family? Were not the disciples of Christ 'turned into' other men on the memorable day of Pentecost? Had not Jesus given them to understand that this was necessary, and that the turning consisted in the Holy Spirit coming

---

[77] E.M. Stanton, 'The Holy Spirit', *TBM* 10.190 (Jan. 1, 1917), p. 4.

[78] Stanton, 'The Holy Spirit', p. 4.

[79] Stanton, 'The Holy Spirit', p. 4.

[80] B.F. Lawrence, 'The Works of God', *WE* 143 (June 10, 1916), pp. 4-7 (5). The article is listed under 'B.F. Lawrence' in the header, but lists 'W. Bernard' in the subscripted sign-off. Also, it wrongly gives the Biblical text for this account as 1 Sam. 10.18-24.

[81] A.W. Orwig, '"Turned Into another Man"', *WE* 148 (July 15, 1916), p. 8.

upon them in further cleansing and the enduement of power from on high? And if they needed a greater degree of heart purity and effectiveness for service, is not the same necessary for all who enter the Christian life.[82]

Orwig would seem to be contending for Saul as an example of the sanctified life as part of his doctrine of the baptism in the Holy Spirit.

The 1920 editors of *PE* offer a contrary reading to Orwig's 1916 article. The Spirit of God is regarded as not normally forcing 'His way against man's will to a position of rule, except in special circumstances' like that of Saul seeking the lives of David and Samuel.[83]

> That event was a signal proof that God could, when He chose, overpower the spirit of man, but there was no moral or spiritual value in such overpowering. Saul was not a whit better man for it all. There was no fellowship between God and man's spirit in such an experience. It proved that no man could resist the overmastering force of the Spirit, but God wanted men who would **welcome** that overmastering energy, who would **glory** in it as their highest honor.[84]

Indeed, the unnamed author of this article contends that 'Saul had indeed been "amongst the prophets" *against* his will'.[85]

S.C. Perry gives an extended treatment on the subject, 'Is Saul Also Among the Prophets?' He points out that while Israel rejoiced over Saul, the question was asked 'Who is their father?' leading Perry to surmise that this is comparable to feeling something is wrong with a profession of faith followed by the proof of failure after several weeks.[86] Further, Perry contends that Saul (and Israel) are not wrong in choosing outright rebellion from the beginning, but of allowing themselves to be sidetracked from God's perfect will. 'How many today who have not tarried before God and received the fullness of the blessing and power to win, but like old king Saul "force themselves" along. You may keep up for awhile [sic], my brother, but it will not

---

[82] Orwig, "'Turned Into another Man'", p. 8.

[83] 'Back to Pentecost', *PE* 360-361 (Oct. 2, 1920), pp. 1-2 (1).

[84] 'Back to Pentecost', pp. 1-2 (1), original emphasis.

[85] 'Back to Pentecost', pp. 1-2 (1), emphasis added.

[86] S.C. Perry, "'Is Saul Also Among the Prophets?'" *CGE* 8.51 (Dec. 29, 1917), p. 3.

last you until the judgment. Be warned.'[87] Perry continues by tracing the sad end of Saul who failed to conquer the Philistines and who suffered a terrible fate leading Israel as well into trouble. This is, for Perry, a word to leaders within the church: 'A career of pride, or self-exaltation or wrong doing or teaching on any line may bring wreck to many others as well as to ourselves. And remember we may hold out for a time and keep up appearances as did king Saul, but a terrible end awaits if we miss God's way. "IS SAUL ALSO AMONG OUR PROPHETS?"'[88]

R.M. Evans, also writing for *CGE*, contends against the notion that 'Satan speaks in tongues' by pointing to Saul who prophesied 'after the Spirit of the Lord had left him' and clarifies that the Scripture 'plainly says that "the Spirit of God was upon him and he went on and prophesied"'.[89]

A 1919 author for *CGE*, R.L. Cotnam, argues that prophets in the early period of Israelite history

> were changed by God's Spirit, were sometimes agitated in a violent manner, these were called motions of prophecy, which persons exhibited, who were filled with a good or evil Spirit [sic]. For example, Saul being moved by an evil spirit, prophesied in his house (1 Sam. 18:10.) [sic] That is, he was agitated with violence and used strange and unusual gestures, signs, and speeches as the prophets did.[90]

He continues by contrasting this with the 'most usual way' of God inspiring the prophets, particularly the writing prophets, by 'dictat[ing] his will to them'.[91]

According to G.F. Taylor in a 1920 article in *PHA*, it was Saul's disobedience that

> led to hatred, envy, strife, and many other evils in his heart. These evils controlled him, and caused him to do many things that he would not have done otherwise. He was so controlled by the evil

---

[87] Perry, '"Is Saul Also Among the Prophets?"', p. 3.

[88] Perry, '"Is Saul Also Among the Prophets?"', p. 3, original emphasis.

[89] R.M. Evans, 'Does Satan Speak in Tongues?' *CGE* 9.25 (June 22, 1918), p. 4.

[90] R.L. Cotnam, 'Prophet and Prophecy: Is this Confined to Man?' *CGE* 10.40 (Oct. 4, 1919), p. 4.

[91] Cotnam, 'Prophet and Prophecy', p. 4.

spirit that he was practically crazy at times. He would come to himself, and resolve to do right, but the evil spirit would soon overcome him again.[92]

This was suggestive of the state of any who refused absolute obedience to the Lord.

In similar fashion, a sermon delivered by W.W. Pelton at Stone Church in Chicago in 1919 argues Saul began as 'a man of humility; yea a righteous man' who fell into disobedience.[93] At Saul's anointing, the Spirit was upon him, he prophesied and drove 'out all the spiritualists. He set up the worship of Jehovah and made great strides for a time, but he fell.'[94] It was the 'spirit of jealousy' at hearing the songs of the women celebrating David's ten thousands and Saul's thousands. This led Saul to allow the place for sin in his life and his eventual suicide in the grips of fear. Such is the 'warning' for those who do not deal quickly with 'something in your life that is wrong and sinful'.[95]

In all of the various appraisals and uses of Saul (negative and positive), there remains a move toward another who would replace him should he not persist as he had begun. In this manner, a 1915 Sunday School lesson declares: 'Saul had failed the Lord and when one instrument fails to do His work, it is set aside for another'.[96] David would be that other instrument for the Spirit.

These early Pentecostal engagements with the Spirit in relation to Saul provide a number of trajectories for understanding the Spirit. (1) The Spirit empowers the humble. (2) The Spirit remains on the faithful. (3) The Spirit alone must be listened to, sought, and obeyed. (4) The Spirit puts all carnality and sin to death. (5) The Spirit once endowed upon an individual should not be treated lightly even if the Spirit does not remain with them. (6) The Spirit is true even if the vessel of the Spirit proves to be false. (7) The Spirit preserves through, and gives joy in the midst of, persecution. (8) The Spirit anoints to give witness to the Lord. (9) The Spirit will not tolerate

---

[92] G.F. Taylor, 'Sunday School Lesson', *PHA* 4.4 (May 27, 1920), pp. 5-6 (5).

[93] W.W. Pelton, 'Failing God! Small Sins Spell Disaster', *LRE* 11.12 (Sept. 1919), pp. 21-24 (22).

[94] Pelton, 'Failing God!', pp. 21-24 (22).

[95] Pelton, 'Failing God!', pp. 21-24 (22).

[96] 'Sunday School: April 11, 1915. David Anointed King', *WE* 84 (Apr. 3, 1915), p. 2.

sin, but instead convicts of sin, along with regenerating and sanctify-ing the individual. (10) The Spirit manifests physically as a witness. (11) The Spirit may overcome individuals against their will, but does not normally do so. (12) The Spirit abandons the unfaithful. (13) The Spirit gives prophetic gifts, even sometimes violently, but most often through clear and self-controlled revelation of God's will.

David

As a shepherd boy tending the flocks of his father, *LRE* heralds Da-vid as already moved by 'God's Spirit'.[97] Thus, David the shepherd boy receives the anointing to be king in Saul's place. As one anointed and moved by the Spirit, David is empowered to do mighty deeds. For T.B. Barratt, the baptism in the Holy Spirit functions as the 'per-sonal experience' of knowing where David received his strength.[98] A 1911 missionary in Ceylon[99] writes to *TBM*, 'We only see our poverty and weakness, but in Him we go in the Spirit of David in boldness and power, clad in the armour of God to fight the fight of faith against the mighty'.[100]

For one contributor to *TP* in 1909, the anointing of David is as the baptism in the Spirit: 'a sign and seal,' 'the earnest' of 'divine choice', and 'authority'.[101] A.E. Luce cites 1 Sam. 16.13 with regard to David's anointing as king and the Spirit of the Lord coming upon him as a type for those who are anointed by God to be kings endowed with help of the baptism of the Spirit.[102] *LRE* (1915) contends the same anointing which Saul had received to be king was poured over David, '[t]he same old oil in the same old way was poured on David's

---

[97] K. White, 'The Life Triumphant: A Sweet Savor of Christ', *LRE* (May 1913), pp. 15-18 (17).

[98] T.B. Barratt, 'Baptized in New York', *AF* 1.4 (Dec. 1906), p. 3; and E.A. Sexton cites the testimony of Barrett, '"Who Hath Believed Our Report? And to Whom Is the Arm of the Lord Revealed?"', *TBM* 1.15 (June 1, 1908), p. 1; and the following article re-printed the previous testimony of Barratt as evidence of the Spirit's work through the years, B.F. Lawrence, 'Apostolic Faith Restored', *WE* 135 (Apr. 15, 1916), pp. 4-5 (4).

[99] Now known as Sri Lanka.

[100] D.E. Dias-Wanigasekera, 'From Ceylon', *TBM* 4.92 (Aug. 15, 1911), p. 1.

[101] A.S. Copley, 'Pentecost in Type', *TP* 1.10 (Sept. 15, 1909), pp. 5-6 (6).

[102] A.E. Luce, 'Pictures of Pentecost in the Old Testament', *WE* 187 (Apr. 28, 1917), p. 2.

head, and the Holy Spirit came on David in the same way [as Saul]'.[103] G.F. Taylor of *PHA* in 1920 uses 1 Sam. 16.13 – 'The Spirit of Jehovah came mightily upon David from that day forward' (KJV) – as one of his primary texts for a weekly Sunday school lesson in order to contend for the initiatory nature of the baptism.[104] Later that summer, Taylor indicates that David was anointed 'king of Israel many years before he reached the throne,' so 'we are anointed with the Holy Ghost' because 'the Lord wants to make us kings in the future ages'.[105]

A 1916 Sunday School lesson offers a suggestive question, distinguishing between the two containers for anointing Saul (a vial) and David (a horn), which are believed to be instructive concerning the reader's own potential level of 'unction and fragrance of the blessed Holy Spirit'.[106] E.M. Stanton of *TBM* also understood the baptism as that anointing of preparation for service.

> Samuel anointed David with the holy oil in the midst of his brethren, and the Spirit of the Lord came upon him. No man is prepared for rulership, in church or state, except he be God's anointed. The baptism with the Holy Spirit is God's anointing for service. The Spirit taking up His abode in the individual anoints by the very act.[107]

Mrs. B.L. Shepherd in *CGE* believes likewise 'the blessed oil of the Holy Spirit, the holy anointing oil, must be upon us and between us constantly'.[108]

W.W. Simpson declares that the failure of those who have received the baptism in the Holy Spirit and wandered away does not negate the trustworthiness of the experience of the baptism as truly from

---

[103] W.W. Simpson, '"At This Time as at First": What the Baptism in the Holy Spirit Meant upon the Life of a Missionary', *LRE* (Nov. 1915), pp. 2-6 (5-6).

[104] G.F. Taylor, 'Sunday School Lesson', *PHA* 4.5 (June 3, 1920), pp. 3-4 (3). Notably he never addresses this actual verse in the text of his lesson and what it might mean for the Spirit to remain on David.

[105] G.F. Taylor, 'Editorial Thoughts', *PHA* 4.13 (July 29, 1920), p. 1.

[106] 'Sunday School', *WE* 84 (Apr. 3, 1915), p. 2.

[107] E.M. Stanton, 'The Holy Spirit', *TBM* 10.191 (Feb. 1, 1917), p. 4.

[108] Mrs. B.L. Shepherd, 'Jewel Joints', *CGE* 11.8 (Feb. 21, 1920), p. 3.

God.[109] Thus, the faithfulness of the original outpouring is not negated by failing to remain filled with the Spirit despite whatever challenges one might face. Some early Pentecostal missionaries seem to have understood those challenges as relating to their fullness of the Spirit. They wrote that they were abandoned by those who had pledged support, leading those who remained faithful despite such circumstances, to experience the sustaining blessings of the 'constant reanointings with the fresh oil ... as David found out'.[110]

David's defeat of Goliath and ultimate victory over the Philistines becomes a battle cry for embracing and walking in the fullness of the Spirit. According to A.B. Simpson in 1909, just as the Philistines sought after David after his crowning, 'so when you get Christ within your heart [sic] the baptism in the Holy Ghost, or some mighty, new gift from heaven, then look out for the devil'.[111] S.H. Frodsham declares David was equipped to defeat Goliath with a sling and stones, but 'when Jesus sent his disciples out to defeat a greater enemy than Goliath, He gave them the baptism in the Holy Ghost as a sling, and the five small stones that are found in Mark 16:17 and 18, the signs that are to follow them that believe'.[112] For A.J. Tomlinson, the persistent faith of David as he faced Goliath denotes all '[b]arriers, oppositions [sic] spurious teachings, divisions and faithlessness can all be swept away by one light stroke of the power of the Holy Ghost'.[113]

The preparation of David also is noted with regard to the empowerment of the Spirit. David refusing Saul's armor and weapon becomes an example to A.W. Orwig (1919) in *CE* of those who recognize that 'college and theological equipment' is insufficient alone to the task of ministering in victory which requires 'a pure heart and the baptism with the Holy Ghost' added to 'the highest order of human equipment possible'.[114] Mrs. Nellie Lincoln writes in *LRE* concerning the need for preparatory times that while David was '[h]idden

---

109 W.W. Simpson, '"At This Time as at First": What the Baptism in the Holy Spirit Meant upon the Life of a Missionary', *LRE* (Nov. 1915), pp. 2-6 (5-6).

110 E. Sisson, 'A Plea for Our Missionaries', *WE* 209 (Oct. 6, 1917), pp. 2-3 (2).

111 A.B. Simpson, 'The Double Portion: Striking Lessons from the Life of Elisha', *LRE* 2.2 (Nov. 1909), pp. 5-13 (9).

112 S.H. Frodsham, 'The Last Commission', *WE* 156 (Sept. 9, 1916), pp. 6-7 (6).

113 A.J. Tomlinson, 'Persistent Faith', *CGE* 7.51 (Dec. 16, 1916), pp. 1-2 (1).

114 A.W. Orwig, '"I Cannot Go With These"', *CE* 302-303 (Aug. 23, 1919), p. 7.

away among Judea's hills, he became "a cunning player on the harp," so when God caused him to stand before Saul, the rapturous music he played drove the evil spirit away'.[115] This preparation meant David could hear the Spirit speaking and respond appropriately. Such is the case when the Day of Pentecost and receiving the baptism in the Holy Spirit is likened by A. Semple McPherson in *BC* to David listening to the word of God to 'tarry until the rushing wind came from heaven, and cause the sound of a going to be heard in the tops of the mulberry trees' signaled that 'victory was theirs through the power of the Lord'.[116]

While preparation, proper equipment, and learning to the listen to the Spirit were illustrated by David, so was the joy of the Spirit-filled worshipper who might dance before the Lord like David. Instead of quenching or grieving the Spirit, *CGE* readers in 1910 are encouraged to 'do or say like David when criticised [sic] by his wife for dancing before the Lord'.[117] In the same way, '[e]very child of God should stand fast in the liberty they had when the Holy Spirit came to abide'.[118] A. Semple McPherson also defends 'dancing in the Spirit' by pointing to David's dancing before the Ark of the Covenant.[119] She states that those who reject such a 'manifestation of the power of God' might become like Michal who was 'stricken with barrenness and leanness'. In the midst of a home revival service in 1915, V.W. Kennedy says, it 'seemed like streams of heavenly music sounded … [and] there were great manifestations of the Spirit. As they danced it made me think of the time that David the king danced before the Lord.'[120] In 1920, A.J. Tomlinson calls for the Church of God in the

---

[115] Mrs. N. Lincoln, 'God's Chosen Vessels: Humiliating Lessons in the Preparation Days', *LRE* (Feb. 1916), pp. 8-11 (10). In an editorial defense of healing in the atonement, *The Bridegroom's Messenger* also points to the spirit induced ailment of Saul and the Spirit-ed treatment by David (1 Sam. 16.14-23), 'Editorial: Healing for All in the Atonement', *TBM* 6.126 (Feb. 1, 1913), p. 1.

[116] A. Semple McPherson, 'The Holy Spirit – Who Is He and Why Receive Him?' *BC* 4.6 (Nov. 1920), pp. 7-9 (7).

[117] A.J. Tomlinson, 'Better Obey God Than Listen to Man', *CGE* 1.6 (May 15, 1910), pp. 1-3 (2).

[118] Tomlinson, 'Better Obey God Than Listen to Man', pp. 1-3 (2).

[119] A. Semple McPherson, 'What About Those Manifestations? Dancing, Shouting, Shaking, Falling Prostrate under the Power, Speaking in Tongues, Interpretation', *BC* 2.8 (Jan. 1919), pp. 2-6 (3).

[120] V.W. Kennedy, 'Report from V.W. Kennedy', *CGE* 6.3 (Jan. 16, 1915), p. 3.

face of naysayers of the Pentecostal experience to enter yet more fervently into singing and dancing after the illustration of David as those who 'give yourselves anew to the Holy Ghost for service. Go into it with all your might like David of old.'[121]

W.T. Gaston, writing for a 1913 issue of *WW*, describes a camp meeting experiencing 'wave after wave of power' where some 'like David of old, "danced before the Lord"' as the Spirit moved them.[122] Miss Elizabeth Sisson contends for the validity of tongues in the face of its potential for shamefulness by pointing to David dancing 'under the demonstration of the Spirit'.[123] Z.R. Thomas praises God 'that when the Spirit of God gets into our feet to make us dance [like David] we can dance with joy and with all our might'.[124] A Sunday School lesson on David bringing the ark of the covenant up to Jerusalem in 2 Sam. 6.12-15 notes dancing and shouting as 'the suggestion of Pentecostal blessing in O.T. dispensation here in vs. 14, 15'.[125]

The Spirit in relation to David was regarded in the following ways. (1) The Spirit empowers to do mighty deeds and fight faithfully. (2) The Spirit on David is comparable to the baptism in the Holy Spirit. (3) The Spirit anoints and prepares for service and kingship. (4) The Spirit does not remain with those who do not persist in faithfulness. (5) The Spirit not remaining does not negate the trustworthiness of the initial Spirit baptism. (6) The Spirit must be constantly sought for fresh fillings. (7) The Spirit gives victory to those maintaining the fullness of the Spirit upon receiving the baptism. (8) The Spirit speaks to the saints and teaches them to listen in order to live overcoming lives. (9) The Spirit gives victory songs and dances to the faithful.

The lessons of Saul and David with regard to the Spirit could thus enable the Pentecostals to think through issues pertaining to their Full Gospel experiences and proclamations. The tales of these anointed kings offered fresh visions of salvation and healing, sanctification and the baptism, and finally the embodied joys of these signs as testimony of the King who was coming in power and victory. No

---

[121] A.J. Tomlinson, 'Music and Dancing', *CGE* 11.18 (May 1, 1920), p. 1.

[122] W.T. Gaston, 'Refreshing Times at Oklahoma Camp', *WW* 9.9 (Sept. 20, 1913), p. 1.

[123] E. Sisson, 'Tongues = Their Use', *LRE* 6.3 (Dec. 1913), pp. 18-22 (18-19).

[124] Z.R. Thomas, 'Operations of the Holy Spirit', *CGE* 5.24 (June 13, 1914), pp. 5, 8 (5).

[125] 'Sunday School', *WE* 91 (May 22, 1915), p. 2.

spirit of the age could keep the kingdom of God from coming to victory by the Spirit of the Lord upon His anointed. Nor could any power stop the Spirit from speaking and acting through His saints to see the kingdom come and the many blessings rain down.

1-2 Kings

These early Pentecostal journals offer far more pertaining to the lives of Elijah and Elisha and their relation to the Spirit than other sections of the Former Prophets. As an example of their prominence in the theological ideas of early Pentecostals, the inaugural issue of *LRE* declares itself to offer the 'Voice of the Spirit' as heard in 'Elijah's ministry' to determine whom people will serve.[126] This picture of one who prays and works earnestly for the rain of the Spirit's blessings to fall on a people turned from sin to righteousness looms large in the Pentecostal perception.

Micaiah

While chapters seventeen through nineteen of First Kings portray the ministry of Elijah and include the initial calling of Elisha, the Elisha narrative is not taken up in full until Second Kings (and specifically the Spirit text in 2 Kings 2). In the interim several prophets appear, but one in particular – Micaiah ben Imlah (1 Kings 22) – takes up the language of the Spirit and the early Pentecostals found in him another example for Pentecostal experiences.

According to A.E. Street writing in *CGE* in 1914, Micaiah ben Imlah is treated as an Old Testament example of one exercising the gift of 'discerning of spirits' which is used to demonstrate that such a gift of the Spirit is not itself indicative of 'Pentecost'.[127] Micaiah is also an example of one to whom the Spirit gave information concerning future events.[128] F.J. Lee points to lying spirits present in contemporary liars and makes use of Micaiah countering those into whom 'a lying spirit' entered 'causing them to tell and act out a [sic]

---

[126] 'A Latter Rain Sermon: "Go Forward": Reinforced by the Voice of the Spirit: Launching the Latter Rain Evangel', *LRE* 1.1 (Oct. 1908), pp. 7-13 (12).

[127] A.E. Street, 'What Is Pentecost?' *CGE* 5.29 (July 18, 1914), p. 8.

[128] A.E. Luce, 'Physical Manifestations of the Spirit', *CE* 248-249 (July 27, 1918), pp. 2-3 (2).

false'.[129] While not specifically referring to Micaiah, E.N. Bell regards those who prophesy falsely (or speak in tongues then interpret falsely) as opening themselves potentially to being 'possessed' by the same 'lying spirits' as he finds referenced among the false prophets who opposed Micaiah.[130]

G.F. Taylor proposes that the gifts attributed to the Spirit may in fact 'come from Satan' if they are 'without divine love'.[131] As his example, he points to the 'evil spirit' that came

> upon certain of the prophets [of the Old Testament], and they prophesied falsely. Even so, one today may be under the influence of an evil spirit, even by permission of God, and he may speak in tongues and of angles [sic], and yet be without divine love. God is love, and those who are void of love, are void of God; and it is impossible to think of a person possessing the gifts of the Holy Spirit, and being void of divine love. Love is obtained in conversion, a greater measure of this love is obtained in sanctification, and a still greater measure in the baptism of the Holy Spirit. You can not [sic] have the gifts of the Spirit without divine love.[132]

Taylor has here conflated the 'evil spirit' of texts like that concerning Saul and the 'lying spirit' which belongs to the story of Micaiah. Despite the potential conflation, Taylor is indicating that 'divine love' must rule the one experiencing the fullness of the Spirit. The danger of not yielding to the Spirit in every way is always present and Micaiah illustrates this in his accusation of the false prophets. It also remains a constant reminder in the early Pentecostal readings of the Judges, of Saul and David, and Elijah and Elisha.

These readings of the Spirit in the Former Prophets concerned with the Micaiah account offer several orientations for understanding the role of the Spirit. (1) The Spirit enables to discern between spirits and the Spirit. (2) The Spirit gives supernatural knowledge, understanding, and prophetic insight. (3) The Spirit pours out divine love as purifying evidence of the charismatic gifts of the Spirit.

---

[129] F.J. Lee, 'Another Characteristic of Satan – A Liar (Demonology)', *CGE* 11.19 (May 8, 1920), p. 3.

[130] E.N. Bell, 'Questions and Answers', *CE* 298-299 (July 26, 1919), p. 5.

[131] G.F. Taylor, 'Sunday School Lesson', *PHA* 3.7-8 (June 12, 19, 1919), pp. 2-3 (2).

[132] Taylor, 'Sunday School Lesson', p. 2.

Elijah and Elisha

AF attempts to make plain a distinction between the experiences of Elijah and the Pentecostal experience of the baptism in the Holy Spirit, but also emphasizes the manner of likeness for empowerment in order to encourage seeking the baptism and its results. In a 1906 article, a defense of the uniqueness of being baptized with the Spirit as distinguished from being filled with the Spirit, it is confessed that the 'Holy Ghost ... was with ... Elijah ... and many other men of God, but He was not poured out upon all flesh till the day of pentecost [sic]'.[133] An article in January 1908 states, the Spirit is testified as present from the creation of the world and being '*with* Elijah' and other men of God who 'spoke as they were moved by the Holy Ghost,' yet it was not until Pentecost that the Spirit was '*in*' the saints to 'abide with us forever'.[134] Indeed, Pentecostals must 'pray through ... [like how] Elijah prayed for rain' until 'we get a witness by the power of the Holy Ghost'.[135] Also an article in April 1908, the mantle of Elijah falling upon Elisha 'is a type of receiving the baptism with the Holy Ghost, for Elijah prayed for a double portion of the spirit of Elijah'.[136] Finally, in May 1908, *AF* declares, 'Elijah was a power in himself through the Holy Ghost. He brought down fire from heaven. So when we get the power of the Holy Ghost, we will see the heavens open and the Holy Ghost power falling on earth, power over sickness, diseases and death.'[137] Thus this article can conclude, 'You have power with God as Elijah had'.[138]

Writing for *WE*, A.P. Collins offers 'Special Prayers in the Old Testament'[139] as a Bible study plan to embrace the prayers of Scripture noting Elijah's two prayers on Mount Carmel (1 Kgs 18.36, 42). The first prayer was for 'God to witness to His power on Mt. Carmel. Obey God and look for results'; and the second, for rain, noting that 'he prayed seven times, and James said he prayed earnestly. Pray

---

[133] 'The Enduement of Power', *AF* 1.4 (Dec. 1906), p. 2.

[134] 'The Baptism with the Holy Ghost', *AF* 1.11 (Oct. 1907-Jan. 1908), p. 4, emphasis added.

[135] 'Prayer', *AF* 1.12 (Jan. 1908), p. 3.

[136] 'Digging for Oil', *AF* 1.6 (Feb.-Mar. 1907), p. 2.

[137] 'The Holy Ghost Is Power', *AF* 2.13 (May 1908), p. 3.

[138] 'The Holy Ghost Is Power', p. 3.

[139] A.P. Collins, 'Pentecostal Bible Course: Lesson 13, Special Prayers in the Old Testament', *WE* 181 (Mar. 17, 1917), p. 13.

earnestly for revival, the latter rain.'[140] Elisha prayed for 'the double portion of the Spirit that was on Elijah,' for 'his servant's eyes to be opened. What did he see? Look up and see the hosts of heaven around you,' and that 'the enemy may be blinded. God is able – omniscient, omnipotent, omnipresent' (2 Kgs 2.9; 6.17, 18).[141]

The preparation for the baptism in the Holy Spirit is indicated by the earnestness of both Elijah and Elisha.[142] F.F. Bosworth, in several publications between 1915 and 1918, also states that one must be 'like Elisha' who will relentlessly pursue the 'double portion' in order to receive the 'fullness of the Spirit,' the 'Baptism in the Spirit'.[143] In order to receive 'enduement with power' reflection upon 1 Kgs 19.11-13 is expected. Here one finds Elijah in a cave seeking the Lord. He only found the Lord in 'the still small voice'. This is taken to indicate the need for quieting oneself and not working oneself into a frenzied state in preparation for the 'power'.[144] An earnest

---

[140] Collins, 'Pentecostal Bible Course', p. 13. This page is improperly dated March 24, 1917, only at the top of page 13. One week prior to this issue, Collins had posted a call on the cover of *WE* for unceasing prayers like Elijah's to be offered for 'all good papers' and 'revival', *WE* 180 (Mar. 10, 1917), p. 1. Expanding on this along similar lines, see also, A.E. Luce, 'Pictures of Pentecost in the Old Testament', *WE* 191 (May 26, 1917), p. 5; and A.J. Tomlinson, 'Consecration to God: And the Service Necessary to Earn and Honest Living', *CGE* 7.6 (Feb. 5, 1916), p. 1. Both Elijah raising the widow's son and Elisha opening the eyes of his servant are indicated as unceasing prayers of faith, W.D. Briggs, 'Prayer', *CGE* 7.22 (May 27, 1916), p. 2.

[141] Collins, 'Pentecostal Bible Course', p. 13.

[142] Even the Shunnamite woman becomes an example of persistence. One may be in 'the true grip of Pentecost' by becoming like the Shunnamite woman who would not be satisfied with any but Elisha coming to raise her son, or Elisha pledging never to leave Elijah. Indeed, 'that soul will surely be baptized', D.W. Myland, 'How the Latter Rain May Be Restored: A Setting Forth of the Seven-Fold Condition', *LRE* 1.10 (July 1909), pp. 15-22 (18).

[143] F.F. Bosworth, 'The Enthronement of Self the Great Sin: Demons Have No Power over a Will Surrendered to God', *LRE* 4.11 (Aug. 1915), pp. 2-6 (5); 'Nothing Can Hinder a Revival in the Church That Prays: "According to the Power That Worketh in Us"', *LRE* (Dec. 1915), pp. 2-7 (2); 'The Promise of the Father: Rain the Remedy for a Spiritual Death', *LRE* (Feb. 1916), pp. 2-7 (6-7); and 'How to Get Latter Rain', *WE* 231 (Mar. 16, 1918), p. 6.

[144] A.S. Copley, 'Power From On High', *TBM* 2.26 (Nov. 15, 1908), p. 2. See also, Mrs. N. Lincoln, 'God's Chosen Vessels: Humiliating Lessons in the Preparation Days', *LRE* (Feb. 1916), pp. 8-11 (10-11); and 'Pentecostal Bible Course: Lesson 12, First and Second Kings', *WE* (Mar. 10, 1917), p. 13.

seeker of the baptism was thus not one who worked themselves into a frenzied state, but one who quieted themselves to seek with faith. A.R. Flower writes, 'All ye who would only see God's moving in the wind and the fire – tarry awhile for that gentle voice of God'.[145] Two weeks later she adds, 'All ye who would have the fire of God descend in your midst mark carefully the conditions as Elijah met them. Our God still answers with fire. Hallelujah!'[146] Elijah himself 'shared the privations of the long three and a half years of drought before faith was given for the open heavens' as an example to tarry 'for the blessing' of the 'Spirit's fulness [sic]'.[147]

The results of the baptism are also likened to Elijah's experiences. J.O. Lehman argues against thinking that 'going and doing' is the only way one accomplishes anything. He contends that the baptism in the Holy Spirit as a deep abiding through prayer and a living sacrifice is demonstrated in Elijah fed by ravens near the Cherith brook which 'kept him in a living sacrifice, and brought him forth just at the right time to meet the hundreds of false prophets at Mt. Carmel'.[148] M.W. Plummer argues in 1910 that one needs the 'spirit of Elijah' to have the 'power of Elijah' knowing that 'the same measure of divine power is for us'.[149] He continues, 'The same burning zeal and mighty faith would effect like results today'.[150] A decade later, A. Semple McPherson calls for the Church to receive the promise of the Spirit being poured out in the last days by praying like Elijah 'till the mighty rushing wind comes from Heaven bringing with it clouds of latter rain'.[151] Mrs. B.L. Shepard reminds those who 'pour out their hearts and lives to God as Elijah did' will likewise experience the inward renewal of the Holy Spirit as intercessor.[152]

---

[145] A.R. Flower, 'Sunday School', *WE* 106 (Sept. 4, 1915), p. 2.

[146] A.R. Flower, 'Sunday School', *WE* 108 (Sept. 18, 1915), p. 2.

[147] A.E. Doering, 'On the Trail of the Double Blessing: Through the Blasts of Adversity', *LRE* (May 1916), pp. 5-8 (6-7).

[148] J.O. Lehman, 'South Africa', *TBM* 6.135 (June 15, 1913), p. 2.

[149] M.W. Plummer, 'A Little Light on the Problem of Power', *TBM* 4.74 (Nov. 15, 1910), p. 4.

[150] Plummer, 'A Little Light on the Problem of Power', p. 4.

[151] A. Semple McPherson, 'The Holy Spirit – Who Is He and Why Receive Him?' *BC* 4.6 (Nov. 1920), pp. 7-9 (7).

[152] Mrs. B.L. Shepherd, 'Jewel Joints', *CGE* 11.8 (Feb. 21, 1920), p. 3.

It was persistent prayer that opened the heavens. One writer in the *PHA* mixes the accounts of Elijah to portray the need to be persistent in prayer in order to experience the fullness of the Spirit. Like Elijah who prayed 'seven times till he got the answer ... may our Pentecostal peoples ... each call on God until the fire falls on our souls and others will be blessed'.[153] B. McCafferty explains that the drought of Elijah's days and the rain for which Elijah prayed fervently are illustrations of the need to pray for the 'latter rain' of the Spirit following the 'Season of Drouth [sic] between the Rains' of Pentecost in Acts and the Latter Rain outpouring of the Holy Spirit.[154] A 1914 call to pray as ceaselessly for a revival in Bombay as Elijah praying until the cloud appeared would give the assurance of coming rain.[155] A call is issued for intercessors in 1920 who will be 'spiritual Elijahs in these days to tap the reservoirs for the deluge, the floods of spiritual rain,' also called 'a double portion ... at the period of the end'.[156] Another article in that same issue of *PE* holds out the hope that the conditions of their day are identical to that of Elijah and thus ready for 'a great rain' of revival.[157]

The same signs which testified to the authenticity of the God of Elijah are expected for the Pentecostal outpourings.[158] Reviewing what the Lord has done 'in all the centuries past' functions for those praying 'for this pentecostal [sic] work' to align them with words of Elisha, 'Where is the God of Elijah?' and then 'to see our privileges in Jesus Christ as we have never seen them before'.[159] In the midst of the 'Pentecostal outpouring' it is necessary to have the 'fire' of the Holy Spirit to fall on us like it did 'when the sacrifice [of Elijah] was on the altar'.[160] According to his wife, W.M. Piper, founder of Stone

---

[153] J.T. Baker, 'Our Weekly Sermon: A Little Farther', *PHA* 1.52 (Apr. 25, 1918), pp. 2-3 (2).

[154] B. McCafferty, 'The Time of the Latter Rain', *WE* 188 (May 5, 1917), pp. 4-5 (5).

[155] M. Clark, 'Sister Margaret Clark Writes', *TBM* 7.52 (Mar. 15, 1914), p. 2.

[156] 'Tapping the Reservoirs of Heaven', *PE* 366-367 (Nov. 13, 1920), p. 3.

[157] 'Sounds of Abundance of Rain', *PE* 366-367 (Nov. 13, 1920), p. 3.

[158] A.P. Collins, 'Pentecostal Bible Course: Lesson 12, First and Second Kings', *WE* 180 (Mar. 10, 1917), p. 13.

[159] 'To God Be Praise', *TP* 2.3 (Feb. 1, 1910), p. 4.

[160] J. Paul, 'Three Essential Points of Pentecost', *LRE* 4.11 (Aug. 1912), pp. 3-6 (3).

Church in Chicago, 'set his face [in 1906] steadfastly toward heaven and, as the servant of Elijah looked for the token of the coming rain, he looked with the eye of faith for a Pentecostal fulness [sic] of bless-ing'.[161] A former Salvation Army officer encountered Pentecostals and 'became a seeker after all God had' and 'looked for rain from heaven and prayed for it like Elijah and so it came with a mighty rushing wind, March 19, 1910, and shook the whole house and filled the temple, praise His holy name. The Comforter came to abide and as He entered in spoke in other tongues.'[162]

For E.N. Bell, as the contest on Carmel demonstrated the god that was truly God, so the sign of the baptism in the Holy Spirit was being given as testimony to the trustworthiness of the Pentecostal witness of Jesus.[163] Several testified that revival meetings became the 'spir-itual' meat of attendees who felt sustained like Elijah for what lay ahead.[164] The editorial of one issue of *CE* in 1919 laments, 'An im-poverished world believes that an impoverished church indicates an impoverished God. Where is the God of Elijah? God wants Elishas to prove that Elijah and the God of Elijah are alive, the God that answers by fire – the fire of the Holy Ghost.'[165] The 'same Spirit' that was in Elijah 'is still in the world' to embolden the Church of God to preach without fear or wavering as found, according to A.J. Tom-linson, week after week in the testimonial pages of the *CGE*.[166]

A call for fresh outpourings following initial baptism in the Holy Spirit is also issued with regard to the examples of Elijah and Elisha. Already in 1909, J.E. Sawders could bemoan that the 'Pentecostal work to-day in many places seems to be passing through a sort of Sahara desert experience' and he attributes this in part to the 'FLESHLY MANIFESTATIONS' that are typified by the wind,

---

[161] L.M. Piper, 'After Seven Years – A Retrospect', *LRE* 6.1 (Oct. 1913), pp. 7-9 (8).

[162] P. Heckman, 'Testimony of a Salvation Army Officer', *TBM* 5.118 (Sept. 15, 1912), p. 3.

[163] E.N. Bell, 'The Need of the Hour', *CE* 53 (Aug. 8, 1914), p. 1.

[164] Mrs. W.F.E. Story, 'Portion of a Personal Letter', *TBM* 7.162 (Sept. 15, 1914), p. 2; also, M.M.T., 'Benton, Tenn.', *CGE* 6.9 (Feb. 27, 1915), p. 3.

[165] 'The Need of a Fire Baptized Church', *CE* 308-309 (Oct. 4, 1919), p. 4.

[166] A.J. Tomlinson, 'Do It Again and Again', *CGE* 10.14 (Apr. 5, 1919), p. 1.

earthquake, and fire to Elijah.[167] Instead, Sawders argues that 'to one of spiritual discernment' the Lord is in the 'still, small voice'.[168] He believes it is missed because of the 'fuss' and 'flesh' which have led many to have 'gone away [from Pentecost] disappointed and renounced the whole thing. As a natural consequence, the Spirit has not been poured out, and the gifts and supernatural power could not be trusted amidst such a state of confusion.'[169] One testimony believes 'greater manifestations than have yet been seen' will occur once 'we all get to the place Elijah did, where we can hear, the small, sweet voice'.[170] F. Bartleman contends that 'Elijah needs another divinely prepared meal. He has run long enough in the strength of a Pentecost lately realized. We must tarry again.' Thus, he believes '"Baptisms" can only be multiplied and continued that way'.[171]

The enabling of the Spirit to enact sustaining hope in the face of trouble and sorrow is indicated at several points. The statement from the Lord to Elijah, 'What doest thou here, Elijah? Arise from the juniper tree. Go forth and stand upon the mount,' functions as a call not to mope in 'self-dejection' but to 'abound in hope through the power of the Holy Spirit'.[172] When Elijah was threatened by Jezebel he became 'discouraged' because 'he had gotten out of God's order, for he ran not only ahead of the chariot but also ahead of the Spirit. It was not his mission to run ahead of the chariot.'[173] This functions to call the Church not to 'carry even a good thing beyond the bounds of its mission'.[174] The Pentecostal work in South Africa is prophetically declared to be coming into victory: 'Like Elijah's servant we see a cloud about the size of a hand and soon there will be the sound of

---

[167] J.E. Sawders, 'A Much Needed Lesson: God's Order Essential to God's Power', *LRE* 1.8 (May 1909), p. 11, original emphasis.

[168] Sawders, 'A Much Needed Lesson', p. 11. A.B. Simpson similarly argues that the 'still, small voice' was gentleness and meekness, 'The Double Portion: Striking Lessons From the Life of Elisha', *LRE* 2.2 (Nov. 1909), pp. 5-13 (10).

[169] Sawders, 'A Much Needed Lesson', p. 11.

[170] E.W. Vinton, 'Will You Stand the Test?' *TBM* 2.37 (May 1, 1909), p. 4.

[171] F. Bartleman, 'Report of Camp Meeting, Alliance, Ohio', *TBM* 1.18 (July 15, 1908), p. 2.

[172] 'Disapproval of Self-Dejection', *TP* 2.9-10 (Sept.-Oct. 1910), p. 5.

[173] D.W. Myland, 'The Book of the Revelation of Jesus Christ: The Messages to the Churches – Continued', *LRE* 3.6 (Mar. 1911), pp. 2-6 (5).

[174] Myland, 'The Book of the Revelation of Jesus Christ', pp. 2-6 (5).

abundance of rain. Hallelujah!'[175] Concerning the support of Pentecostal missionaries to deliver 'The Whole Gospel for the Whole World,' S.C. Perry writes, 'Elijah's God is still alive, and has as many interests in earth as ever and as much power to protect His own, vindicate this cause and supply their needs as in olden times'.[176]

Elijah running ahead of Ahab's chariot becomes a defense for Pentecostals running in the Spirit. It is regarded in 1908 in *TBM* as a testimony of the seeming 'eccentricities of devout worshippers' that after the defeat of the prophets of Baal, 'the Holy Spirit got into Elijah's legs' so that he outran Ahab's chariot.[177] A 1913 missionary in India testified to the readers of *TBM* that a word from the Spirit had strengthened him 'like Elijah [who] was under the juniper tree and was enabled to run several days'.[178] Elijah empowered by the Spirit to run is an evidence of the happenings of a Church of God worship service in 1914 being true to the Scriptures.[179]

WE seems to have been taken by the image of the whirlwind that caught up Elijah. The 'wind of God ... the whirlwind of the Spirit' can bring either destruction or blessing to 'raise you above the dust and turmoil of the world' like Elijah taken up to heaven.[180] The cover article also points to the 'whirlwind' that caught up Elijah as likened to 'the individual power for every saint'.[181] Elsewhere, the nature of the dual function of blessing and wrath is joined in the thunderstorms of Elijah.[182]

---

[175] L.O. Lehman, 'God Is Working', *TBM* 3.58 (Mar. 15, 1910), p. 4.

[176] S.C. Perry, 'The Whole Gospel for the Whole World', *CGE* 6.1 (Jan. 2, 1915), p. 3; and S.C. Perry, 'Line of Separation', *CGE* 6.47 (Nov. 20, 1915), p. 2.

[177] V.P. Simmons, 'Eccentricities of Devout Worshippers', *TBM* 1.16 (June 15, 1908), p. 4. A.R. Flower also notes that it seems that often 'God has used some untutored eccentric character to convey His message', 'Sunday School', *WE* 104 (Aug. 21, 1915), p. 2.

[178] R.E. Massey, 'Letter from Brother R.E. Massey and Wife', *TBM* 6.127 (Feb. 15, 1913), p. 3; and again in R.E. Massey, 'India', *TBM* 5.100 (May 1, 1913), p. 3.

[179] Z.R. Thomas, 'Operations of the Holy Spirit', *CGE* 5.24 (June 13, 1914), pp. 5, 8 (5).

[180] 'Messages of the Moment: The Army of the King', *WE* 169 (Dec. 16, 1916), p. 6.

[181] 'The Soon Coming of Christ', *WE* 213 (Nov. 3, 1917), p. 1.

[182] Bro. Bender, 'A Little Cloud Out of the Sea the Size of a Man's Hand', *CE* 286-287 (May 3, 1919), p. 4.

A 1917 author for *WE* discusses the likeness of the wind and fire to the likeness of Pentecost. 'Elijah was charged with fire before he came to the altar. He lived in touch with the fire, and he had to have a chariot of fire to take him home to glory. The man of fire calls on God, who answers by fire.'[183] This is then likened to 'an individual tongue of fire for every saint who will wait on Him, and will pay the price'.[184] The writer goes on to ask,

> What was the characteristic of Elijah before translation? It was restlessness and activity. He could not stay long in one place, but was urged forward, on, and on, and on. The Spirit was urging and he could not lodge and settle down. The Spirit was urging and lifting him till at last the Spirit had the mastery. He got into the whirlwind. The whirlwind encircled him and lifted him right into the chariot, and the chariot of fire did not burn him, because the Spirit of fire was already in his heart and in his body.[185]

Just as Elijah exercised 'the gifts of the Spirit,' so also, 'before the second advent God is working through Elijahs, and manifesting the supernatural through His various servants all around the world. They represent Elijah that He promised to send.'[186]

An article by Sister Aimee in 1920 testifies to the baptism of fire as a witness to God of Scripture being the God of Pentecostals:

> They who have received the Spirit ... and have walked in His paths can testify to a 'baptism of fire.' Fire that burns the dross, consumes self and selfishness with a fiery zeal for souls – fire that kindles love and melts the ice of coldness and formality – fire that falls from heaven and consumes the sacrifice – fire that falls upon re-builded altars and wood that is put in order under a whole burnt-offering – fire that proves Elijah's God still lives today, and answers still by fire.[187]

A.W. Frodsham is accredited with the following 'prophecy':

---

[183] 'The Need of Fire', *WE* 205 (Sept. 1, 1917), p. 4.

[184] 'The Need of Fire', p. 4.

[185] 'The Need of Fire', p. 4.

[186] 'The Need of Fire', p. 4.

[187] A. Semple McPherson, 'The Holy Spirit – Who is He and Why We Receive Him?' *BC* 4.6 (Nov. 1920), pp. 7-9 (8).

Elijah walked on and on with God. He walked in the spirit and the Spirit walked in him. At last the Spirit got the mastery and had his way. The spirit of the world was not strong enough for the spirit of heaven. Elijah was taken. Superabundance of spirit brings about translation.[188]

This idea of translation following the fullness of the Spirit is echoed elsewhere. According to one author, it was the 'chariot of fire … [that] kept back the enemy [Death] from Elijah. The fire to keep back the enemy and the whirlwind to lift up the prophet! Both will be used again. Both are necessary, both are precious. The Holy Ghost and *fire!* The rushing mighty wind and the cloven tongues of fire!'[189] Elijah is believed to have realized in his translation into heaven the force and power of the Holy Spirit as the wind.[190] Contrary to this positive notion of Elijah being translated as one yielded to the Spirit, F. Bartleman believes that Elijah being taken was because he had come to think he 'was the only one left and that the whole thing depended on him'. Elijah 'represents the old liners' (the holiness preachers not coming into Pentecost) because he could not see through to the new thing of Pentecost which would be given to the Elishas. Like Elisha, Bartleman was able to 'slay the oxen, break the plow up, make the sacrifice, and go on with the mantle of the Lord' with the leaving behind of his 'old theology' and those who held to it.[191]

According to an extended treatment by A.B. Simpson in *LRE* (1909), the double portion of the Spirit which Elisha requested from Elijah was 'the fulness [sic] of the Holy Spirit, for the inheritance of the saints of God'.[192] Simpson contends this was 'out of date,' because it was not intended until 'the Christian age' and thus the sign of Elijah translated to heaven was also 'not due until the end of the Christian age'.[193] He hears Elijah saying to Elisha, 'I have overlapped

---

[188] M. Wood, 'Super-Abundance of Spirit Brings About Translation', *TBM* 10.198 (Apr. 1, 1917), p. 4.

[189] 'The Translation of Elijah', *WE* 223 (Jan. 19, 1918), p. 8, original emphasis.

[190] 'The Rushing Mighty Wind', *CE* 260-261 (Nov. 2, 1918), p. 4.

[191] 'God's Onward March through the Centuries: The Pentecostal Experience Opens to Us a New Realm', *LRE* 2.10 (July 1910), pp. 2-8 (4-5).

[192] A.B. Simpson, 'The Double Portion: Striking Lessons from the Life of Elisha', *LRE* 2.2 (Nov. 1909), pp. 5-13 (6).

[193] Simpson, 'The Double Portion', p. 6.

the ages, and I am going up centuries before the translation of the saints is due, and if you see me when I go, you can take a step in advance too; you may get ahead of the ages and get the Holy Ghost before the time just as I get my translation before the time'.[194] Others have also claimed that Elijah was one 'ahead of his time', and was a testimony to our own translation into the heavens.[195] Elisha's life is considered

> the fullest type and sample of the Gospel Age, a life that antici-pated as no other did, the New Testament. For Elisha was wholly different from Elijah. Elijah was the Old Testament; Elisha from start to finish is what his name means, 'the salvation of God.' Just as Elijah got ahead of his time, got ahead of the law and leaped into the Gospel with one bound, so Elisha's life was just the Gos-pel life, just grace; grace, victorious grace from beginning to end.[196]

Simpson again picks this up:

> Elijah came in the spirit of the law; Elisha came in the Spirit of the Gospel; Elijah came like John the Baptist, Elisha came like Jesus of Nazareth; Elijah came like lightning, smiting and destroy-ing; Elisha came like light, illuminating, guiding and cheering with its soft and genial radiance. Elijah came eccentric, Elisha came normal and natural.[197]

Simpson continues contrasting Elijah and Elisha. While Elijah was a loner and eccentric, Elisha 'was a man of the people, he was a man among his fellow-men. He lived a normal life, a simple life, a helpful life, a human life.'[198] This exemplifies the Spirit-filled life where one is made 'a better man and a sweeter woman; more human as well as more divine'.[199] Simpson holds that there is a 'place for Elijah's min-istry,' but it is temporary.[200] The enduring ministry is that of Elisha

---

[194] Simpson, 'The Double Portion', p. 6.

[195] A.H. Argue, 'The Patient: His Coming Draweth Nigh: Present Day Condi-tions Portrayed in Prophecy', *LRE* 5.11 (Aug. 1913), pp. 17-19 (18).

[196] Simpson, 'The Double Portion', p. 9.

[197] Simpson, 'The Double Portion', p. 10.

[198] Simpson, 'The Double Portion', p. 9.

[199] Simpson, 'The Double Portion', p. 10.

[200] Simpson, 'The Double Portion', p. 10.

whose 'life was beneficent'.[201] There are 'young Elijahs all along the way, people that would rather criticize than encourage, people that thought they were called to cursing rather than blessing,' but Simpson points to the account of Jesus' disciples who wrongfully longed to be like Elijah calling down fire from heaven.[202] This misses what others have noted, that Elisha called down a curse on the 'children' of Bethel and thus was precisely not like Christ contending 'God the Spirit … alone has the right to kill and to make alive'.[203]

For Simpson 'even in these days of immanence we may anticipate a little bit the coming age and overlap until we get a glimpse into the heavens and a little of the glory of the days that are yet to come'.[204] One must 'tarry' in order to 'stand the test' and must have a 'faith that will not let go' like that of Elisha who would not leave Elijah.[205] Simpson presents the disrobing of Elisha as the removal of all he held dear and of his own righteousness. When Elisha received the mantle of Elijah 'it fell at his feet, and with his own arms he had to put it on and use it … [just as] you have to take the Holy Ghost by faith'.[206] The mantle as the 'symbol' of the Holy Spirit functions to remind of the nearness of God to act in the here and now.[207]

Elisha testifies to every 'gift and every manifestation' as 'worthless unless it leads to practical power, practical fruit, to practical service, to the salvation of men, the evangelization of the world and to the hastening of the coming of the Lord'.[208] Instead, we must be like Elisha whose life 'was mighty in its simplicity'. It was 'full of help in little temporal things. He touched the ordinary needs of the poor widow in debt, the soldiers that were famishing for water, the farmers who [sic] bread had failed; he came right down to the circumstances of a life of trial and emergency.'[209]

Elisha becomes the 'type' of Christ who 'holds our hands and teaches us how to shoot the arrows of prayer, the Holy Ghost comes

---

[201] Simpson, 'The Double Portion', p. 11.
[202] Simpson, 'The Double Portion', p. 11.
[203] E.H. Booker, 'The Abuse of Power', *LRE* 2.5 (Feb. 1910), p. 17.
[204] Simpson, 'The Double Portion', p. 6.
[205] Simpson, 'The Double Portion', p. 7.
[206] Simpson, 'The Double Portion', p. 8.
[207] Simpson, 'The Double Portion', pp. 8-9.
[208] Simpson, 'The Double Portion', p. 10.
[209] Simpson, 'The Double Portion', p. 11.

and bends the bow with the migthy [sic] momentum of heavenly intercession, and you feel the glow of that heavenly intercession'.[210] Simpson writes, 'I know nothing more delightful than to have the spirit of prayer come upon us. I believe the great purpose of all these mighty outpourings of the Holy Ghost today, whether in the gift of tongues or the baptism of power in other ways is for intercession, for prayer.'[211] Finally, Simpson notes the 'posthumous ministry' of Elisha, who though dead, still ministered life.[212] This is used as a witness to have 'enough of the Holy Ghost' still to reach loved ones with the good news even when we are dead and gone.[213] Finally, Simpson notes the 'critical eyes' of the sons of the prophets upon Elisha that 'always watch us' as being the work of the devil to try those who have just had a blessing.[214]

A.A. Boddy, in *LRE* (1912), preaches, 'Elijah is a type of the Lord Jesus' in his being taken to heaven, but 'Elisha is a type of the undiscouraged saint of God … [that] is determined to press on and get God's best'.[215] Elisha asked for the eldest son's 'double portion, a Pentecostal outpouring of the blessed Holy Spirit worked so mightily in pre-Pentecostal times in Elisha and others'.[216] Elisha seeing Elijah taken is likened to the work of the Spirit to give us 'continually … a vision of Jesus'.[217] Elisha refusing to give in to the discouraging sons of the prophets 'pressed on' to receive the blessing as a witness to tarry. The mantle of Elijah 'came down upon [Elisha] … and clothed him with power from on high. There is a difference between having the Holy Ghost and the Holy Ghost falling on you.'[218]

A.A. Boddy can say, 'The falling of Elijah's mantle upon Elisha was a picture of the coming of the Holy Spirit, the Pentecostal baptism'.[219] It was necessary 'to have a pure Baptism of the Holy Ghost' first for Elisha to pass through the Jordan as a type of death as it is

---

[210] Simpson, 'The Double Portion', pp. 12-13.
[211] Simpson, 'The Double Portion', p. 13.
[212] Simpson, 'The Double Portion', p. 13.
[213] Simpson, 'The Double Portion', p. 13.
[214] Simpson, 'The Double Portion', p. 9.
[215] A.A. Boddy, 'They Two Went On', *LRE* (Oct. 1912), pp. 2-7 (3).
[216] Boddy, 'They Two Went On', p. 3.
[217] Boddy, 'They Two Went On', p. 4.
[218] Boddy, 'They Two Went On', p. 4.
[219] Boddy, 'They Two Went On', p. 4.

for all believers as this is 'the secret of the Pentecostal work'.[220] Returning to the Jordan, Elisha was now able to turn back the waters having been made a new man. He could now sweeten bitter waters, cause an axe head to float, and deliver the armies of Israel, Judah, and Edom by minstreled music to accompany his prophesying and bringing about the miraculous provisions. The further signs, offered by Boddy, of the raising of the Shunammite's dead son, the cleansing of Naaman from leprosy, and even the very bones of Elisha raising a dead man testified to the 'wonder-working power' of a man who 'had received his baptism'.[221]

A.R. Flower sees the journey of Elisha from Gilgal to the other side of the Jordan as a spiritual journey akin to the Pentecostal journey. Before Elisha could receive the double portion spirit of Elijah, he had to overcome the flesh (Gilgal), worship by the Spirit (Bethel), overcome sin through the triumph of faith (Jericho), and then to the Jordan as 'the place of absolute consecration, death to the world and flesh'.[222] A.E. Luce pleads with those who are tested in passing from Gilgal to Bethel, Bethel to Jericho, and Jericho to the Jordan, 'Dear saved one, seeking the baptism of the Holy Ghost, are you ready to go all the way?'[223] You must be 'in the position of Elisha, ready to follow all the way'.[224]

A.E. Luce offers numerous articles (taken from her book *Pictures of Pentecost in the Old Testament*) in *WE* and *PE* on Elijah as a type in Scripture of the Baptism in the Holy Spirit.[225] As the altar that was

---

[220] Boddy, 'They Two Went On', p. 4.

[221] Boddy, 'They Two Went On', p. 5.

[222] A.R. Flower, 'Sunday School', *WE* 110 (Oct. 2, 1915), p. 2. A.E. Luce, similarly traces the path of Elijah and Elisha pointing to Gilgal as dealing with sin, Bethel as consecration, Jericho as overcoming, and the Jordan as death, 'Pictures of Pentecost in the Old Testament', *WE* 192 (June 2, 1917), pp. 4-5 (5).

[223] Luce, 'Pictures of Pentecost in the Old Testament', WE 192 (June 2, 1917), pp. 4-5 (5).

[224] Luce, 'Pictures of Pentecost in the Old Testament', WE 192 (June 2, 1917), pp. 4-5 (5).

[225] Luce, 'Pictures of Pentecost in the Old Testament', *WE* 190 (May 19, 1917), pp. 2, 8; A.E. Luce, 'Pictures of Pentecost in the Old Testament', *WE* 191 (May 26, 1917), p. 5; A.E. Luce, 'Pictures of Pentecost in the Old Testament', *WE* 192 (June 2, 1917), pp. 4-5; A.E. Luce, 'Pictures of Pentecost in the Old Testament', *WE* 193 (June 9, 1917), pp. 2, 6. These were put together and reprinted in 1920 as a single article, A.E. Luce, 'Fire from Heaven and Abundance of Rain', *PE* 342-

built and soaked in water by Elijah, so must the life of the seeker of the Baptism in the Holy Spirit be offered entirely in humility before the 'fire from heaven [falls] that convinces the world in this day ... [that] "The Lord, He is God"'.[226] It is not necessary to 'keep on begging and beseeching God to baptise [sic] you as if He were unwilling'. Instead, offer prayers like 'the calm confidence of Elijah's prayer'.[227] The fire that falls demonstrates the 'acceptance of the Sacrifice [sic],' 'cleansing from dross,' and 'an impelling force' to bear witness to God.[228] A.E. Luce goes on to encourage 'Spirit-filled people not only to stand courageously and testify for [the Lord] before the multitude, bringing down the fire from heaven, but also to be faithful in the hours of persevering prayer in secret'.[229] 'The Lord is seeking for such prophets [as interceding Elijah] today, who will not only be faithful in public, when surrounded by the helpful influence of others, but who will yield to the call of the Spirit.'[230]

Luce believes that the account of Elijah and Elisha's journey to the east of the Jordan, Elijah's ascent and Elisha's mantling is 'one of the most deeply instructive types of the death, resurrection, ascension and glorification of the Lord Jesus, and of the subsequent descent of the Spirit of Power'.[231] The passing through the Jordan ('everywhere in Scripture ... is a picture of death') is akin to 'tarrying for the baptism in the Holy Ghost'.[232] Thus, the response of Elisha to Elijah concerning what might be done for him must be the same response of those to whom Jesus asks likewise in order that they might receive 'the baptism in the Holy Ghost, or a fresh infilling and anointing'.[233] If the seeker will fix their eyes on the Master, 'it will not be long before, like Elisha, you receive the descending mantle of

---

343 (May 29, 1920), pp. 1-2, 5. This last complete article is not cited in the footnotes which follow as the earlier citation covers the original periodical publication.

[226] Luce, 'Pictures of Pentecost in the Old Testament', *WE* 190, pp. 2, 8 (2).
[227] Luce, 'Pictures of Pentecost in the Old Testament', *WE* 190, pp. 2, 8 (2).
[228] Luce, 'Pictures of Pentecost in the Old Testament', *WE* 190, pp. 2, 8.
[229] Luce, 'Pictures of Pentecost in the Old Testament', *WE* 191, p. 5.
[230] Luce, 'Pictures of Pentecost in the Old Testament', *WE* 191, p. 5.
[231] Luce, 'Pictures of Pentecost in the Old Testament', *WE* 192, pp. 4-5 (4).
[232] Luce, 'Pictures of Pentecost in the Old Testament', *WE* 193, pp. 2, 6 (2).
[233] Luce, 'Pictures of Pentecost in the Old Testament', *WE* 193, pp. 2, 6 (2).

Power'.[234] Like Elisha we must act in faith once we've received the 'mantle' of the baptism and do what Jesus would do and did.

Luce further likens the 'the chariot and horses of fire, and the whirlwind which carried Elijah away into heaven' to 'the two symbols on the day of Pentecost': wind and fire.[235] The same connection is noted by an unnamed author where it is specifically noted that the wind and fire are in reverse order between Elijah's experience and the Day of Pentecost.[236] Both Elisha and the disciples of Jesus had to learn to 'get on without that master-hand which had so long helped and guided them'.[237] She develops this further, stating, 'The same lesson which Elisha and the disciples had to learn is for us ... [better] than the corporeal presence of Jesus among men, is the abiding of His Spirit within them'.[238]

A.L. Sisler[239] contends that Elijah stands as a figure of like endowment with the Spirit as the Church baptized in the Spirit and thus as one who stood apart for his day as a testimony to this day.[240] This endowment is not to be confused with the reception of the Spirit which all who 'come to Jesus' have received.[241] It is 'over and beyond this ordinary grace, which all believers must have ... [and] is a blessed anointing of the Holy Spirit which gives special equipment and fitness for service. Elijah had it.'[242] In fact, Sisler contends that it was only by Elijah being 'filled with the Spirit ... that Carmel itself, with all its heroic deeds, was gloriously possible'.[243] It was by Elijah giving himself to 'deep meditation' upon the Word of God that he maintained the fullness of the Spirit as an example to our age in order to

---

[234] Luce, 'Pictures of Pentecost in the Old Testament', *WE* 193, pp. 2, 6 (2).

[235] Luce, 'Pictures of Pentecost in the Old Testament', *WE* 193, pp. 2, 6 (2).

[236] 'Forerunners of Jesus', *WE* 210 (Oct. 13, 1917), p. 6.

[237] Luce, 'Pictures of Pentecost in the Old Testament', *WE* 193, pp. 2, 6 (2).

[238] Luce, 'Pictures of Pentecost in the Old Testament', *WE* 193, pp. 2, 6 (2).

[239] A.L. Sisler was wrongly attributed with the following articles, but corrected this by a personal letter to the editor stating the author of these articles was in fact F.M. Myers and that they were taken from Myers' book *Elijah and the Secret of His Power*, 'Notice', *PHA* 3.12-13 (July 17, 24, 1919), p. 6. I have chosen to maintain Sisler's name throughout what follows because it is his name attributed in the *PHA* articles as cited.

[240] Sisler, '1 Kings 17 Chapter', *PHA* 3.7-8 (June 12, 19, 1919), pp. 3-5 (3-4).

[241] Sisler, '1 Kings 17 Chapter', pp. 3-4.

[242] Sisler, '1 Kings 17 Chapter', p. 4.

[243] Sisler, '1 Kings 17 Chapter', p. 4.

empower for a redeeming witness.[244] The editor, G.F. Taylor, adds a brief clarifying editorial note just after this article proposing that Sisler does not mean 'Elijah had the Pentecostal baptism,' but 'was filled with the Spirit according to the measure of the Spirit given in his day' because 'no one had the Baptism of the Spirit until the day of Pentecost'.[245] G.F. Taylor continues to emphasize through a later editorial a distinction between the Baptism of Pentecost and the likes of Elijah.[246] Later that summer Sisler affirmed Taylor's editorial note on Elijah's fullness of the Spirit.[247]

This early Pentecostal hearing of the Spirit in the Former Prophets offers extensive points concerning the role of the Spirit. (1) The Spirit was *with* the Old Testament saints and is now *in* Pentecostal saints. (2) The Spirit testifies with power for those who seek the Lord in faith. (3) The Spirit baptism is typified by the double portion of the Spirit on Elisha. (4) The Spirit empowers to overcome sickness, disease, and death. (5) The Spirit is given in fullness, as the Baptism, to those who earnestly tarry in quietness. (6) The Spirit renews as an indwelling intercessor. (7) The Spirit is poured out like rain to revive those who intercede for the outpouring. (8) The Spirit falls like fire on those prepared to receive. (9) The Spirit baptizes as a testimony to the trustworthiness of the Pentecostal witness to Jesus. (10) The Spirit sustains hope in the midst of opposition. (11) The Spirit is present in the still, small, and quiet. (12) The Spirit is needed for regular outpourings. (13) The Spirit supplies every faithful kingdom worker's needs. (14) The Spirit testifies by the energizing of the saints to run. (15) The Spirit baptizes with fire as testimony to the same God of the Old Testament sanctifying and empowering saints. (16) The Spirit transforms and translates to glory those committed to faithfulness. (17) The Spirit makes people truly human and in conformity to the good news of Jesus. (18) The Spirit is only received by faith. (19) The Spirit is the nearness of God to act in the present. (20) The Spirit guarantees life giving ministry beyond the life of any individual saint. (21) The Spirit baptism signifies the double portion of the eldest son as the one to receive fullest inheritance. (22) The Spirit reveals Jesus

---

[244] Sisler, '1 Kings 17th Chapter', *PHA* 3.9 (June 26, 1919), pp. 5-7 (5).

[245] Sisler, '1 Kings 17th Chapter', pp. 6-7: editorial note.

[246] 'Editorial: Speaking in Tongues', *PHA* 3.11 (July 10, 1919), pp. 8-10 (8).

[247] A.L. Sisler, 'Dear Brother Taylor and Advocate Family', PHA 3.14 (July 31, 1919), p. 12.

unceasingly. (23) The Spirit mortifies the sinful nature. (24) The Spirit baptism is received only by those properly prepared to receive. (25) The Spirit is the abiding presence of Jesus.

The Double Portion

The double portion of the Spirit of Elijah that came upon Elisha bears special discussion. According to W.J. Seymour (1907), the 'double portion' of the Holy Spirit is Spirit baptism that prepares one to be taken for the 'marriage supper of the Lamb' and such persons are the 'wise virgins' having been saved, sanctified, and baptized in the Holy Spirit.[248] A 1910 *CGE* editorial, presumably written by A.J. Tomlinson, does not see it the same way. The editorial states,

> Some saints are going to be taken up soon to meet Jesus in the air, and if I am not one that goes like Elijah I want to be like Elisha, so close to some that do go that I can receive a double portion of their spirit to enable me to endure successfully the awful persecutions, trials and afflictions that will be poured out during the tribulation days.[249]

While Seymour envisions the rapturing of those receiving the 'double portion', Tomlinson seems to believe the rapturing may not happen, but the double portion will yet be necessary to have for faithful abiding. One recent convert to Pentecostalism writes in *AF*: 'I want a double portion of His Spirit, so that I may overcome all the temptations that come'.[250]

The double portion Spirit also serves to empower for the task of preaching the Full Gospel. The 'faithful few' who are willing to 'obey and follow' the Lord in partnering with Him in His work are receiving 'a double portion of His Spirit'.[251] H. Tower (1910) testifies that he had 'received the "double portion" according to Acts 4:29-31' along with two of his gospel co-workers in order to proclaim the Word with boldness and signs following.[252] Similarly, Lucy Leatherman

---

[248] W.J. Seymour, '"Receive Ye the Holy Ghost"', *AF* 1.5 (Jan. 1907), p. 2; and W.J. Seymour, '"Behold the Bridegroom Cometh"', *AF* 1.5 (Jan. 1907), p. 2.

[249] 'Warning and Advice: Divers and Strange Doctrines to Be Avoided', *CGE* 1.12 (Aug. 15, 1910), pp. 1-3 (3).

[250] H. Ward, 'Parmele, N.C.', *TBM* 1.11 (Apr. 1, 1908), p. 3.

[251] Mrs. B.L. Shepherd, 'Calling Us Deeper', *CGE* 9.6 (Feb. 9, 1918), p. 4.

[252] H. Tower, 'News from Gainesville, N.Y.', *LRE* 3.1 (Oct. 1910), p. 14.

(1912) of London, England, testifies to 'praying for the "Double portion," Acts 4.31, where they were shaken the second time', apparently looking for a greater filling as one who already testifies to 'speaking and singing in tongues … [even while] praying for the "Double portion" and the more excellent way'.[253] In 1910, a missionary band heading to China ministered in Berlin, Ontario,[254] where they testify that 'the brethren laid hands upon us and prayed the Lord to give us a double portion of His Spirit'.[255] A missionary to India in 1919 who recently lost her husband is affirmed by the confession of S. Coxe that the Lord 'will put a double portion of His Spirit upon our dear Sister Schoonmaker' to further the work of the gospel.[256]

Similar to the prayer for 'Sister Schoonmaker' to receive the 'double portion' of the Spirit that was on her now deceased husband, several others likewise mourn the passing of leading Pentecostal workers and desire their 'double portion'. O.M. Hilburn mourns the loss of Pentecostal Holiness Superintendent P.Z. McKenzie and catches himself 'sobbing in tears. Elisha like, desiring a double portion of his spirit'.[257]

With the passing of leading Pentecostal Holiness minister N.J. Holmes an entire issue of the *PHA* was issued that included numerous tributes. One of those included a call for 'the double portion of the spirit of Elijah [that] rested upon Elisha, so we trust that the double portion of the spirit of dear Brother Holmes may rest upon those who shall succeed him'.[258]

The double portioned Spirit functions for the early Pentecostal in numerous ways. (1) It signifies Spirit baptism. (2) This Spirit baptism is preparatory for the rapture of the Church. (3) The Spirit enables for faithful abiding in the midst of persecution. (4) The Spirit

---

[253] L.M. Leatherman, 'From Lucy M. Leatherman', *TBM* 5.102 (Jan. 15, 1912), p. 2.

[254] The city had been founded as Berlin as it was founded by German born immigrants, but due to anti-German sentiment during the First World War, a 1916 referendum was called, and the city's name was voted by a narrow margin to be changed. Later that year the city officially became known as Kitchener.

[255] F. Denney, C. Denney, and B. Appleby, 'From Out-Going Missionaries', *TBM* 4.72 (Oct. 15, 1910), p. 2.

[256] S. Coxe, 'He Fought a Good Fight', *LRE* 11.8 (May 1919), pp. 15-17 (15).

[257] O.M. Hilburn, 'Rev. P.Z. McKenzie', *PHA* 2.47 (Mar. 20, 1919), pp. 5-6 (6); and O.M. Hilburn, 'Rev. P.Z. McKenzie', *PHA* 3.3 (May 15, 1919), p. 12.

[258] H.V. Dempsey, 'By Henry V. Dempsey', *PHA* 3.39 (Jan. 22, 1920), p. 13.

empowers the faithful to overcome temptations. (5) The Spirit empowers for the preaching of the Full Gospel message with signs following for those faithfully committed to the work of the kingdom. (6) The Spirit carries on the work even after faithful workers are taken away by anointing others.

The Sons of the Prophets

While the double portion serves a positive function regarding the Spirit, the sons of the prophets are used in both negative and positive ways. A 1914 issue of *CGE* portrays the sons of the prophets as a negative Old Testament example of why one should not use the term 'Pentecostal' as simply 'a mighty manifestation of the working of the Holy Spirit'.[259] Such a usage of 'Pentecostal' fails to account for the peculiarity of the happenings of the Day of Pentecost and that since such persons as the sons of the prophets were also 'favored by the presence of the Spirit' then some other manifestation must be particular to 'Pentecost'.[260]

An article in *CE* (1919) also portrays them negatively: 'The sons of the prophets are generally at hand to exercise a depressing influence by standing in the way of lambs who seek the Shepherd's arms and blessing'.[261] They are the ones exercising an 'unkind spirit' and failing to allow the 'Holy Spirit' to witness 'to our spirits that we are **children of God**' and therefore beloved in our humility.[262]

In the same year, *LRE* regards them negatively. The sons of the prophets are a type of those in the world and the Church who believe that things 'become too straight for us'.[263] This is the way of those 'filled with higher criticism' and 'infidelity' who find the way of Jesus to be too 'straight'.[264] They are discontent with where they are and seek a different place. In the loss of the axe head into the depths of the river they exemplify the 'downward' way of every person 'left to

---

[259] A.E. Street, 'What Is Pentecost?' *CGE* 5.29 (July 18, 1914), p. 8.

[260] Street, 'What Is Pentecost?', p. 8.

[261] A.J. Howden, 'The Secret of True Prayer: A Few Thoughts on Luke 18', *CE* 274-275 (Feb. 8, 1919), p. 7.

[262] Howden, 'The Secret of True Prayer', p. 7, original emphasis.

[263] J. Saunders, '"And the Iron Did Swim": At the Touch of the Despised Stick', *LRE* 12.3 (Dec. 1919), pp. 5-7 (5).

[264] Saunders, '"And the Iron Did Swim"', pp. 5-7 (5).

himself'. That it was a borrowed axe indicates our being 'bought with a price'. Jesus, himself, is 'the Stick that causes the iron to swim'.[265]

Several positive uses for the idea of the sons of the prophets occur in the early establishment of schools within the Pentecostal movement. Sometime around 1909 beginning in Houston, Texas, a Pentecostal 'school' was started by 'a company of Apostolic Faith preachers and workers' which was called 'The School of the Prophets'.[266] This spread to 'different cities of Texas, Mississippi, Alabama, Missouri ... Iowa ... and Arkansas'.[267] The reason for this name was to

> honor the Holy Spirit as General Superintendent, Teacher and Leader. We court the supernatural. We have learned from actual experience that the student learns more in one hour under the power and inspiration of the Holy Spirit than in five under the ordinary methods of study. Hence we stand for the liberty of the Spirit throughout the work.[268]

The one other positive use occurs several times with regard to the need for attending a certain Bible conference being held by the Pentecostal Holiness Church and featuring the Pentecostal ministry of J.H. King. As such, F.A. Dail believed, 'If it was necessary for the young prophets in old times to be trained in the schools of the prophets, how much more is it necessary for the young preachers and old ones too to attend'.[269]

The sons of the prophets provided the early Pentecostals with several insights concerning the Spirit in the Former Prophets. (1) The Spirit can be present with those who are unfaithful. (2) The

---

[265] Saunders, '"And the Iron Did Swim"', p. 5.

[266] D.C.O. Opperman, 'Ozark Bible and Literary School', *WW* 12.8 (Aug. 1915), p. 4; see also a similar ad for the same school opening in Eureka Springs, Arkansas listed in *WE* 131 (Mar. 18, 1916), p. 13. The Mount Tabor Bible Training School in Chicago described themselves also as a 'faith school' that utilizes the notion of the 'schools of the prophets' wherein there is 'manual work connected with the school' to aid in funding, see 'Mount Tabor Bible Training School', *WE* 215 (Nov. 17, 1917), pp. 15-16 (16).

[267] Opperman, 'Ozark Bible and Literary School', p. 4.

[268] Opperman, 'Ozark Bible and Literary School', p. 4.

[269] F.A. Dail, 'Notice of Bible Conference', *PHA* 1.51 (Apr. 18, 1918), p. 11; 'Notice of Bible Conference', *PHA* 1.52 (Apr. 25, 1918), p. 12, 'Notice of Bible Conference', *PHA* 2.1 (May 2, 1918), p. 4.

experience of the Spirit in the Former Prophets is distinguishable from the Pentecostal experience. (3) The Spirit testifies concerning those who are true sons of God. (4) The Spirit superintends, leads, and teaches in power, inspiration, and liberation.

Conclusion

The early Pentecostal readings of the Spirit in the Former Prophets offer several points for overall reflection. The need for empowered leadership is repeated throughout. This leadership is given in preaching and teaching, mission, and testimony. The empowering means the deliverance from fleshliness, sin, and the power of the devil. Conflict is the result of the Spirit outpoured, but more so, deliverance through the conflict by enabling one to persist in faithfulness if they will abide in the Spirit. This is manifest in divine love toward the saints and even toward those who once enjoyed the blessings of Pentecost but have wavered. It is also manifest in the freedom in the Spirit to speak in tongues, prophesy, sing, run, and dance, even in the face of antagonism and troubles.

Noting the similarities (and differences), S.P. Jacobs, writing in *TBM* in 1911, and making this article out of a chapter from his book (*The Real Christian*), contends that the Spirit was said to '"come upon" and "rest upon" [Old Testament] believers' (Othniel, Judg. 3.10; Gideon, Judg. 6.34; Jephthah, Judg. 11.29; and Samson, Judg. 15.14; 16.17).[270] Jacobs concludes this point stating, 'Such unsullied purity and constant fellowship with the Holy Spirit imply complete salvation from sin'. They were 'regenerated' by and prophesied by the Spirit (noting Saul for both, 1 Sam. 10.6 and 10.10 respectively).[271]

He summarizes his work with the following:

> We have here, during many centuries before Pentecost, the Holy Spirit coming upon, being in, filling, teaching, guiding, regenerating, and cleansing believers, empowering them for prophecy, etc. These operations of the Holy Spirit cannot be ignored in order to make place for Christianity. Whatever Christianity is, it must be something more than these operations of the Spirit manifested

---

[270] S.P. Jacobs, 'The Spirit before Pentecost', *TBM* 5.99 (Dec. 1, 1911), p. 4. In the article, Jephthah is mis-spelled 'Jepthah' and Samson as 'Sampson'.

[271] Jacobs, 'The Spirit before Pentecost', p. 4.

prior to Pentecost. Contrary to all this, modern tradition affirms that these operations of the Holy Spirit are really Pentecostal, and were projected back to the favored few, and that Pentecost simply made possible for all what had been the privilege of the few ... To confound the personal incoming of the Holy Spirit at Pentecost with His coming, quickening, guiding, cleansing, and empowering operations before Pentecost, is an error equal to confounding Christ's personal coming at Bethlehem with His ministrations under former dispensations (1 Cor. x:4; Ex. iii:2; xiv:19). Wonderful as are the foregoing operations of the Holy Spirit, long prior to Pentecost, they rank far below Pentecostal grace.[272]

Jacobs is intent to note that the Pentecostal experiences are something unique, yet remarkably similar, in the Pentecostal dispensation.

In this fashion the early Pentecostals found assurances in the similarities (and differences) of their own days to that of the Former Prophets and particularly to their experiences *of the Spirit* to that described in the Former Prophets. Provision for needs; an overcoming faith, hope, and love. And all of these by the same Spirit who anointed judges, kings, and prophets of old. Still they found themselves enjoying an ever-deepening relation to that same Spirit – a more abiding effect and a more powerful experience – if only they would give themselves to tarrying and obedience.

Several larger categories are helpful for understanding the many ways in which these texts were heard by the early Pentecostals. First, the Baptism in the Holy Spirit is the most predominant use throughout the literature with every publication offering some connection to the Spirit in the Former Prophets as giving witness to their experience of the Baptism. The Elijah/Elisha account looms exceptionally large with the language of the 'double portion' which begins to function for these readers as a type of the Baptism. This functioned testimonially that the Spirit who was at work previously is at work still and in the fullest measure.

Second, the power (often associated with the Baptism) of the Spirit is present to overcome, deliver, enable witness, heal, prepare, and make provision. The testimonies that are given throughout liken present experiences to the experiences of the Former Prophets. Some highlight only the likeness, but several (*PE* and *PHA*)

---

[272] Jacobs, 'The Spirit before Pentecost', p. 4.

specifically separate their experiences as truer than those of the Former Prophets. Again, all of the periodicals take this idea up likely due to its connection to the Baptism even when not explicitly connected to such. Particularly, the power to bear witness is highlighted. In fact, the Baptism is testimony that the Spirit is carrying forward the plans of God.

Third, prayer functions as primary to the experience of the Spirit for all of these journals. The Spirit is received by prayer and enlivens prayer. Particularly through the example of Elijah's persistent praying, the Spirit is believed to fall in the same manner. Prayer then functions as a way of abiding in the Spirit in their reading of the Former Prophets. Prayer is affirmed if it is done in an attitude of humility. Further there must be an earnest seeking to receive the promised outpouring of the Spirit without selfish motivation.

Fourth, every journal affirms that the Spirit can be lost through faithlessness. Saul is the primary example they draw upon and his turn to 'Spiritism' is the primary culprit named (*TBM, CGE, PE, PHA*). While he began well, he did not end well. He was prideful and failed to die to himself and his sinful ways. This serves as a call to purity by the Spirit in order to continue to enjoy the presence of the Spirit. The Spirit could endanger as well as protect depending upon the orientation of the recipient toward the Spirit. This is also why the narrative flow of Elijah/Elisha passing through the towns west of the Jordan and finally the Jordan functions as steps in the journey of the believer involving death to self and the sanctifying/cleansing work of the Spirit leading to the Baptism.

Fifth, the texts of the Former Prophets serve an apologetic function for the early Pentecostals. They hear defense of their experiences of the Spirit in such things as dancing and running (*TBM, CGE, WW* and *BC*) and the various charismatic gifts of the Spirit like speaking in tongues, interpretations, and the prophetic (*CGE, LRE, PE*). It was important that an answer be offered without defending every practice.

Sixth, several contend for (divine) love in relation to the Spirit (*LRE, PE,* and *PHA*). This love was enjoined with the endowment of the Spirit and required a persistent abiding. One could be clothed as Gideon by this divine love through the outpoured Holy Spirit or lose the Spirit through abandoning their first love like Samson.

Seventh, the Spirit in the Former Prophets bears witness in several explicit Pentecostal testimonies to being the Spirit of Christ (*TBM*, *CGE*, *PE*). This Christological orientation for interpreting the Spirit is implied throughout the literature with the language of 'anointing' tied to the likes of Saul and David to kingship. It is also confessed that Christ Jesus offers a better anointing as one more full of the Spirit than those endowed in the Former Prophets. Further, it is the Spirit outpoured by Christ that prepares for the rule of the soon coming King.

In brief, the hearing of the Spirit in the Former Prophets functioned to affirm the early Pentecostals in their new-found experiences and interpretations of Scripture in the following ways even as it provided critique. (1) The Spirit is wholly faithful and persistent in offering an overcoming witness through the Baptism. (2) The Spirit fully enables, sanctifies, anoints, empowers, and remains with those faithful who themselves give faithful witness in the face of persecution and temptations. (3) Finally, the Spirit reveals God's will in Jesus for creating a kingdom of the faithful – and faith-filled – prepared for these last days. This hearing of the Spirit in the early Pentecostal periodicals prepares the way for the hermeneutic proposed in chapter two of a close literary and theological hearing of the Spirit in the Former Prophets that unfolds over the four chapters that follow.

4

THE LIBERATING SPIRIT OF JUDGES (OTHNIEL, GIDEON, JEPHTHAH, AND SAMSON)

Introduction

The endowment of the רוח of Judges sets a trajectory for 1 Samuel and the anointing of Saul to be king of Israel who brings about deliverance in the fashion of the judges' own endowments. Othniel (3.10), Gideon (6.34), Jephthah (11.29), and Samson (13.25; 14.6, 19; 15.14) are each particularly noted as endowed with the Spirit of Yahweh. It is these four accounts which will be heard as offering a liberating S/spirit in the book of Judges for Pentecostal hearings. This Spirit of Yahweh upon these judges 'appears as an efficient cause in the calling of a charismatic minister' (citing Judg. 6.34; 11.29; 13.25; 14.6, 19; 1 Sam. 11.6; and 16.13) and certainly serves that function in Judges (and on into 1 Samuel).[1]

There are ten occurrences of רוח in Judges (3.10; 6.34; 8.3; 9.23; 11.29; 13.25; 14.6, 19; 15.14, 19), but only seven occur in the construct form with Yahweh. The three others consist of two which refer to a personal state of being (the Ephraimites' 'anger': 8.3; and the 'strength' or 'breath' of Samson: 15.19) and one in the construct state with God as the 'troubling spirit' (רוח רעה) sent by God between Abimelech and the leadership of Shechem (9.23). The other seven

---

[1] J.A. Soggin notes that Saul serves as a sort of judge/king linking the texts of Judges/Samuel, *Judges, A Commentary* (OTL; Philadelphia, PA: Westminster, 1981), p. 46.

are scattered among four of the judges: Othniel (3.10), Gideon (6.34), Jephthah (11.29), and Samson (13.25; 14.6, 19; 15.14). E.J. Hamori contends that the troubling spirit in 9.23 is 'not merely ... to signify mood or inclination,' but actually refers to a spirit.[2] However, for the sake of this work the 'spirit' here is indicative of an attitude which is incurred by the influence of Yahweh with potential implication of relation to the Spirit of Yahweh, but deemed sufficiently ambiguous to be excluded from this study. Among other reasons for excluding this text from the study is that it is not in construct with either 'God' or 'Yahweh', even though it is specified as 'sent' by 'God'.

While there are no occurrences of 'S/spirit' within either the introductory material of Judges (1.1-3.6) or the concluding materials (Judges 17-21), the spread of occurrences include the first (Othniel) and last (Samson) judges and two of the extended intermediating accounts (Gideon and Jephthah). The following brief outline of Judges indicates in bold the explicitly Spirit empowered characters.

1. Introductory Accounts (Judg. 1.1-3.6)
2. **Othniel** (Judg. 3.7-11)
3. Ehud and Minor Judge (Judg. 3.12-31)
4. Deborah (Judg. 4.1-5.31)
5. **Gideon** (Judg. 6.1-8.32)
6. Abimelech and Minor Judges (Judg. 8.33-10.5)
7. **Jephthah** (Judg. 10.6-12.7)
8. Minor Judges (Judg. 12.8-15)
9. **Samson** (Judg. 13.1-16.31)
10. Concluding Accounts (Judg. 17.1-21.25)

This literary structure is suggestive of the central (even paradigmatic) role of the Spirit in the book of Judges. The placement of the explicit Spirit texts would sufficiently indicate to the readers that the implication is the other judges were likewise endowed with the Spirit. 'The empowering of the Spirit is crucial in Judges ... and down to the time of David it remained the mark of God's chosen [person]'.[3]

---

[2] E. Hamori, 'The Spirit of Falsehood', *CBQ* 72 (2010), pp. 15-30 (21, 23, 27). On this 'spirit' as 'Agency/Agent of Disaster' that is not to be identified as the Holy Spirit, see Block, 'Empowered by the Spirit of God', pp. 50-51.

[3] H. Wolf, 'Judges' in F.E. Gaebelein (ed.), *Deuteronomy-2 Samuel* (EBC 3; Grand Rapids, MI: Zondervan, 1992), p. 398.

The opening Spirit salvo 'The Spirit of the LORD came upon him' (Judg. 3.10) in the account of Othniel gives overall direction for understanding of the Spirit in the Old Testament with regard to leadership in the Former Prophets. This Spirit endowment marked individuals as carrying forward the redemptive plans of the faithful God of Israel in spite of the lack of the faithfulness of Israel.

The Spirit Testifies: Othniel (Judges 3.10)

After documenting a number of the specific sins of Israel, Judges declares that Yahweh handed Israel over to King Cushan-rishathaim of Aram of Mesopotamia for eight years until Israel's cry for a savior was answered in Othniel.

ותהי עליו רוח־יהוה וישפט את־ישראל ויצא למלחמה

ויתן יהוה בידו את־כושן רשעתים מלך ארם

ותעז ידו על כושן רשעתים

'And the Spirit of Yahweh came upon him, and he judged Israel and he marched out to war. [And] Yahweh gave King Cushan-rishathaim of Aram into his hand and his hand prevailed against Cushan-rishathaim' (Judg. 3.10).[4]

Prior to this Spirit empowering text concerning Othniel, he is introduced to the readers in the first chapter of Judges as one who is already a military leader having courageously conquered Kiriath Sepher and thus receiving the daughter of his uncle Caleb as reward (1.13).[5] Othniel has demonstrated his military prowess and his faithfulness to obey Yahweh. Only now in the text (3.10) is explicit mention of the Spirit upon Othniel. Is this because the Spirit was not previously necessary for Othniel's exploits? Or is it only at this point necessary for the text to clarify that the Spirit had been behind the

---

[4] All translations are my own unless indicated otherwise.

[5] K.L. Younger Jr. misreads the account as if Othniel is not an ethnic Israelite and follows this up by suggesting all the greater contrast to the other Israelites in the introductory chapters who inter-marry Canaanite women instead of an Israelite woman, *Judges and Ruth: From Biblical Text … to Contemporary Life* (NIVAC; Grand Rapids, MI: Zondervan, 2002), p. 108.

work of Othniel to call Israel to respond in faithfulness?[6] Such a 'testimonial function' may actually be a key to understanding the explicit Spirit passages in Judges rather than its function being to indicate only punctiliar experiences of Spirit endowment that exclude deliverers who are not named as being Spirit endowed or even suggesting to the readers that the judges only experienced the Spirit at those key moments. Thus the readers would likely perceive the Othniel account as a way of providing the reader with 'a stock example' including particularly the emphasis on the Spirit coming upon the deliverer.[7] Indeed, he appears to be the 'paradigmatic deliverer in the book of Judges'.[8] At a literary level, Othniel lacks the flaws of the other judges and functions as 'the paragon by which the other major or cyclical judges are assessed'.[9] The key factors indicating his ideal function are the 'completeness of the elements in the cyclical pattern, the brevity of the story, and the flawless performance' of Othniel in carrying

---

[6] D. Firth argues (without textual support) that Othniel had not previously needed the Spirit for empowerment noting that Othniel was militarily successful without any mention of the Spirit in Judg. 1.12-15. This presumes that any mention of the Spirit coming upon an individual is absolute rather than notable by the text for specific referential purposes. Yet, Firth also wants to contend for the Spirit on Ehud and Deborah without any explicit mention of the Spirit because 'both are already recognized as deliverers' and thus there is 'no need for the testimonial function of the Spirit'. D. Firth, 'The Historical Books', pp. 12-23 in Burke and Warrington, *A Biblical Theology of the Holy Spirit*, p. 15, and see especially p. 15 n. 14; and also in a previous writing, D.G. Firth, 'The Spirit and Leadership: Testimony, Empowerment and Purpose', pp. 259-80 in Firth and Wegner (eds.), *Presence, Power and Promise*, pp. 270-71.

[7] J.D. Martin, *The Book of Judges: Commentary* (Cambridge: Cambridge University Press, 1975), p. 42.

[8] L.R. Martin, 'Power to Save!?: The Role of the Spirit of the Lord in the Book of Judges', *JPT* 16.1 (2008), pp. 21-50 (24), also T. Butler, *Judges* (WBC 8; Nashville, TN: Thomas Nelson, 2009), pp. 66-8. P.E. Satterthwaite provides a helpful chart comparing the elements of the Othniel account to the other major judge accounts as he likewise regards Othniel to be the ideal judge offering a framework to compare and judge the others, 'Judges', pp. 580-92 in Arnold and Williamson (eds.), *DOT:HB*, p. 583. In a similar fashion, R.G. Boling argues for the 'exemplary character intended by this representation' and renounces all other occasions in Judges as indicating deviances 'from the Othniel standard', R.G. Boling, *Judges* (AB; Garden City, NY: Doubleday, 1975), pp. 81, 83.

[9] Younger, *Judges and Ruth*, pp. 105-10. Younger also cites R.H. O'Connell, *The Rhetoric of the Book of Judges* (VTSup 63; Leiden: Brill, 1996), p. 83, as an idyllic judge when compared to the other judges' characterizations.

out the task of Yahweh through the empowering Spirit of Yahweh.[10] The completeness of the cyclical pattern refers to the 'formulae' of Judg. 2.11-19 of which Othniel serves as a prime example.[11]

A feature which would not be missed by the reader: Othniel's Judahite marriage to Acsah (in Judges 1) contrasts with the Israelites who disobey Yahweh in the following narrative by taking Canaanite wives for themselves (3.5-6) and placing this statement just prior to re-introducing Othniel as now the Spirit endowed judge bringing about the salvation of Israel.[12] Though he is a Judahite, the narrative describes him as bringing about the salvation of Israel. His enablement is not simply to the benefit of his own tribe, but for all of the tribes. In contrast to this, the other judges rally forces only from individual tribes or coalitions of the various tribes.

There may be some ambiguity as to the basis for the liberation from the oppressors in the Othniel narrative whether the narrative states Othniel or Yahweh works the deliverance. However, there need not be a decision between whether Othniel or Yahweh saved Israel. The text seems sufficiently ambiguous to allow for both to be identified in the deliverance even as the readers would understand Yahweh to be the primary cause via Yahweh's Spirit empowered human agent.[13]

Indeed, the Spirit of Yahweh is testifying to the saving power of Yahweh to act on behalf of Israel even after the passing of Moses and Joshua (which is carefully noted in Judges 1-2). Yahweh is able to raise up Spirit-endowed leaders who were to guide in victory vouchsafing the life of Israel in the land. With regard to the account of Othniel it might be said that 'God imparts His Spirit for enablement on those who walk carefully before Him in a life of obedience'.[14] However, the readers would soon encounter Spirit

---

[10] Martin, 'Power to Save!?', p. 24.

[11] D.G. Firth suggests that this account of Othniel is intended to set the standard by which all later judges would themselves be judged by arguing that it may itself be 'drawn almost entirely from formulae in Judges 2:11-19'. See also D. Firth, 'The Historical Books', pp. 12-23 in Burke and Warrington, *A Biblical Theology of the Holy Spirit*, pp. 15-16; and D.G. Firth, 'The Spirit and Leadership', pp. 259-80 in Firth and Wegner, *Presence, Power and Promise*, p. 271.

[12] Younger, *Judges and Ruth*, p. 108.

[13] Younger, *Judges and Ruth*, p. 103.

[14] L.J. Wood, *Distressing Days of the Judges* (Grand Rapids, MI: Zondervan, 1975), p. 169.

empowered judges (Gideon, Jephthah and Samson) who seem to fall further and further from this ideal and yet receive the Spirit of Yahweh. Thus, while Othniel should serve as an ideal, Yahweh would deliver through those far less than ideal. The plan of Yahweh for and through Israel was much bigger than any individual judge and that judge's individual righteousness.

The Spirit Clothes: Gideon (Judges 6.34)

Some years later, the vast coalition armies of Midian, Amalek, and the men of the east gathers together against the tribes of Israel in the valley of Jezreel. Israel cries out to Yahweh and receives prophetic answer. A man named Gideon receives a divine call (with signs confirming) to work the deliverance of Israel. His immediate task finds him assaulting the idolatry of his hometown and of his own father (even if at night) and receiving the nickname Jerubbaal (meaning 'Let Baal contend [with him]').

Just as the armies of the east cross the Jordan, the text declares that וְרוּחַ יהוה לָבְשָׁה אֶת־גִּדְעוֹן וַיִּתְקַע בַּשּׁוֹפָר וַיִּזָּעֵק אֲבִיעֶזֶר אַחֲרָיו 'the Spirit of Yahweh clothed Gideon, and he sounded the shofar, and assembled Abiezer behind him' (Judg. 6.34). He proceeds to assemble the armies of Manasseh, Asher, Zebulun, and Naphtali via messengers. From here he inquires of God concerning the guarantee of victory, receives two signs indicating God's power and presence, followed by a testing of Gideon by Yahweh. Finally, victory is won at the hands of 300 men armed with covered torches and shofars. Following the narrative flow, this victory commenced by the Spirit of Yahweh was not simply a momentary enablement, but a process of calling, assembling, testing, sifting, spying, gathering, supplying, and following through. The Spirit empowerment at this point seems to suggest a prolonged clothing of Gideon to carry out the deliverance of Israel even if the text only highlights the initial moment of response.

The Spirit of Yahweh[15] לבשה ('clothed') Gideon is translated in several ways: 'came over',[16] 'took possession of',[17] 'clothed',[18] 'clothed itself with',[19] and was an 'investment of',[20] The readers would likely hear that Gideon has been *clothed by*,[21] and thus overcome by the Spirit

---

[15] The LXX[A] reads πνεῦμα θεοῦ.

[16] Soggin, *Judges*, p. 129. Soggin indicates (incorrectly) that LXX[BA] have ἐνεδυνάμωσεν meaning 'empowered'. While LXX[B] does indeed use this term, which is suggestive of another Hebrew *Vorlage* (to which Soggin provides several potentials), LXX[A] translates with ἐνέδυσεν meaning 'clothed', which is further supported by the first recension of the Lucianic LXX, the Old Latin, the Syriac, and the Targum.

[17] C.F. Burney, *The Book of Judges, with Introduction and Notes, and Notes on the Hebrew Text of the Books of Kings, with an Introduction and Appendix* (New York: KTAV Pub. House, 1970), p. 203; Gray, *Joshua, Judges, Ruth* (Grand Rapids, MI: Eerdmans, 1986), p. 233; J.D. Martin, *The Book of Judges*, pp. 90-91; G.F. Moore, *A Critical and Exegetical Commentary on Judges* (ICC; Edinburgh: T&T Clark, 1966), p. 197.

[18] Boling, *Judges*, p. 138; Butler, *Judges*, p. 183; J. Gray, *Joshua, Judges, Ruth*, p. 233; Wolf, 'Judges' in Gaebelein (ed.), *Deuteronomy-2 Samuel*, p. 423.

[19] Martin, *The Book of Judges*, p. 90, see footnote which indicates the 'lit[eral]' translation of the Hebrew. Despite Martin's note on p. 90, he states that 'a more accurate literal rendering of the Hebrew than the one suggested in the note' is 'clothed', p. 91; Burney, *The Book of Judges*, p. 203. Or 'puts him on' according to B.G. Webb, *Judges* (NICOT; Grand Rapids, MI: Eerdmans, 2012), p. 237 n. 51. S.M. Horton spends several pages discussing the interpretations of this verb and concludes that it can 'only mean that the Spirit filled Gideon. Gideon did not put on the Spirit; the Spirit put on Gideon', *What the Bible Says About the Holy Spirit*, pp. 38-39.

[20] Gray, *Joshua, Judges, Ruth*, p. 233.

[21] N.M. Waldman argues from certain ANE cognate uses that לבש in the Qal stem here is not functioning according to its traditional syntax, but rather that of the ANE notion of being 'overwhelmed'. Contrary to this, if the traditional Qal function is followed, this suggests that the Spirit is on the inside of Gideon, that is, being 'clothed' with Gideon, 'The Imagery of Clothing, Covering, and Overpowering', *JANES* 19 (1989), pp. 161-70 (165-67). If one hears the Spirit putting Gideon on, this might find further support in the inward language of 2 Sam. 23.2 where David prophetically declares, 'The Spirit of the LORD speaks *in* me' (רוח יהוה דבר־בי). Admittedly the ב preposition is likelier read as 'through' rather than 'in' despite that the more predominant usage in the HB is 'in, by, with'. However, this is not likely the case due to other terms offering a more fitting reading of the Spirit being *in* Gideon, the Spirit functions more appropriately as the 'clothing', the Spirit remains as the subject of the verb, the Qal passive stem can mean 'clothed' rather than 'put on', and elsewhere the subject of the verb for clothing means to 'clothe' or 'cover', see Martin, 'Power to Save!?', pp. 35-36.

at this particular point,[22] despite his concerns requiring two tests with wool and dew along with the revelation of a dream of terror striking the hearts of the enemy. The Spirit likely is mentioned here because this process of assembling for deliverance needed enablement at each step since he would now carry out a public deliverance instead of a night attack on the local shrine.[23] Gideon would need to act publicly with boldness to bear witness to the plans of Yahweh. Gideon is clothed by the Spirit in a fashion akin to the other texts of the Former Prophets that speak of the Spirit as being/rushing upon/on the charismatic leader (Judg. 3.10; 11.29; 14.6, 19; 15.14; 1 Sam. 10.6, 10; 11.6; 16.13; 18.10).[24]

The readers would likely hear the 'clothing' of Gideon as functionally no different than the Spirit coming upon Othniel before him in the narrative.[25] From a literary perspective, the verbal choice may be significant in that the Spirit is 'clothing' Gideon in contrast with Gideon later making an ephod (an article of sacred clothing) by the end of the Gideon narrative (8.27).[26] This would certainly create a sense of irony with regard to the manner in which Yahweh had determined to lead the people of Israel: by the Spirit clothing.

The Spirit and Promise: Jephthah (Judges 11.29)

At this point in the narrative the normal cycle of Israel in trouble for unfaithfulness does not surprise. This time extended words of instruction and reminders of the previous faithfulness of Yahweh and faithlessness of Israel ensues (10.6-12). Yahweh declares that Israel can now call on other gods for help – those gods which Israel has perversely turned to instead of Yahweh (including the gods of the Ammonites who now trouble them). Further, Yahweh declares he will no longer answer Israel. Israel persists in repentance and crying

---

[22] D. Moody argues for a psychological reading of the Spirit in Judges (particularly with regard to Gideon) as being 'possessed' and having their 'ordinary ego' replaced by a 'new ego' of the Spirit, see his *Spirit of the Living God*, p. 15.

[23] Martin, 'Power to Save!?', p. 34.

[24] Younger, *Judges and Ruth*, pp. 185-86.

[25] Firth, 'The Spirit and Leadership', pp. 259-80 in Firth and Wegner, *Presence, Power and Promise*, p. 273.

[26] This was suggested by wordplay, according to Younger, *Judges and Ruth*, p. 185 n. 28. See also Martin, 'Power to Save!?', p. 37.

out to Yahweh for help. Yahweh's answer comes in the form of an unseemly character with troubling provenance introduced in chapter 11: Jephthah. The elders of Gilead promise to follow Jephthah if he will deliver Israel (11.10). Jephthah's initial response is to seek peace with Ammon through a re-telling of the relationship of Ammon, Moab, and Israel (11.15-27). The strategies of Jephthah were for peace with the enemy, but Yahweh would have peace only through military victory that bears clear evidence of the Spirit bringing about the victory.[27]

The Ammonite king spurns the gesture of Jephthah,

ותהי על־יפתח רוח יהוה ויעבר את־הגלעד ואת־מנשה
ויעבר את־מצפה גלעד וממצפה גלעד עבר בני עמון

'And the Spirit of Yahweh came upon Jephthah, and he passed through Gilead and Manasseh, and passed through Mizpah of Gilead, and from Mizpah of Gilead he passed over to the Ammonites' (Judg. 11.29). Jephthah's Spirit endowed successful warpath is immediately followed by an unnecessary and unsought for vow resulting in the memorialized sacrifice of his daughter as if to make guarantee of victory over Ammon (11.30-31, 34-40).[28] The reader is here again confronted by a character less than ideal and yet the Spirit of Yahweh comes upon him.

When the Spirit Stirs: Samson (Judges 13.25; 14.6, 19; 15.14)

Judges 13 reiterates that Israel again לעשׂות הרע בעיני יהוה 'did evil in the eyes of Yahweh' and were handed over to the Philistines for forty years. Without any textual indication of repentance or prayers from Israel at this immediate point, Yahweh answers with the supernatural

---

[27] Martin, 'Power to Save!?', p. 39.

[28] Reading the vow as intended to manipulate divine response wherein God is depicted as intentionally removed from the narrative, see J.C. Exum, 'On Judges 11', pp. 131-44 in A. Brenner (ed.), *A Feminist Companion to Judges* (The Feminist Companion to the Bible 4; Sheffield: Sheffield Academic, 1993); and 'The Centre Cannot Hold: Thematic and Textual Instabilities in Judges', *CBQ* 52 (1990), pp. 410-31. I owe this insight to L.R. Martin from a conversation, followed by a rereading of portions of his monograph: *The Unheard Voice of God*, pp. 9-10.

announcement of a child from the tribe of Dan especially dedicated to Yahweh from birth, who would begin to deliver Israel from the Philistines. Upon the birth and naming of this boy, the child immediately enjoyed the blessing of Yahweh.[29]

ותחל רוח יהוה לפעמו במחנה־דן בין צרעה ובין אשתאל

'And the Spirit of Yahweh began to stir him at Mahaneh-Dan between Zorah and Eshtaol.'

When the Spirit תחל ... לפעמו 'began ... to stir him'[30] to action in Judg. 13.25 it appears to function as a way of motivating him to call for Israelite response to the Philistine aggression. The readers have come to anticipate a response (even if diminishing or more problematic). However, no Israelite response is forthcoming, but only the stirring of an individual to (questionable) action. The hiphil form of the verb חלל (here translated 'began') carries the meaning of 'began', but in its other forms it carries the idea of 'profane'.[31] Would the readers hear some wordplay irony in the use of a term sounding antithetical to the sacred? In fact, this term was a significant part of the promise of Yahweh concerning this boy who would 'begin' to deliver Israel from the Philistines (13.5). This boy was dedicated to Yahweh from birth and to חלל the deliverance. By chapter sixteen the readers encounter Samson חלל to be afflicted[32] by Delilah as she cut his hair (v. 19) and he remained subdued until his hair חלל to grow back (16.22).

---

[29] Soggin contends that the Spirit was not present with Samson from birth, but only the Nazirite blessing, *Judges*, p. 235.

[30] The LXX reads that the Spirit of the LORD συνεκπορεύεσθαι (LXX[B]) or συμπορεύεσθαι (LXX[A]) meaning 'to accompany' him, rather than as the MT reads, 'to stir/move' him. The Targumim reads the LORD לתקפותיה 'strengthened' him. The LXX (and the Vulgate's *esse cum eo*) suggests a much more mutually participatory role between the Spirit and Samson. D.G. Firth reads this verb as 'direct' rather than stirring or agitating, 'The Spirit and Leadership', pp. 259-80 in Firth and Wegner, *Presence, Power and Promise*, p. 275.

[31] According to D.F. O'Kennedy, 'חלל', pp. 145-50 in VanGemeren (ed.), *NIDOTTE* vol. 2 (Grand Rapids, MI: Zondervan, 1997), pp. 146, 150. However, my count of the occurrences of the hiphil of the first entry of חלל is 56 with every one of these occurrences carrying some idea of 'begin' except for Ezek. 39.7 which reads 'profane' much like every occurrence of the niphal, piel, and pual.

[32] My reading follows the MT reading ותחל לענותו. The LXX[B] καὶ ἤρξατο ταπεινῶσαι is consistent with the MT, but LXX[A] καὶ ἤρξατο ταπεινοῦσθαι makes the verb passive: 'and he began to be weakened'.

Thus, there is a literary resonance between the use of the hiphil stem of חלל here in Judg. 13.25, where the Spirit 'began ... to stir him' (having previously promised he would 'begin' to deliver Israel from the Philistines: 13.5), and by the end of the Samson narrative in 16.19 and 22 where the text says Delilah 'began to afflict him' and his hair 'began' to grow.

The 'stirring' or 'troubling'[33] (פעם) by the Spirit of Yahweh (13.25) also sets a trajectory for the turmoil of the Samson narrative that follows where this qal verb's cognate noun form appears again and again within the Samson narrative of Judg. 16 (vv. 15, 18, 20 [2x], 28) signifying 'occurrence' or 'time' and culminating in his fateful end.[34] From this initial stirring by the Spirit to take action to the end of his life Samson was a provocative deliverer who carried out plans against the Philistines that even Samson's own parents (and likely the readers) could not envision as the plan of Yahweh apart from a special revelation *ex eventu*. This explains the editorial comment that Samson's actions were indeed the opportunity for Yahweh to confront the Philistines (14.4).

As the narrative unfolds, a lion confronts Samson on his way to fetch a Philistine wife from Timnah.

ותצלח עליו רוח יהוה וישסעהו כשסע הגדי ומאומה אין בידו
ולא הגיד לאביו ולאמו את אשר עשה

'And the Spirit of Yahweh came powerfully upon him, and he tore it with his bare hands like the tearing of a young goat, but he did not tell either his father or his mother what he had done' (Judg. 14.6). The 'seizing' (צלח) of Samson is used in each of the following times with the Spirit in relation to Samson (14.19 and 15.14) and later also

---

[33] This latter term might more effectively draw upon the 'troubling' nature of the Samson account altogether and give emphasis to the 'troubling' nature of the Spirit. See Martin, 'Power to Save!?', p. 44.

[34] See the similar comment by Webb, *Judges*, p. 359, and also 359 n. 28. D.G. Firth notes this reoccurrence as well, but believes it 'is difficult to draw clear conclusions from such a limited sample ... [even though] it is possible that it is chosen here to suggest that the direction of the Spirit was not Samson's own choice', 'The Spirit and Leadership', pp. 259-80 in Firth and Wegner, *Presence, Power and Promise*, p. 275 n. 37.

for Saul (1 Sam. 10.10) and David (1 Sam. 16.13). This 'seizing'[35] of Samson by the Spirit 'is not simply a strongman act, but part of God's overall plan to free his people from Philistine oppression'[36] or better, to *begin* to free them.[37]

The Spirit rushing with power on Samson to kill the lion (14.6) functions literarily to open the way for his wedding riddle and the Spirit-ed angry response of Samson to his betrothed's betrayal by killing thirty Philistines from Ashkelon (14.19).

ותצלח עליו רוח יהוה
וירד אשקלון ויך מהם שלשים איש
ויקח את־חליצותם ויתן החליפות למגידי החידה
ויחר אפו ויעל בית אביהו

And the Spirit of Yahweh came powerfully upon him, and he went down to Ashkelon and killed thirty of their men. And he took their clothes and gave the garments to those who had answered the riddle. And he burned with anger and he went up to his father's house (14.19).

These two accounts thus function to interpret one another by the first setting the stage for the second which then serves as the point of beginning the deliverance from the Philistines that the narrator has clarified just previously in verse four.[38] Readers would encounter the Spirit coming upon Samson in 14.19 as not only to empower him to get the victory in general, but to authorize and enable him to

---

[35] The MT has this strong language, the LXX[A] reads much more mutually participatory again by offering that the Spirit κατηύθυνεν 'guided/led' him. T. Butler translates this here and elsewhere in the Samson account (14.19) as 'came straight to', *Judges*, p. 314. The LXX[B] reads that the Spirit ἥλατο 'leapt' upon him.

[36] Martin, *The Book of Judges*, p. 165.

[37] G.F. Moore regards this seizing as 'irresistible' in giving Samson 'access' to 'divine rage'; 'irresistible' may be an overstatement except on the part of the character's own sense of empowerment own unleashed against the enemies, *Judges*, p. 331. G. Bush reads צלח as indicating 'a peculiar *urgency*, an *impelling influence* on the part of the Spirit', *Joshua and Judges*, p. 183, original emphasis. C.F. Burney also notes the impelling force of the Spirit upon Samson, *The Book of Judges*, p. 66. However, L.R. Martin notes the uses of צלח in relation to the Spirit on an individual (as noted above) and seems to conclude rightly 'nothing in the text suggests that the Spirit negates Samson's power of volition', 'Power to Save!?', p. 44.

[38] Firth, 'The Spirit and Leadership', pp. 259-80 in Firth and Wegner, *Presence, Power and Promise*, p. 275.

conquer this specific enemy (the Philistines at Ashkelon).[39] As the Spirit of Yahweh had powerfully enabled Samson to overcome the lion, so the Spirit of Yahweh powerfully enabled Samson to overcome the Philistines. The narrative thus vindicates Samson's actions by identifying them with Yahweh's own actions against any who would seek the undoing of his people. Samson, seized by the Spirit, seems to inhabit 'the borderlands between the civilized and the wild, between man and beast'.[40] The narrative offers a shocking contrast between Samson's self-will and the Spirit's role to work deliverance. The Spirit empowered deliverers move further from the center of the community and become both outcasts and loners even as the Spirit provokes them to further action on the behalf of the community. The Spirit of Yahweh would preserve the life of Israel even at the cost of the lives of enemies and even when Israel resists the very deliverance wrought for them by binding and handing Samson over to an army of Philistines once Samson again provoked the Philistines through an enflaming of their fields by pairs of fire-wielding foxes (15.1-13).

Not only does Samson fail to call Israel to action by the Spirit, but he also becomes the target of Israelite (specifically Judahite) aggression seeking to make nice with their oppressors instead of casting off their bonds. Readers thus find the Philistines approach to take hold of the newly bound Samson.

הוא־בא עד־לחי ופלשתים הריעו לקראתו ותצלח עליו רוח יהוה
ותהיינה העבתים אשר על־זרועותיו כפשתים אשר בערו באש
וימסו אסוריו מעל ידיו

When he came to Lehi, the Philistines triumphantly shouted at him, and the Spirit of Yahweh powerfully seized him[41] and the ropes which were on his arms were like flax that is burned with fire and his bonds disintegrated from his hands (Judg. 15.14).

He grabs a nearby fresh jawbone of a donkey and kills a thousand Philistines. This would have dealt a heavy blow again to the Philistines. However, it does not appear to inspire any form of action on

---

[39] Bush, *Joshua and Judges*, p. 195.

[40] Webb, *Judges*, p. 368.

[41] 'A Cairo Genizah fragment does not contain "the Spirit of Yahweh broke in upon him"', according to Butler, *Judges*, p. 315.

Israel's part other than for Samson to compose a poem about it and the people to rename the place. Samson does not even find his spirit lifted by this but falls into a morose despair about lacking water from Yahweh, which he receives miraculously. The narrative continues with no further explicit mentions of the Spirit of Yahweh despite Samson lifting and removing of the gates of Gaza, casting off the various traps of Delilah, and his final suicidal destruction of three thousand Philistines and the temple of Dagon at Gaza.

Conclusion

The Spirit appears to effect deliverance throughout Judges, however, the 'progression from Othniel to Samson suggests diminishing faithfulness on the part of the judges upon whom the spirit comes ... This diminishing faithfulness is paralleled by diminishing returns, in terms of deliverance.'[42] While Othniel gathers Israel as loosely connected tribes together to join in the deliverance, Samson antagonizes as an individual only motivating his own people to hand him over. The interceding tales of Gideon and Jephthah both entail inter-tribal conflicts resulting immediately as a result of the deliverance from an external enemy and both result in the judges carrying out perversions by the end of their stories which became memorialized in Israel for generations. In what ways might the readers understand the function of the Spirit in relation to these judges as examples?

First, the Spirit is identified so clearly with the work of Yahweh that the Spirit in Judges functions as Yahweh in relating to the judges. The Spirit of Judges should not be relegated to an 'impersonal force'[43] only related to Yahweh in some unclear fashion, but identified with the very movements of Yahweh, as Yahweh's own Spirit, to work out the redeeming liberation of Israel through the chosen

---

[42] J.C. McCann, *Judges* (Interpretation; Louisville, KY: John Knox, 2002), p. 82. This is also noted by Butler, *Judges*, p. 287.

[43] R.G. Boling believes that in Judges 'the expression [רוח] stands for an impersonal power or force which can be absorbed or can so envelop a man that he becomes capable of extraordinary deeds. This spirit is distinguishable from other spirits in that it is a Yahwistic one and thus lends itself to correlation with the administrative freedom of Israel's sovereign', *Judges*, p. 81. See also his discussion of the 'Yahweh spirit' in *Judges*, pp. 25-26.

judge. Further, while some readers might contend that this Spirit so overwhelms the individual that personality is lost, the narrative suggests rather that the 'Spirit's power is something that can be drawn upon ... not something that overcomes the judge' as if to make an automaton. [44]

Second, the function of the Spirit in Judges serves to guarantee that Israel will continue to enjoy life in the land. The Spirit enables Israel to remain in the land and enjoy 'peace' for periods of time that would include well-being and wholeness in a holistic fashion. The deliverance does not function simply to allow for life as it was prior to the deliverance where Israel served other gods and married foreign women. Readers note that the purpose of the clothing of Gideon functions to allow for the life of Israel to continue by enabling Gideon to lead the tribes in enacting their deliverance by his *and* their acts of faith. The community is being enabled by the Spirit to be delivered even though the individual judge is highlighted as the one empowered by the Spirit. However, not every time (e.g. Samson) the Spirit of Yahweh comes upon a judge does it culminate in calling the people to take up arms to work out their own salvation. [45]

Third, these Spirit texts seem not only to serve for guaranteeing the continuing life of Israel in the land by delivering from enemies (even if only partially and temporarily), but also by indicating the leadership chosen by Yahweh had already, prior to noted Spirit empowerment, functioned as leaders. [46] The Spirit highlighted those appointed to lead Israel into seasons of peace. Such an endowment would require the leader to discern the will of Yahweh with implications of the Spirit remaining and enabling beyond simply the mustering of Israel to battle or the tearing of a lion. The readers might

---

[44] Firth, 'The Historical Books', pp. 12-23 in Burke and Warrington, *A Biblical Theology of the Holy Spirit*, p. 16.

[45] J.H. Walton, V.H. Matthews, and M.C. Chavalas, *The IVP Bible Background Commentary: Old Testament* (Downers Grove, IL: IVP Academic, 2000), p. 255. T. Butler suggests as much and also cites Walton, Matthews, and Chavalas, but fails to address any problem inherent in such a proposal, *Judges*, p. 208. He also fails to note that Walton, Matthews, and Chavalas indicate a difference of the function for the Spirit on Samson than the Othniel, Gideon, and Jephthah regarding the empowerment to muster the armies of Israel, p. 267.

[46] Firth, 'The Spirit and Leadership', pp. 259-80 in Firth and Wegner, *Presence, Power and Promise*, pp. 276-77

understand the explicated Spirit texts thus to indicate the presence of the Spirit of Yahweh even prior to and following the notable endowments of the Spirit to carry out functions of specific deliverance.[47]

Fourth, the Spirit of Yahweh transforms individuals, but does not so overpower them as to annul their ability to be unfaithful. The judges were given power, but the expectation was that this would be included with a life of purity as well (for Israel and for the judge). The emphasis upon empowering in the Book of Judges should not miss the equal (though often neglected) emphasis on purity in Judges as a key component of the overall function of the book. The narrative is replete with the impurity of Israel to live according to the purposes of Yahweh. Yet this notion is the very purpose of the judge's deliverance from enemies as also entailing a call back to faithfulness toward Yahweh. The Spirit's empowering serves to save, but also to call back to righteousness (or so it would seem to have been intended and functioned for the readers). The Spirit was no guarantee of purity in every fashion. The careful readers would not miss this inference.[48]

Contrary to what readers might have anticipated after encountering the story of Othniel, the Spirit's relationship to Gideon is not one of transforming morality or a demonstration of the spirituality of Gideon, but only a sign of the LORD's 'sovereign will to set things in motion for the deliverance he has planned'.[49] '[T]he Spirit's power is

---

[47] Rea, *The Holy Spirit in the Bible*, p. 54.

[48] It is not surprising that many readers of Judges are bothered by the distinction between purity and power (including many Pentecostal readers). See the discussion by Martin, *The Unheard Voice of God*, pp. 3-8, and especially footnotes 11-14. As an example of just such an issue with the relation between purity and power, H. Wolf views the role of the Spirit in Judges as a 'problem' due to the endowment of individuals not regarded as moral exemplars. Instead, he proposes (as others as well) that the Spirit was only a temporary endowment in Judges and not like the 'NT experience of the permanent indwelling of the Holy Spirit' which he believes was unknown in the OT period, 'Judges' in Gaebelein (ed.), *Deuteronomy-2 Samuel*, p. 381. This presumes at least two things: (1) that the NT experience of Spirit endowment necessitated a sanctified life free of any ability to sin, whereas the OT experience allowed for individuals to experience salvation apart from this sanctifying work, and (2) that the Spirit is experienced in a different manner apart from the Christological orientation of the outpoured Spirit in the NT.

[49] Younger, *Judges and Ruth*, p. 187. See also, D.I. Block, 'The Period of the Judges: Religious Disintegration under Tribal Rule', in A. Gileadi (ed.), *Israel's*

available for the specific purpose of delivering the nation, but that does not represent a transformation of the one empowered by the Spirit.'[50] Power is not to be confused with purity. Certainly, neither Jephthah nor especially Samson would be considered exemplars of Spirit empowered holiness.

Fifth, and related directly to the fourth function, the Spirit does not vouchsafe every action of the one who is Spirit endowed, but is noted instead to bring about deliverance regarding the immediate needs of the individual and community. This punctiliar notice does not rule out a continuing presence of the Spirit upon the judges or that the other named judges throughout the book were devoid of the Spirit. As the text of the Former Prophets follows into First Samuel, Yahweh will similarly 'seize' another who will actually be transformed by his Spirit (Saul), even if temporarily, to continue the delivering work of Samson. This time the Spirit endowed will call all Israel to response as Othniel at the beginning.

Several points regarding Jephthah bear reflection. Some have pointed out that it is only after Jephthah begins his role as a military deliverer that he is endowed with the Spirit.[51] Once again, the delayed explicit statement of the Spirit of Yahweh coming upon a judge does not require that this is the first experience of the Spirit upon the judge. In fact, the language of 'seizing' might be heard by readers as a significant enablement in contrast to the regular enablement. The explicit statement of the Spirit enabling one already adept at warfare serves to highlight the witness of Yahweh compelling the community to action. It also may be saying too much to claim that Yahweh had not already made the decision for a deliverer when Yahweh finally 'grew tired of the suffering of Israel' (Judg. 10.16).[52] Though Yahweh had just previously said he would not answer, now Yahweh declares he will answer. This answer appears in Judges 11 with the choice of

---

Apostasy and Restoration: Essays in Honor of Roland K. Harrison (Grand Rapids, MI: Baker, 1988), p. 52.

[50] Firth, 'The Historical Books', pp. 12-23 in Burke and Warrington (eds.), *A Biblical Theology of the Holy Spirit*, p. 16.

[51] Gray, *Joshua, Judges, Ruth*, pp. 179, 255; and Martin, *The Book of Judges*, p. 144. Contra this, C.F. Burney, through a complex discussion of the various editings of Judges contends that the actual full mustering did not happen until after the Spirit of the LORD came upon Jephthah, *The Book of Judges*, p. 318.

[52] Contrary to Martin, 'Power to Save!?', pp. 38-39.

Jephthah confirmed by the Spirit of Yahweh's endowment. Judges 10.16 and 11.28 might actually better be read as two ways of describing the same thing rather than as distinct accounts: the first being general, while the latter is specific. Yahweh's response to the repentant cries is witnessed in his Spirit coming upon Jephthah to work deliverance.

The endowment[53] functions to provide Jephthah 'convincing testimony that his cause was good'.[54] It was given not, however, to vouchsafe any and every decision he made as if all he did was sanctified by Yahweh.[55] 'Yahweh … shows himself once again to be the God of surprising grace and sends his empowering Spirit upon Jephthah'. The fulfillment of Jephthah's rash vow and the ensuing tribal war against Ephraim makes the deliverance from Ammon seem questionable moving forward since it brings into question the righteousness of any judge by turning Jephthah from 'deliverer into [just] another oppressor'.[56] However, this Spirit enablement of an outlaw and rash vow-maker clarifies that Yahweh is more concerned about the preservation of Israel than about the means of their deliverance.[57] This would play out again with the (beginning of the) deliverance from the Philistines whose oppression was first noted in Judg. 10.7 alongside Ammon and who would be answered in the prayers of Israel by Spirit empowerment of Samson. Indeed, it is a strange matter (though likely encouraging to the readers) that by Samson's weaknesses 'the Spirit works' to bring about the LORD's purposes.[58] The endowment of the Spirit of Yahweh accomplishes the work of Yahweh despite the sanctity of the recipient though much more could have been done had purity been laid hold of by these wayward deliverers.

Finally, a careful reading would notice the irony of Samson himself returning again and again to self-imposed bondage all the while believing victory would be available. His impurity (as one set aside

---

[53] Soggin uses the language of 'possession' with regard to Jephthah and the Spirit, *Judges*, p. 219. He also uses this language for Samson, p. 247.

[54] Bush, *Joshua and Judges*, p. 150.

[55] Younger, *Judges and Ruth*, p. 261.

[56] Younger, *Judges and Ruth*, p. 266.

[57] Martin, 'Power to Save!?', pp. 38-39.

[58] Firth, 'The Spirit and Leadership', in Firth and Wegner (eds.), *Presence, Power and Promise*, p. 275

for specific purity) and unbelievable failings (contrasted with unbelievable victories) function to affirm the Spirit's role as the gracious and merciful hand of Yahweh despite all of this. The Spirit is not given to perfect individuals nor does the Spirit guarantee perfection or obedience. The Spirit simply enables the endowed opportunities for a fresh obedience whether pursued or not. Could it be that readers might hear the continuing saga of Samson as ensuing without the Spirit's enablement? This does not seem likely. The more probable explanation is that the Spirit is simply named at points to set a precedence for such an unlikely and unseemly character to be known as one empowered by the Spirit of Yahweh.[59] There would not be a need to 'always explicate what was commonly understood' and sufficiently highlighted in the text.[60]

---

[59] As such L.J. Wood proposes that Samson maintained the continuing endowment of the Spirit over the course of his judging role, but that the several occasions where the Spirit is noted to enable him are unique moments of extraordinary enablement, *Distressing Days of the Judges*, pp. 311-12.

[60] Hildebrandt, *An Old Testament Theology*, p. 118.

5

STRINGS OF THE SPIRIT: WHEN PROPHETS PLAY THE LYRE

Introduction

A recurring notion in 1 Samuel (chapters 10, 16, 18-19) appears to highlight the relation of kings Saul and David to the Spirit, prophesying, and the playing of the lyre. Saul initially receives the Spirit of Yahweh and begins to prophesy as predicted by Samuel once Saul hears the music of the prophets at Gibeah. Later, the Spirit of Yahweh departs from Saul and comes upon David (who later claims to prophesy in psalms). With the departure of the Spirit of Yahweh from Saul a 'troubling spirit of God' comes upon him causing sudden violent outbreaks. The only relief from the troubling spirit is the music of Spirit-endowed David on the lyre. Further, the 'prophets prophesying' appears to function musically throughout this literary unit being included with the overcoming of Saul twice to 'prophesy' when encountering a group of prophets prophesying (in the first instance explicitly with music and suggestive in the second). A literary and theological interpretation of the relevant texts is offered for discerning the role of the Spirit in the instrumentation of the prophetic in 1 Samuel.

One finds the Benjamite Saul, son of Kish, overwhelmed by the Spirit again and again in the first book of Samuel (and David's melodic prophetic relation to the Spirit from 1 to 2 Samuel). These troubling texts offer a melody for hearing the Spirit's relation to Saul and David and the music of the Spirit-ed: 1 Sam.10.1-12; 16.13-23; 18.6-14; and 19.8-24. Saul is promised to be made new. Saul is tasked to act once the Spirit descends. Saul is overwhelmed by the lyres and cymbals and finds himself joining the prophetic band. Saul is troubled and only finds relief in the rests offered at the hands of Spirit-empowered David strumming songs of deliverance. At the repeating crescendo, Saul finds himself utterly overcome with the dissonant spirit and seeking to end the ministering minstrel but is cast down in a parody of his son Jonathan intermingled with his first encounter as concluding cadence. How should one read the Spirit in these accounts?

Though much could be said about the therapeutic nature of music (as much has already been said in numerous volumes),[1] this does not seem the point of these texts. In fact, the musical instrumentation is just that: instrumental. It is the Spirit who carries forward the movements. One might in fact surmise from these texts that it is Yahweh who plays the instruments by his Spirit to will and do what Yahweh desires. And these instruments in the hands of Yahweh can be played to lift and relieve the spirit or to compel the spirit to melancholy notes of despair. How one might respond to the strings of the Spirit's strumming finds one voice in these troubling and relieving accounts.

---

[1] For a comprehensive discussion of music therapies with extensive bibliography see, T. Wigram, I. Nygaard Pedersen, and L.O. Bonde (eds.), *A Comprehensive Guide to Music Therapy: Theory, Clinical Practice, Research and Training* (London: Jessica Kingsley Publishers, 2004). Several articles which speak to the use of music therapy related to the Church and drawing on several of the following passages can be found in C.O. Aluede, 'Music Therapy in Traditional African Societies: Origin, Basis and Application in Nigeria', *Journal of Human Ecology* 20.1 (2006), pp. 31-35; 'F. Adedeji, 'The Theology and Practice of Music Therapy in Nigerian Indigenous Churches: Christ Apostolic Church as a Case Study', *Asia Journal of Theology* 22.1 (2008), pp. 142-54; 'Some Reflections on the Future of Music Therapy in Nigeria', *The Journal of Language, Technology & Entrepeneurship in Africa* 2.1 (2010), p. 36; 'F. Adedeji and A. Ogunleye, 'Music as a Form of Medicine for the Church: A Theomusicological Study and Application in I Samuel 16:14-23', *Ogbomoso Journal of Theology* 18.1 (2013), pp. 27-49; A.O. Ricketts, 'Employing Music as an Aid for Healing in the Church', *Ogbomoso Journal of Theology* 18.2 (2013), pp. 102-11. Several books addressing this topic include the following E.W. Nelson, *Music and Worship* (TX: Baptist Spanish Publishing House, 1985); D.P. Hustard, *Jubilate II: Church Music in Worship and Renewal* (Carol Stream, IL: Hope, 1989); M. Coleman and L. Indquise (eds.), *Come and Worship* (New Jersey: Choose Books, 1989); J.N. Corbitt, *The Sound of Harvest* (Grand Rapids, MI: Baker, 1998).

The Music Begins: Saul's Charismatic Anointing (1 Samuel 10.1-12; 11.6)

Israel demands a king like the other nations around them to fight their battles and make them to have a great name. Yahweh grants them a king, Saul, from among the Benjamites, the son of Kish. The prophet of Yahweh who has been introduced as hearing the word of Yahweh, previous to this account, is Samuel whom Yahweh entrusts to anoint this king. Saul was thus anointed by Samuel לנגיד 'to rule' Israel and a primary function of this rulership would be carried out when והושיע את־עמי מיד פלשתים 'he will save my people from the hand of the Philistines' (1 Sam. 9.16; 10.1).[2] It is notable that the use of the vial (פך) of oil for the anointing of Saul is the same term used for the container poured over Jehu at his anointing (2 Kgs 9.1, 3). This offers a suggestive literary contrast to the horn (קרן) used for David (1 Sam. 16.1, 13) and Solomon (1 Kgs 1.39). The reader might note this linkage anticipating Jehu, who was also intended to deliver Israel from her enemies, yet himself faces the ultimate rejection as king by Yahweh.[3] Perhaps the nature of the vial (earthenware) and that of the horn are also meant to contrast in the length of their usefulness: the former breaks easily and irreparably, while the latter endures.[4]

The Spirit coming upon an individual to indicate kingship was for the deliverance and salvation of Israel. It was thus for the sake of vouchsafing the community to enjoy the blessings of Yahweh through faithful obedience.[5] However, while this is true of Saul's

---

[2] The LXX reiterates the note on saving from the Philistines at 10.1, while the MT does not include the addition.

[3] Auld, *I & II Samuel: A Commentary* (Louisville, KY: Westminster John Knox Press, 2011), pp. 110, 113; K. Bodner, *1 Samuel: A Narrative Commentary* (Sheffield: Sheffield Phoenix Press, 2008), pp. 92-93. This literary link is further strengthened by both Jehu and Saul hiding their anointing from immediate inquiries.

[4] Y. Weinberger, *I Samuel: A New Translation with a Commentary Anthologized from Talmudic, Midrashic, and Rabbinic Sources* (Brooklyn, NY: Mesorah Publications, 2011), p. 166.

[5] W. Brueggemann goes so far as to say, 'The act of kingmaking is soteriological. Saul is *to save*. The act is also ecclesiological. It is for the sake of the *community*. Saul is to save and to make this community freshly possible', *First and Second Samuel* (Louisville, KY: John Knox Press, 1990), p. 74, original emphasis.

king-making it would also be true of the judges to whom Saul seems to stand as a Janus-like figure between other delivering and community guaranteeing judges and kings. Three signs would confirm for Saul that he was to be the appointed ruler and deliverer of Israel: two men giving direction to find the lost donkeys near Rachel's tomb at Zilzah,[6] three men ascending to Bethel with offerings to share, and minstreling prophets descending from Gibeah (which is significantly noted as near a Philistine garrison). The three signs that Saul was Yahweh's anointed would happen among the 'familiar settings of a tomb and a tree and a town'.[7] The sacred spaces and acts of the signs would be followed by the 'rush' or 'come powerfully' (צלח) of the transforming Spirit upon him to empower him to act to deliver and vouchsafe the community.

The reader is emphatically informed that Saul was changed into 'a new man' with לב אחר 'a different heart' at the point which he left Samuel rather than after meeting the prophets and prophesying with them (10.9).[8] Samuel had stated this change would happen after the three signs, yet it is not stated that Saul is changed after the signs despite the fulfillment narrative following. The narrative clarifies that everything stated by Samuel about Saul was fulfilled even if not in the way thought at first.

The readers notice a priestly or cultic notion in connection with the second sign for Saul where he receives the לחם 'bread' given for sacrificial offering to the priests (clarified as such by the LXX), a prophetic connection to Saul's endowment with רוח where he prophesies, and finally a kingly connection since this is his anointing to be king of Israel. Might this proposal be an offer that Saul had at least at this point begun to be a king *and* priest even if only temporarily doing these well? Further, he joins the prophetic band to the proverbial question in the mouth of Israel. This would position Saul as one

---

[6] J. Mauchline, *1 and 2 Samuel* (London: Oliphants, 1971), p. 98, contends that the verbal root of Zelzah (an otherwise unknown location in Benjamin) means 'to rush' and may in fact be a playful way of indicating the nature of the Spirit of God 'rushing' upon Saul.

[7] E.H. Peterson, *First and Second Samuel* (Louisville, KY: Westminster John Knox Press, 1999), p. 64. D.I. Block also notes the three signs given, 'Empowered by the Spirit of God, p. 47.

[8] T.W. Cartledge, *1 & 2 Samuel* (Macon, GA: Smyth & Helwys Pub, 2001), pp. 133-34.

anticipated potentially to function as Moses for Israel in the wilderness.

What does it mean for Saul to be בנביאים 'among the prophets' and to prophesy with that musical band of prophets? 'It is not said explicitly in so many words, but it is suggested that there is a musical component in Saul's new heart with his 'acting the prophet'.[9] Indeed, the nature of the prophetic endowment seems directly connected at times to instrumentation by the Spirit-ed prophets. Readers might anticipate the musical nature of the prophetic as a common feature of ancient Israelite prophetic practice.[10] David would later sing by the Spirit playing the prophet (2 Samuel 22-23) and it would seem he did likewise in his early ministrations singing such soothing tones for Saul's troubled spirit. Further, Elisha would call for instrumentation to give prophetic instruction in 2 Kgs 3.15.

The readers are meant to appraise Saul positively (at this point) as איש אחר 'a different man' who has been charismatically endowed by the Spirit of God to lead Israel even if we must wait for Saul to respond to the Spirit's moving again to take action to deliver (11.6).[11] Sadly, 'having first been a charismatic king, Saul will become the reverse [by the end of his story], a demonically haunted despot'.[12] At this point the readers find a bumbling Benjamite to be changed of heart by God.[13] The narrative reports Samuel as saying that when the Spirit of Yahweh rushes upon Saul he is עשה לך אשר תמצא ידך 'do whatever your hand finds to do' but with the restriction of waiting for Samuel to come after a time. As such, he is both freed and bound

---

[9] Auld, *I & II Samuel*, p. 112.

[10] A. Phillips argues for ecstasy resulting in gibberish as typical of the band Saul encounters, Saul's own prophetic instrumentation and then later the 'sons of the prophets', but this is not found in the text itself, 'The Ecstatics' Father', pp. 183-94 in P.R. Ackroyd and B. Lindars (eds.), *Words and Meanings: Essays Presented to David Winton Thomas* (Cambridge: Cambridge University, 2009), pp. 187-93.

[11] F.A. Murphy suggests that if one follows an overall negative appraisal of Saul by the narrator of the Former Prophets, then the 'six repetitions of "prophesy" and "prophet" could be mocking' Saul as failing to do what the Spirit was known to equip leaders to do: militarily deliver. However, the opposite might also hold at some level, *1 Samuel* (Grand Rapids, MI: Brazos Press, 2010), p. 82.

[12] Murphy, *1 Samuel*, p. 83.

[13] 'Here, at the edge of Israel's newness, is the gift (charisma) of freedom, ecstasy, and self-transcendence yielding to a purpose beyond Saul's own self', Brueggemann, *First and Second Samuel*, p. 75.

by the words of Samuel.[14] The narrative clarifies this binding as the suggestive nearby location of the Philistine garrison for Saul to conquer by the empowering transforming Spirit and the timeline for Saul to abide by.[15] If he is a אַחֵר אִישׁ 'new man' who is equipped as deliverer then here is his opportunity which is only later taken up specifically by his son Jonathan, but decidedly missed by Saul (1 Samuel 14). The careful reader notices that Samuel has offered this clue as to just what Saul should have put his hand to do by offering a side comment about the nearby Philistine garrison (even if Samuel immediately binds the hand of Saul to wait at Gilgal). One is left wondering just what Saul's hand will find instead to do with the onrush of the Spirit of Yahweh.

In v. 11, the readers encounter Israel inquiring whether Saul is הֲגַם בַּנְּבִיאִים ... 'really'[16] among the prophets'. An unnamed man answers by asking, מִי אֲבִיהֶם 'Who is *their*[17] father?' Is Saul to be under the fatherhood of another over Israel? Should the readers assume Yahweh is that 'father' as represented through the leader of the prophetic band? Should it be understood in much the way that Elijah and later

---

[14] Brueggemann, *First and Second Samuel,* p. 75; D. Jobling, *1 Samuel* (Collegeville, MN: Liturgical Press, 1998), pp. 60, 68; and Murphy, *1 Samuel,* p. 79.

[15] Caquot and Robert offer such a reading concerning the binding words of Samuel to Saul identifying the nearby Philistine encampment:

La mention des «préfets» philistins rapelle l'occupation militaire que connaît le territoire benjaminite (en 13.3 on en trouve un á Guéba) et correspond à l'indication de 9.16. On apprend qu'il s'y trouve un haut-lieu avec une confrérie de prophètes extatiques, dont la transe semble entretenue par la musique. L'action soudaine du souffle de YHWH, exprimée par le verbe צלח se retrouve à propos de Saül en 11.6 dans un contexte guerrier (cf. aussi Samson en Jg. 14.6, 19; 15.14): ici elle se manifeste par la contagion de la transe prophétique, qui semble confirmer que désormais Saül est bien devenu «un autre homme».

A. Caquot and P. de Robert, *Les livres de Samuel* (Genève: Labor et Fides, 1994), p. 128.

[16] V.P. Long, *The Reign and Rejection of King Saul: A Case for Literary and Theological Coherence* (SBLDS 118; Atlanta, GA: Scholars Press, 1989), p. 208 n. 54, contends that the uses of הֲגַם in 10.11 and 19.24 seem best read as 'really' or 'indeed' rather than as 'also'. He notes such a use in all other occasions (Gen. 16.13; 1 Kgs 17.20; Job 41.1 [Eng 41.9]; Est. 7.8; with an ambiguous usage at Ps. 78.20).

[17] The MT records this man as asking, 'Who is *their* father?' while the LXX text records it as 'Who is *his* father?' The former seems to indicate a 'father' of the prophets. The latter reading suggests Saul's relationship to the prophetic leadership. The MT has been followed.

Elisha would be a 'father' to Israel under the authority of Yahweh?[18] It does seem to point toward a narrative theme wherein Samuel tries to maintain the control over Saul despite authorizing Saul to act.[19] At the public anointing of Saul that follows in the narrative, Samuel writes down, commends, and preserves the instructions regarding kings for Israel and Saul to affirm. This would call to mind the instructions of Moses in Deut. 17.14-20. Upon Samuel's dismissal of Israel, some of the warriors who found their 'hearts changed by God' joined themselves to the heart-changed Saul (even as troublers rejected him in scorn).

Saul's transformation and enablement do not lead him any further than the prophetic accompaniment. Saul fails to raise the alarm against the Philistine garrison and never takes action against it until his son Jonathan acts in faith to challenge it (1 Samuel 13). However, 1 Samuel 11 finds Israel oppressed by Nahash king of Ammon. The wailing cry of the people of Gibeah in response to the suffering of the people of Jabesh is heard by Saul (and apparently by God),

ותצלח רוח־אלהים על־שאול בשמעו את־הדברים האלה
ויחר אפו מאד

---

[18] Cartledge, *1 & 2 Samuel*, p. 135, believes this 'father' was actually Samuel who would have been the 'father' of the band of prophets. K. Bodner suggests this question concerns 'divine empowerment' as not being 'a hereditary privilege' despite the fact that the term 'father' is used, *1 Samuel*, p. 96. Auld also suggests a potential link between this account of the band of prophets, where large groups are normally typified negatively in the Former Prophets, and the four hundred in the court of Ahab as Micaiah also introduces the work of the Spirit. In both accounts the Spirit empowers for a special mission: Micaiah to lie like the other prophets and Saul to prophesy like the other prophets, *I & II Samuel*, p. 113.

[19] For an extended treatment of just such a reading of the Samuel/Saul narratives, see J.R. Middleton, 'Samuel Agonistes: A Conflicted Prophet's Resistance to God and Contribution to the Failure of Israel's First King', in M.J. Boda and L.M. Wray Beal (eds.), *Prophets, Prophecy, and Ancient Israelite Historiography* (Winona Lake, IN: Eisenbrauns, 2013), pp. 69-92, and a less extensive though still detailed exposition arguing along the same lines can be read in T. Czövek, *Three Seasons of Charismatic Leadership: A Literary-Critical and Theological Interpretation of the Narrative of Saul, David and Solomon* (Regnum Studies in Mission; Waynesboro, GA: Paternoster, 2006), pp. 66-72.

'and the Spirit of God powerfully seized him when he heard these words and he burned with anger' (1 Sam. 11.6).[20] This Spirit-induced anger leads to a summoning of Israel in vast array to work the deliverance from Ammon. The function of the Spirit coming upon Saul at this point reads like the judges before him who experience the Spirit coming upon them powerfully and are moved to take action by summoning Israel to war to bring about the salvation of the people of God from their enemies. This victory under Saul and solidarity of the tribes of Israel results in a reaffirmation of Saul's kingship and a celebration of Yahweh's fellowship (11.12-15). However, the king and kingdom are soon troubled through disobedience and a change of רוח.

David's Spirit-ed Songs of Deliverance for Saul's Troubling Spirit (1 Samuel 16.13-23; 18.6-14; 2 Samuel 23.1-2)[21]

In the course of the narrative, Saul becomes rejected and David accepted as the next king. Samuel locates Jesse's chosen son to anoint

---

[20] The distinction between the use of 'God' and 'Yahweh' in relation to the Spirit is noted and traced in great detail by J.M. Ragsdale, '*Ruah YHWH, Ruah 'Elohim*'. Ragsdale proposes a literary and theological distinction (per his title) as explanation for the variant uses in the Former Prophets but requires emendation (to Saul's first Spirit encounter recorded at 1 Sam. 10.6) in order to arrive at such consistent uses as he proposes. The literary distinction is noteworthy. However, an explanation is not as simple as that either a variant textual tradition needing emendation is offered here or that Saul is somehow regarded as never enjoying the Spirit of Yahweh, but only the Spirit of God. Ragsdale regards the later as if this were a lesser or more censured experience.

[21] The MT and the LXX texts of 1 Samuel 16-18 show decidedly differing textual traditions with numerous alternate readings including the much longer version of the MT which seems to this writer to be an expansion upon an earlier text form better represented in the LXX text form. For a detailed discussion of the use of the LXX in this extended account of David, see D. Barthélemy (ed.), *The Story of David and Goliath: Textual and Literary Criticism: Papers of a Joint Research Venture* (Fribourg, Suisse: Éditions universitaires, 1986). It should be noted that the MT is used throughout as the base text for this literary reading not necessarily because it offers a more original text at any particular point but for its more fixed nature as a canonically received text form found in the Pentecostal tradition. Several key areas where the MT offers a longer form which is absent from the LXX in the portion below covering 1 Sam. 18.6-14 include: the repetition of the 'troubling spirit from God'

as king and David experiences the 'powerful coming' or 'rush' (צלח)
of the Spirit of Yahweh upon him מהיום ההוא 'from that day onward'
(1 Sam. 16.13).[22] The text moves the reader to hear another change
occurring in Saul at the moment of the Spirit of Yahweh rushing
upon David: ובעתתו רוח־רעה מאת יהוה 'and a troubling[23] spirit from
Yahweh tormented [בעת] him' (v. 14). In the place of this רוח (Spirit),
which empowers for deliverance, Saul receives a troubling רוח (spirit)
to torment. This troubling רוח 'is "bad" because the effects of [Saul's]
possession are negative and destructive' and not because somehow
this is actually an 'evil spirit' as to its character.[24] It reminds careful
readers of the pronouncement in Judg. 2.15 that unfaithfulness on
the part of the people of God that will result in Yahweh actively
bringing 'trouble' against them. This personal active language יד־יהוה
היתה־בם לרעה 'the hand of Yahweh was against them for trouble',
sounds very like the troubling spirit of Yahweh.

---

coming on Saul that had earlier been mentioned in 1 Samuel 16 (18.10), the claim
of Saul prophesying as David played (18.10), and Saul's attempt to spear David
(18.10, 11). The MT seems to offer a more theologically developed explanation of
Saul's attempts on David and David's justification for fleeing. This is one of the
reasons for this text to be included with the passage from 1 Sam. 16.13-23 rather
than to have its own distinct section. The other reason is because it seems to be a
repetition of sorts as explanation for the abandonment of Saul to the troubling
spirit and David's flight.

[22] It is usually contended that the Spirit only came upon individuals for a singular act and that the abiding presence of the Spirit does not happen until the NT
era following Jesus. This verse seems to indicate otherwise. In point of fact, Saul
himself had the Spirit of Yahweh upon him for some time until the readers encounter the anointing and endowment of David. While most commentators seem
to ignore this abiding sense as contradicting the tendency to distinguish the Spirit
between the testaments, Tsumura contends that there is no indication of a 'spas-
modic' endowment of the Spirit upon Saul as the text only now states the Spirit of
the Yahweh left him. He argues for the Spirit also abiding in the OT as evidenced
by both Saul and David. D. Tsumura, *The First Book of Samuel* (NICOT; Grand
Rapids, MI: William B. Eerdmans, 2007), p. 423.

[23] 'Troubling' is a better rendering than 'evil' which carries some moral implications which may or may not be present at various points in these texts.

[24] Block, 'Empowered by the Spirit of God', p. 47; Tsumura, *The First Book of
Samuel*, pp. 426-28, discusses this 'spirit [of Yahweh] which brings forth disaster' as
a better rendering than 'evil spirit' as the grammatical construction is not adjectival,
but a construct chain. J. Rea comments that it 'may not have been a morally evil
demon' but instead is some 'misery' producing spirit, *The Holy Spirit in the Bible*, p.
57.

Would the readers understand this רוח as utterly different S/spirits or as being the same Spirit?[25] The very same source is accredited with sending both the Spirit of Yahweh upon David and the troubling spirit upon Saul in much the same fashion as Micaiah ben Imlah will later testify before Ahab about a lying spirit.[26] Both are attributed to Yahweh (or *God* in 1 Sam. 16.23) even though the language still seems to suggest some differentiation as to their purposes and effects. Both 'fall upon' (צלח + אל; 1 Sam. 16.13; 18.10) and 'come upon' (היה + על; 1 Sam. 16.16; 19.20) individuals. Both 'depart' (סור; 1 Sam. 16.14, 23) from Saul. Both enable the prophetic (1 Sam. 18.10; 19.20).[27] Is there a sense in which the רוח (however characterized) is in fact always bringing about hostility in order to bring life: whether toward those who are truly enemies or those only perceived as such (cf. Judg. 3.10; 6.34; 9.23; 11.29; 14.6, 19; 15.14; 1 Sam. 11.6)? 'Saul encounters God's dark side … Saul … knows … God not only through divine absence, but also, paradoxically, through YHWH's persecuting presence in the form of an evil spirit.'[28] The Spirit of Yahweh would thus not be safe, but always moving in the direction for which one finds themselves oriented: whether to trouble or to life.[29]

How does Saul find[30] relief from this tormenting spirit? His servants suggest the lyre playing David whose instrumentation will make

---

[25] Brueggemann, *First and Second Samuel*, p. 125; R. Routledge, "'An Evil Spirit from the Lord'' – Demonic Influence or Divine Instrument?' *EvQ* 70.1 (Jan-Mar 1998), pp. 4, 5. D. Firth reads this 'baleful spirit' as a human orientation rather than a being, 'The Historical Books', pp. 12-23 in Burke and Warrington (eds.), *A Biblical Theology of the Holy Spirit*, p. 13.

[26] Brueggemann, *First and Second Samuel*, p. 125.

[27] Several of these are noted by E.J. Hamori whose own conclusion is that the relationship between these two רוח and Yahweh is 'unclear', 'The Spirit of Falsehood', p. 20.

[28] Murphy, *1 Samuel*, p. 189. See also, J.C. Exum and J.W. Whedbee, 'Isaac, Samson, and Saul: Reflections of the Comic and Tragic Visions', in Y.T. Radday and A. Brenner (eds.), *On Humour and the Comic in the Hebrew Bible* (Sheffield: Almond, 1990), pp. 117-60 (153). Routledge likewise makes a case for this troubling Spirit being both the result of Saul's rejection of the Spirit of Yahweh and that this not only makes Saul susceptible to the troubling spirit, but also that Yahweh actively sends this troubling spirit upon Saul, Routledge, 'An Evil Spirit from the Lord', pp. 6, 7.

[29] Horton, *What the Bible Says about the Holy Spirit*, pp. 47-48.

[30] The request by Saul that he be 'provided' (ראה) someone to help him find wholeness (1 Sam. 16.17) utilizes the same term for the word of Yahweh to Samuel

Saul feel 'better'. There is a rather ironic twist in that Saul's servants assure him he will feel 'better' (טוב – 1 Sam. 16.16) once the musician comes to bring his relief, even as the very one called to bring his relief had been just previously described by Samuel to Saul as 'better' (טוב – 1 Sam. 15.28) than him. However, Saul does not immediately make the connection that these are one and the same individuals.

There is another play on words, often missed in translation, which adds poignancy to the function of these terms in the narrative.[31] The רוח (spirit) which troubles Saul departs as David would play the lyre and Saul would be given רוח (the verbal form meaning 'to give room/space/relief'). 'Saul's desperate concern was how to have the spirit of life available, rather than the troubling spirit. The narrative makes clear that David makes the spirit of life available to Saul. Saul has life only because David mediates it to him. David is a life giver, even to Saul!'[32] It is the 'healing music'[33] played on the lyre[34] which brings relief (רוח) at this point from the hands of David, but it is also music (of maidens) that later will stir up Saul to seek David's life (1 Sam. 18.7-11).[35] This latter lyric which vexes Saul's spirit seems to be intended in the narrative to celebrate Saul equally alongside David and not actually to aggrandize David more than Saul.[36] Apparently the maiden's praises offer up 'a certain rhythm [that] gives Saul the

---

that Yahweh had 'provided' (ראה) someone to be king for the aid of Israel (1 Sam. 16.1). See Brueggemann, *First and Second Samuel*, p. 125.

[31] R.D. Bergen, 'Evil Spirits and Eccentric Grammar: A Study of the Relationship between Text and Meaning in Hebrew Narrative', in R.D. Bergen (ed.), *Biblical Hebrew and Discourse Linguistics* (Dallas, TX: Summer Institute of Linguistics, 1994), pp. 320-35.

[32] Brueggemann, *First and Second Samuel*, pp. 126-27; see also Auld, *I & II Samuel*, p. 191; and Tsumura, *The First Book of Samuel*, p. 433.

[33] Brueggemann, *First and Second Samuel*, p. 125.

[34] The lyre (כנור) was regarded by some in the ANE as having 'divine power' and was listed among the gods worshiped at Ugarit, though nothing of this sort seems to pertain to ancient Israelite beliefs. On which, see, Tsumura, *The First Book of Samuel*, p. 429; on the Ugaritic texts see *KTU* 1.47:32; 1.118:31.

[35] Bodner, *1 Samuel*, p. 175.

[36] This follows a pattern within Hebrew poetics which is similarly exemplified in Deut. 32.30; 33.17; Mic. 6.7; Ps. 91.7; 144.13, see Bodner, *1 Samuel*, pp. 194, 195; Brueggemann, *First and Second Samuel*, p. 136.

blues'.[37] His hearing of songs of the Spirit is a hearing which carries him in ways he does not seem to appreciate or understand.

David plays well (טוב) for the relief (רוח) of Saul, but one wonders what form of Spirit-ed music might offer such relief? The later texts of Samuel point toward a prophetic song which might itself be indicative of the very type of music played by the Spirit-ed David on such occasions: 2 Samuel 22. This song of David is also displayed in the Psalms (18) and offers several terms of note which are also found in the texts of the Former Prophets (cf. 2 Sam. 22.1-6). The 'terrifying' (בעת) of the 'Spirit from the Lord for troubling', which so bothered Saul, is what David ironically sings about on the day he found deliverance from the hand of Saul (שאול). David sings,

כי אפפני משברי־מות נחלי בליעל יבעתני:

חבלי שאול סבני קדמני מקשי־מות:

'For Death's waves encompass me, Belial's torrents terrify (בעת) me, Sheol's (שאול) cords entangled me, Death's snares entrapped me.'[38] His limerick rings with the words which must have also tormented Saul who believes death always to entrap him and to suffer the terrorizing tunes of the troubling רוח. David, however, knows the one upon whom he must call and who will come to his aid. While Saul calls for a musician, David calls for Yahweh. That both kings had the Spirit of Yahweh upon them did not mean they were kept ever free from the terrors surrounding them. The difference is only in their responses to those terrors. We hear Saul returning to seek his first endowment of the Spirit of Yahweh when he first encountered the instruments of the prophets and himself entered their company (1 Sam. 10.5-10). Yet he seeks only the instrumentation of another, while David becomes the instrumentation.

The psalms of David are the songs of the Spirit.[39] It is such Spirit-ed songs which overcome trouble and make way for new life. David knows this is the manner in which he plays and sings Spirit enabled נאם דוד 'oracles of David' from Yahweh (2 Sam. 23.1). David is the one who sings in the Spirit of Yahweh and embraces the life giving

---

[37] Bodner, *1 Samuel*, p. 195.

[38] 2 Samuel 22.5-6; Ps. 18.5-6 MT, 18.4-5 ETT.

[39] The prophetic nature of the psalms connected to the Spirit is explicated in 11QPs[a] col.27 lines 2-11.

power of such songs. He has learned to attune himself to the Spirit in faith-filled trust. He opens his swansong,

רוח יהוה דבר־בי ומלתו על־לשוני

'The Spirit of Yahweh spoke in[40] me, his word on my tongue' (2 Sam. 23.2). The reader at this point in the text would note that if David could declare prophetically at the end of his life that the Spirit of Yahweh had given him words to speak and lyrics to sing then the readers would be reminded of his earlier singing for Saul in such fashion. David seems to offer here the 'basic (and normative) paradigm of prophetic utterance'.[41]

The inwardness and closer relationship of the Spirit of Yahweh in this text would not be missed by the readers who would note that David had experienced the Spirit of Yahweh אל 'upon' him though the Spirit is regularly described as על 'upon' the judges and Saul. This is not to suggest that the prepositional choice for the judges and Saul implied no personal engagement but only a surface engagement. This is all the clearer as Judg. 2.18 had prefaced the judges endowments by stating that Yahweh would be עם 'with' the judges he would raise up to save them. Saul was made לאיש אחר 'a new man' with לב אחר 'a new heart' by God through the Spirit of Yahweh. However, it does seem to highlight the unique relationship of David to the Spirit of Yahweh who has the words of the Spirit 'in' him and the Spirit mightily 'with' him. It is this enablement that David confesses to give him the words to overcome troubles and persist in faithful confessions of Yahweh.

As Saul sits in his house and David plays the lyre, the troubling Spirit of God which again rushes upon Saul causes him to prophesy.

ויהי ממחרת ותצלח רוח אלהים רעה אל־שאול
ויתנבא בתוך־הבית ודוד מנגן בידו כיום ביום והחנית ביד־שאול

'And it was the next day and the troubling spirit of God came mightily upon Saul and he prophesied in the house, while David played with his hands upon the harp as he [he did] day by day, and Saul had a spear in his hand' (18.10). This seems to happen in a similar fashion

---

[40] Or 'through'.

[41] D.I. Block contends, 'The basic (and normative) paradigm of prophetic utterance is expressed by David' in 2 Sam. 23.1-2, 'Empowered by the Spirit of God', p. 45.

to when the Spirit of Yahweh came upon him at his anointing when he met the minstrel prophets and joined their band (1 Sam. 10.5-10). Are the readers to understand Saul's inner words that he will 'nail David to the wall' as a *false prophecy* since it does not come to pass despite the will to bring it about? Is this an attempt by the troubling spirit to overcome the delivering Spirit? Or is this simply Saul's own demise depicted in his surrender to trouble over life? Perhaps he may sing well enough, but has he given himself fully to the prophetic words which he declares to the strumming of the Spirit-ed David? There is nothing apparent in the text to indicate that Saul 'raved' (ESV, NAS, NLT, NRSV), 'raged' (NAB), or 'fell into a frenzy' (NJB) in his prophesying. The readers would assume (apart from any description) that he was prophesying just as he had when encountering the minstreling prophets at his Spirit endowment.

Despite his failed attempt on David's life, once again the readers will find David soothing Saul until the moment Saul again tries to spear David in 1 Sam. 19.9, 10 and David once for all takes flight.

ותהי רוח יהוה רעה אל־שאול
והוא בביתו יושב וחניתו בידו ודוד מנגן ביד
ויבקש שאול להכות בחנית בדוד ובקיר
ויפטר מפני שאול ויך את־החנית בקיר
ודוד נס וימלט בלילה הוא

And the troubling spirit of Yahweh came upon Saul as he sat in his house with his spear in his hand, and David's hand [was] strumming. And Saul sought to strike with [his] spear into David into the wall. And he escaped from the presence of Saul and [Saul] struck the spear into the wall, but David fled and escaped that night.

A Spirit-ed Finale: Overcoming Songs of the Spirit (1 Samuel 19.8-24)

The readers note the refrain, as in 1 Sam. 18.10-11, that a רוח רעה 'troubling Spirit' (this time of Yahweh)[42] comes upon Saul where he tries once again to spear David playing the lyre to bring Saul relief from this terrorizing (1 Sam. 19.9). Saul sits enthroned with spear in

---

[42] This reading follows the MT. The LXX reads 'of God'.

hand appearing ready to do whatever his hand finds to do as the רוח comes upon him, yet here 'Saul has the proclivity to become a thing, and God is satirizing him through this, through his becoming the javelin in his hand and turning into a human weapon of murder'.[43] The readers would anticipate the singing of David to bring relief, but the Spirit-ed minstreling appears to provoke the troubling spirit on Saul.[44] David escapes to the side of Samuel at Naioth in Ramah where Saul hears he has fled (1 Sam. 19.18-19). Has David fled to Samuel at Ramah seeking the endorsement and protection of the king-making prophet-priest of Israel? Saul enlists his messengers to capture David (and Samuel?) at Naioth in Ramah, but they are overcome by the Spirit of God.

וישלח שאול מלאכים לקחת את־דוד
וירא את־להקת הנביאים נבאים ושמואל עמד נצב עליהם
ותהי על־מלאכי שאול רוח אלהים ויתנבאו גם־המה

'And Saul sent messengers to capture David. And they saw a group of prophets prophesying, and Samuel standing as leader over them, and the Spirit of God came upon the messengers of Saul and they also began to prophesy' (1 Sam. 19.20). Thus, they join the prophetic company.[45] A second troop is sent and likewise they join the prophets. Yet a third group of messengers are sent who also join the band.

At last[46] Saul arrives near Naioth seeking David and Samuel. Even while approaching Naioth, Saul is overcome by the רוח and begins again to prophesy as he continues to Naioth in Ramah. The narrator has already alerted us that Saul would not 'see' Samuel until the day of his death (1 Sam. 15.35) and thus the readers might wonder about this earnest quest for Samuel and just what its end will be. Is Saul seeking his death? However, as Saul arrives at the scene he is overcome (as his three groups before him) by the Spirit and prophesies so as never actually to engage Samuel until the day of his death (fulfilled in an unlikely turn of phantasmic proportions in 1 Samuel 28).

---

[43] Murphy, *1 Samuel*, p. 190.

[44] Block, 'Empowered by the Spirit of God', p. 51.

[45] Verse 20 refers to the 'company' (להקת) of the prophets prophesying which occurs only here in the HB.

[46] It should be of significance that Saul once again fails to understand what he should: they are at Naioth. He seems blind to see what he ought to see throughout the accounts of 1 Samuel and incapable of finding what ought easily to be found.

וילך שם אל־נוית ברמה ותהי עליו גם־הוא רוח אלהים
וילך הלוך ויתנבא עד־באו בנוית ברמה:
ויפשט גם־הוא בגדיו ויתנבא גם־הוא לפני שמואל
ויפל ערם כל־היום ההוא וכל־הלילה
על־כן יאמרו הגם שאול בנביאם:

And he went there to Naioth in Ramah, and the Spirit of God
came upon also, and as he was walking he prophesied until coming
to Ramah, and he even stripped off his garments, and he even
prophesied before Samuel. And he fell undressed all that day and
all night. Thus they say, 'Is even Saul among the prophets?' (1 Sam.
19.23-24).

This overpowering of Saul by the רוח אלהים 'Spirit of God' in 1
Sam. 19.23, 24 (and the three groups sent to seize David in Ramah
preceding this text) echoes back to the earlier overcoming of Saul
following his anointing to lead Israel (1 Sam. 10.9-13). There he was
overcome by the passing minstreling prophets and joined their band.
Here again he is overcome by the Spirit and prophecy (including his
three groups of messengers).[47] In the earlier account this is the beginning of his reticent anointing to the kingship of Israel. Here he is
stripped of the very emblems of kingship which he has come to cling
to with the fingers of a tormented spirit. While the scene of Saul's
being overcome at the meeting of the singing prophets in 1 Sam.
10.9-13 signaled a beginning which seemed to anticipate a Spirit empowered leading of Israel, by 1 Samuel 19 the readers encounter a
Saul given over to being terrorized and terrorizing as he quickly falls
upon his own demise. From beginning to end Saul is overcome by
the Spirit.[48] As Saul falls to the ground before Samuel one is reminded
that Samuel had earlier announced Saul's reign would not תקום 'arise'
(1 Sam. 13.14).[49]

We might best understand the stripping of Saul in prophetic
demonstration as he walks along and finally lay on the ground to be

---

[47] This seems to offer a prescient literary echo for the later attempt by King
Ahaziah to fetch Elijah wherein three bands of men are overcome (in that case by
fire from heaven – 2 Kgs 1.9-14).

[48] See the comments toward this end in Brueggemann, *First and Second Samuel*,
pp. 145-46.

[49] Bodner, *1 Samuel*, p. 211.

a removal of his royal clothes and not about Saul's nudity.[50] Saul in-voluntarily 'takes off' (פשט) his garments before David (1 Sam. 19.24) in direct contrast to his son Jonathan who voluntarily 'takes off' (פשט) his own royal garments for David (1 Sam. 18.4).[51] What Jonathan did out of his love for David, Saul would do only under the unwilling compulsion of the Spirit (or is he made willing by the Spirit?).[52] Saul stands (or better, lies) in stark contrast to his son Jonathan. While Saul must be humbled to remove his royal attire, Jonathan has freely given these emblems to David.[53] Readers might wonder at the way in which the love of Yahweh for David seems to abound, while that for Saul has been given up to another.[54]

In Saul's quest to find David and Samuel, the reader's once again find that Saul is clueless about the whereabouts of that which he seeks. Saul is characterized as being ignorant of the location of the donkeys in 1 Samuel 10 and the location of David and Samuel in 1

---

[50] Tsumura, *The First Book of Samuel*, p. 499, who also notes S.R. Driver as con-tending for just such a reading that does not require absolute nudity, but instead seems to entail the removal of the royal outer garments, in *Notes on the Hebrew Text and the Topography of the Books of Samuel; With an Introduction on Hebrew Palaeography and the Ancient Versions and Facsimiles of Inscriptions and Maps* (Oxford: Clarendon Press, 1913), p. 160. See R.B. Allen on 'naked' (ערם) where it is specified that it was most likely Saul simply divested himself of his royal garments, 'ערם', in R.L. Harris, G.L. Archer Jr, and B.K. Waltke (eds.), *Theological Wordbook of the Old Testament* (vol. 2; Moody Press: Chicago, IL: Moody, 1981), pp. 697-98.

[51] Bodner, *1 Samuel*, p. 210.

[52] J.W.H. Van Wijk-Bos, *Reading Samuel: A Literary and Theological Commentary* (Macon, GA: Smyth & Helwys Pub, 2011), p. 109; of note is a 1918 article in the Church of God Evangel calling for love to knit the church together like Jonathan was to David in this account: 'What an example! We find there was never strife between David and Jonathan after that ... So when we knit together in love it will bring the clothes off of our back for our brother; it will cause us to speak kindly to him, bring down high looks, evil thoughts, strife and envying. You will be com-forted by the power of love and the mystery of God will be acknowledged among you'. J.Q. Myers, 'Knit Together in Love', *CGE* 9.44 (Nov. 2, 1918), p. 3.

[53] Long has previously noted this narrative analogy in *The Reign and Rejection of King Saul*, pp. 40, 41.

[54] W. Brueggemann, 'The narrative suggests that God's transformative spirit is peculiarly allied with and attentive to David. Before that compelling, inscrutable, inexplicable power, Saul is helpless', *First and Second Samuel*, p. 145. However, this presupposes there was no returning to Yahweh for Saul or the potential of David likewise being given over to the troubling spirit should he not persist in proper faithfulness.

Samuel 19. Here again, Samuel is sought while Saul is at a place of water (1 Sam. 9.11-13).[55] Here again three signs are given. Here again Saul is transformed into a different man. Here again the proverb of Saul's association with the prophets is repeated. Here 'Saul's epigraph is repeated at the end of the chapter, as an epitaph'.[56] The 'satirical recapitulation' of 1 Sam. 19.24 serves to indicate that the people did not think Saul to be of the sort to prophesy (themselves regarding the prophets positively).[57] So perhaps Saul's inclusion among the prophets appears more like ridicule as he lays prostrate removed of his regal robes and prophesying ... overwhelmed by רוח. In fact, this state would provide the readers final indication of his removal from kingship as well. However, the reader is consoled that Yahweh (here specifically by his Spirit) both raises up and lays low.

Conclusion

In these stories, Saul has been open to Yahweh's רוח, for good or ill. In the words of Hannah (which frames the books of 1-2 Samuel with the songs of David) יהוה ממית ומחיה מוריד שאול ויעל 'Yahweh kills and gives life, bringing down to Sheol, and he raises up' (1 Sam. 2.6). Saul was raised and has been brought down. At each pivotal turn of the song of his story, רוח from Yahweh is present to give life and to terrify it, to empower for deliverance, to exalt the humble and humble the proud. The instrumentation is the minstreling prophets at the first and last and the Maestro of Judah, son of Jesse. Their Spirit-ed songs overwhelm Saul to make him a new man. They relieve his torments and torment him further. They move him to lay aside his claims to kingship and at the last to declare that the king of Israel must be one endued with and yielding to the רוח of Yahweh to give and assure the life of Israel and Yahweh's abiding presence with them.

Attuned readers note the ways in which the Spirit functions in 1-2 Samuel. These accounts indicate for the readers that the prophets

---

[55] Bodner, *1 Samuel*, p. 210; J.P. Fokkelman, *Narrative Art and Poetry in the Books of Samuel: A Full Interpretation Based on Stylistic and Structural Analyses Vol. 2* (Assen: Van Gorcum, 1986), p. 281.

[56] Murphy, *1 Samuel*, p. 199.

[57] Long, *The Reign and Rejection of King Saul*, pp. 208, 209.

of Yahweh and the state of the רוח by which they ministered might actually best be found in the preserved tunes of the shepherd king David.[58] It is the words of this king who found himself early on composing words of praise and adoration, calling for vindication and deliverance, declaring the blessing upon the messiah of Israel that gives voice to the prophets and their musical prophesying. It is the songs of David that are songs of the Spirit. It is the Spirit singing to transform.

First, the Spirit in 1-2 Samuel strikes chords that transform. Saul is made a new man sufficiently that others find themselves also transformed by him. This transformation is not an overriding of his will, but an enablement to do the will of Yahweh.[59] Thus, he is tormented by the Spirit when he finds he can no longer endure faithfulness to Yahweh. The Spirit-ed singing of David is all that brings him relief to restore to him some sense of his former glory. At the last, it is the songs of the prophetic band that overcome him to lay him low stripped of royalty.

Second, carrying forward the movement of the first function, the Spirit is enjoined by Spirit-ed music. It is not simply spoken words which bring about the endowment of the Spirit. It is the singing with the Spirit that creates an atmosphere for impartation. Readers find their voices caught up in the Spirit-ed songs of David who though troubled and seemingly swallowed by Sheol (much as Saul before him) find their hope resting in Yahweh.

---

[58] Scholarship has tended to portray these accounts as offering a purview into a primitive retelling of earlier times where dervish-like prophets worked in frenzied states and attributed their ministrations to the רוח. For an extended discussion of this proposal and some of its difficulties as well as an attempt counter to the one proposed here, see S. Parker, 'Possession Trance and Prophecy in Pre-Exilic Israel', *VT* 28.3 (July 1978), pp. 271-85. He writes that 'It seems clear that we have to do with some kind of trance state, or altered state of consciousness', p. 272. A similar proposal to Parker can be found in R.R. Wilson, 'Prophecy and Ecstasy: A Reexamination', *JBL* 98.3 (1979), pp. 321-37.

[59] This is contrary to the reading of J. Rea who believes that the transformation must be lasting to be non-superficial, *The Holy Spirit in the Bible*, p. 56. J. Goldingay affirms the idea that the Spirit does not require the recipient to 'act against their nature or will'. He falls short of seeing the enablement as more broadly the ability to obey the will of Yahweh and instead suggests it is only for some dramatic act that would 'otherwise be impossible', *Old Testament Theology: Volume 1: Israel's Gospel* (Downers Grove, IL: IVP, 2003), p. 669.

Third, the Spirit confirms and enables leadership.[60] Saul and David are first anointed by oil and only later is the Spirit said to come upon them (1 Sam. 10.1, 10; 16.13).[61] The outward sign of the anointing oil did not assure the proper choice as king. The Spirit empowerment testified to the choice as being Yahweh's alone. Further, the leadership of these two first kings serves to show that 'the necessary ingredient for kingship' is the Spirit of Yahweh.[62]

Fourth, the Spirit empowered for victory over enemies. Readers might have expected Saul to take action by the Spirit to engage the nearby Philistines, though he does not. Instead, the readers find the Spirit later provoking him to take action against Ammon, to which he succeeds. While the text does not ever clarify the Spirit enabling David to gain victory in military battle with or without summoning Israel, he is preserved and overcomes the attempts on his life by troubled Saul who relentlessly pursues him.

---

[60] 'This narrative is a study in what happens to one man when he is caught up in Yahweh's purpose of powerful rescue and new governance, 'Brueggemann, *First and Second Samuel*, p. 77. See also, J. Rea, *The Holy Spirit in the Bible*, p. 56.

[61] Hildebrandt, *An Old Testament Theology of the Spirit of God*, pp. 124-25; and S.M. Horton, *What the Bible Says about the Holy Spirit*, p. 44.

[62] Hildebrandt, *An Old Testament Theology*, pp. 121, 127.

6

DISCERNING THE SPIRIT (1 KINGS 22)

Introduction

While the texts of 1-2 Samuel (discussed in chapter 5) regarding the Spirit offer some ambiguity with regard to the function (for trouble or life), the Former Prophets carries the need for discernment further in the account of Micaiah ben Imlah of 1 Kings 22. This story belongs to several extended prophetic accounts involving the king of Israel (Ahab son of Omri) interwoven within the tales of the prophet Elijah (1 Kings 17-19, 21; 2 Kings 1-2). While descendants of the prophetic king David rule in the southern kingdom of Judah, the northern kingdom has continued to suffer turmoil politically and spiritually. This culminates in the text of Kings with the stories of Ahab who seeks to destroy even the distorted Yahwistic worship of Jehu from Israel and replaces it with that of Baal and Asherah under the support of his Sidonian wife Jezebel (1 Kgs 16.29-33).

Elijah works from the fringes of the kingdom to demonstrate the faithfulness of Yahweh over and against Baal (1 Kings 17-19). In the dramatic showdown on Carmel, Elijah slaughters the prophets of Baal and Israel declares Yahweh as God. Yet Elijah finds himself fleeing for his life and despairing alone at Horeb following the threats of Jezebel to slaughter him. Yahweh's answer to Elijah refers to three individuals (Hazael, Jehu, and Elisha) who will in sequence bring about the judgment of Ahab and his house and a judgment against Israel for unfaithfulness. Beyond the three, Elijah is informed there are yet 7,000 who had not bowed their knee to Baal but remained faithful to Yahweh and by implication within the context will aid in the plan to work out the judgment of Ahab and his family (1 Kgs 19.18).

Perhaps this is suggestive that the unnamed prophets of chapter 20 and the 400 court prophets (along with Zedekiah and Micaiah) of chapter 22 somehow belong to those who were for and with Yahweh. However, the account involving Micaiah is not so clear. It is laden with ambiguities that seem to beckon for divine discernment. It calls for a faithful hearing to discern not only what Yahweh has said, but also why Yahweh has said it.[1] Arguably 'ambiguity is consonant with the atmosphere of the whole narrative', but this should not leave us without recourse toward Spirit-led discernment.[2]

Can I Get a Witness? (1 Kings 22.1-18)

An unnamed king of Israel seeks to provoke war in a time of peace and extends an invitation to Jehoshaphat king of Judah to join him. The king of Israel in chapter 22 remains unnamed for nearly the entirety of the narrative.[3] However the reader would expect that the king of Israel, Ahab, in the previous two chapters would be this unnamed king. This is highlighted all the more by the use of the name Ahab at the very close of the previous narrative (1 Kgs 21.29). While it eventually is clarified in chapter 22 that this is Ahab, the text intentionally refrains from naming him until a key point in the text.[4] As such the narrative ambiguity is further heightened and suggests this could be another king until clarification in the revelation of Yahweh.

---

[1] This hearing of 1 Kings 22 does not take into account the later retelling of this story with variations in 2 Chronicles 18 as this lies outside of the Former Prophets.

[2] I.W. Provan, *1 and 2 Kings* (NIBC; Peabody, MA: Hendrickson, 1995), p. 165.

[3] The NLT includes the name 'Ahab' throughout the narrative and first introduces it at v. 2. This misses the effect of the king being unnamed.

[4] V.P. Hamilton notes that 'king of Israel' is used seventeen times in this chapter (vv. 2, 3, 4, 5, 6, 8, 9, 10, 18, 26, 29, 30 [2x], 31, 32, 33, 34), 'the king' is used ten times (vv. 12, 13, 15 [2x], 16, 27, 35, 37 [2x]), and the name 'Ahab' is only used six times: once in verse 20, twice in his obituary (vv. 39-40), and three times in relation to the rule of Jehoshaphat and Ahab's son Ahaziah (vv. 41, 49, 51), *Handbook on the Historical Books: Joshua, Judges, Ruth, Samuel, Kings, Chronicles, Ezra-Nehemiah, Esther* (Grand Rapids, MI: Baker Academic, 2001), p. 440.

Further, the reader would expect that the peace enjoyed with Aram is the result of (and will follow likewise) the events of chapter 20, which recounts multiple victories for the king of Israel over Aram by the word of prophets.[5] The reader might expect by the preceding context that victory will come again at the word of the prophets. Though the reader would also remember that the king had just recently averted disaster as well and wonder if this might be yet forthcoming.

This king of Israel may have had proper claims to Ramoth Gilead (Deut. 4.43; 1 Kgs 4.13), but his move to retake it at this point in the narrative becomes a fool's errand leading to his end.[6] Though the reader might have been inclined to consider the union of the kingdoms of Judah and Israel in retaking 'promised land' a positive, there are reasons to doubt this conclusion. In his move to retake Ramoth, this king fails to abide by the instructions of the ideal king 'seated on the throne' (ישב על כסא) in Deut. 17.14-20 who does not act in self-interest nor out of pride.[7] Specifically, Ahab fails this ideal by: (a) his quest for power, (b) acquiring many horses, and (c) not committing the words of the Torah to heart. He seems to be grasping for power in his attempt at Ramoth Gilead in similar fashion to the acquisition of Naboth's vineyard in the previous chapter for which Ahab faced judgment and received mercy for repentance (1 Kings 21). Second, the king of Israel receives the addition of Jehoshaphat's cavalry to supplement his own (1 Kgs 22.4) against the large number of chariots in Aram (1 Kgs 22.31), as if this was the means to guarantee a successful campaign. Finally, the king of Israel needs another (enter Jehoshaphat) to instruct him to seek a 'word' (דבר) from Yahweh, though he ought to have already known the 'words' (דברים) of Yahweh, because the narrative (echoing Deuteronomy) indicates each king 'sat on his throne' (ישבים ... על-כסאו; 1 Kgs 22.10) and as such was required to know and write these kingly instructions.

---

[5] R. Nelson, *First and Second Kings* (Interpretation; Atlanta, GA: John Knox, 1987), pp. 145-46.

[6] J.M. Hamilton, 'Caught in the Nets of Prophecy? The Death of King Ahab and the Character of God', *CBQ* 56.4 (1994), pp. 649-63 (651-52).

[7] These are all noted by G. Miller, 'The Wiles of the Lord: Divine Deception, Subtlety, and Mercy in I Reg 22', *ZAW* 126.1 (2014), pp. 45-58 (55).

While Jehoshaphat initially commits himself fully to the king of Israel for this war (22.4), he first desires a word specifically from Yahweh (22.5). It would appear that Jehoshaphat is compelling the Israelite king to seek 'the patron deity of all Israel' and may in fact assume a victory at the hands of Yahweh.[8] The king's response is to summon 400 prophets who unanimously offer a word of victory. Jehoshaphat remains unconvinced and inquires if there might be *another* prophet of Yahweh to speak. Jehoshaphat asks if there is '*another* prophet of Yahweh' (נביא ליהוה עוד) suggesting these also are prophets of Yahweh from his perspective (22.7).[9] Is the reader to note the particle עוד ('another') as indicating that these 400 were to be regarded as prophets of Yahweh?[10] How then did they survive Jezebel's censure (1 Kgs 18.4, 13)? Do they belong to Baal? If so, how did they survive Elijah's cleansing on Carmel (1 Kgs 18.40) and then find their way into the counsel of the king of Israel?

However, the narrative does not refer to them as prophets of Yahweh specifically, but allows for such claims only in the mouths of characters like Jehoshaphat (22.7; who seems readily duped on multiple occasions in the narrative), the king of Israel (22.8; who is portrayed as untrustworthy), and Zedekiah along with the 400 prophets themselves (22.11-12; who are also suggestively portrayed as untrustworthy by the end of the narrative). Such characters do not seem necessarily to be reliable sources of information in the narrative overall by the end. The narrative also offers another vagary as to their relation to Yahweh by not including 'Yahweh' in their victory pronouncement, but changing this to a word from אדני 'Adonai' (22.6).[11]

---

[8] D.I. Block, 'What Has Delphi to Do with Samaria? Ambiguity and Delusion in Israelite Prophecy', pp. 189-216 in P. Bienkowski, C. Mee, and E. Slater (eds.), *Writing and Ancient Near East Society: Essays in Honor of Alan Millard* (New York: T & T Clark, 2005), p. 194.

[9] R.W.L. Moberly, 'Does God Lie to His Prophets? The Story of Micaiah ben Imlah as a Test Case', *HTR* 96.1 (2003), pp. 1-23 (5).

[10] Moberly, 'Does God Lie to His Prophets?', p. 5.

[11] This is following the MT represented in *BHS*. However, many Hebrew manuscripts, Aquila, Symmachus, Theodotion, and the Targums read 'Yahweh' instead of 'Adonai/Lord', on which see J. Gray, *I & II Kings* (OTL; Philadelphia, PA: The Westminster Press, 2nd rev. edn, 1970), p. 445 n. c. This is also noted by A.H. Konkel who leaves open the possibility that the Targums and many of the MT have simply harmonized their readings to the rest of the text, *1 & 2 Kings* (NIVAC; Grand Rapids, M: Zondervan, 2006), pp. 351-52 n. 5.

The change of reference to the deity responding is noteworthy for the reader.[12] Whether the 400 prophets are at the last true or false is not the issue – even though the reader 'ought to be suspicious when four hundred preachers agree on anything! Inspired individuals seldom appear in droves.'[13] Perhaps this is part of the reason Jehoshaphat has requested *another*.[14] In either case the text seems to read that their 'words are, in essence, Yahweh's words' in the explanations that follow in the narrative even if not with the same intent as assumed earlier.[15]

The readers would not be able to discern who speaks for Yahweh in this account prematurely since vagaries and subterfuges abound. Thus the reader is confronted by a narrative ambiguity of whether this prophet is another prophet of Yahweh *inclusive with* the 400 or whether this prophet should be distinguished as actually a prophet of Yahweh *in contrast to* the 400. Such ambiguity is a call for discernment. It becomes clear through this narrative that 'integrity is the key to [such] discernment' for the characters and thus is suggestive for discernment for the readers.[16]

As the text continues to unfold, the king of Israel relents by sending for a prophet of Yahweh named Micaiah ben Imlah who the king conceives as only prophesying trouble (רע) for him. Jehoshaphat rebukes the king and the king sends immediately for Micaiah. The very name Micaiah ('Who is like Yah?') suggests this individual at least claims Yahweh as patron deity and offers the hope of a clarifying word from Yahweh.

A royal court scene follows where the king of Israel and Jehoshaphat sit enthroned in regalia near the gate of Samaria with the 400 prophets prophesying before them. Among them is one named Zedekiah ('Yah is just/righteous') who also bears the name of Yahweh. Both Zedekiah and Micaiah bear the name of Yahweh in their personal names which seems a strange matter given the former purging

---

[12] Block, 'What Has Delphi to Do with Samaria?', in Bienkowski, Mee, and Slater (eds.), *Writing and Ancient Near East Society*, p. 202.

[13] Hamilton, *Handbook on the Historical Books*, p. 441. Targum Jonathan and Josephus both refer to the 400 prophets as being 'false' as cited by D.I. Block, 'What Has Delphi to Do with Samaria?', in Bienkowski, Mee, and Slater (eds.), *Writing and Ancient Near East Society*, p. 195 n. 20.

[14] Nelson, *First and Second Kings*, p. 148.

[15] Miller, 'The Wiles of the Lord', p. 49 n. 18.

[16] Moberly, 'Does God Lie to His Prophets?', p. 15.

of Yahwistic prophets and worship from Israel under Ahab at the instigation of Jezebel. Perhaps we might understand a resurgence of Yahwistic worship following the confrontation on Carmel? Could it really be that the king of Israel is known at this point to entertain the prophecies of men who bear the name of Yahweh and therefore would be considered prophets of Yahweh?

While Micaiah is fetched, Zedekiah speaks for the 400 with his use of iron horns prophetically to demonstrate victory over the Arameans. The other prophets all resound with affirmations (now in the name of Yahweh). Meanwhile the messenger from the king of Israel informs Micaiah about the words of the other prophets and demands agreement with them. Micaiah's response is unambiguous (at first blush). Micaiah emphatically states he will only say what Yahweh tells him to say. However, upon arriving at the court of the kings and being questioned as to whether to go to war or hold back, Micaiah answers 'Go up and succeed! Yahweh has given [victory] into the king's hand' (עלה והצלח ונתן יהוה ביד המלך; 1 Kgs 22.15). The reader would remember that an unnamed prophet in chapter 20 told Ahab concerning Aram that Yahweh will 'give it into your hand' (נתנו בידך; 1 Kgs 20.13) as a prophetic word of victory. In 1 Kgs 22.12 and 15, the 400 prophets and then Micaiah (by the instruction of the messenger) prophesy an echo of this earlier message that Yahweh will 'give [Aram] into the hand of the king' (נתן ... ביד המלך). A word that sounds suspiciously similar might in fact ring true in the ears of the king (and to the reader), but in the mouth of Micaiah it leads to questions for the king who only ever expects רעה 'trouble' from Micaiah.[17] In a turn of the tables, the king of Israel demands the truth from Micaiah's mouth concerning the word of Yahweh, though moments before he had seemed all too ready to be affirmed in his previously intended plans.[18] Even the king suspects subterfuge.

The king of Israel does not believe Micaiah, but demands he

לא־תדבר אלי רק־אמת בשם יהוה

'speak only the truth to me in the name of Yahweh' (22.16). Micaiah offers a vision of

---

[17] This is indicated by G. Miller only with regard to Micaiah altering the words, but this misses that Micaiah is mimicking the very words of the 400 prophets before him, 'The Wiles of the Lord', pp. 50-51.

[18] Moberly, 'Does God Lie to His Prophets?', p. 7.

כל־ישראל נפצים אל־ההרים כצאן אשר אין־להם רעה

'all of Israel scattered upon the mountains like sheep without their shepherd' to which Yahweh says,

לא־אדנים לאלה ישובו איש־לביתו בשלום

'These have no master, let each one return to his home in peace' (22.17). The reader would remember that in chapter 20, the armies of Israel like חשפי עזים 'flocks of goats' (20.27) routed Aram upon the הרים 'mountains' (20.23), but here one finds no positive reference to the same imagery (22.17).[19] This offers a clear literary echo where the expected victory that had been pronounced in pastoral imagery is referenced now as a promise of defeat where no shepherd (the image of the king) remains. Such a shift from both the initial word of Micaiah to the king and now a use of similar terms and imagery from a previous account seem to beckon for a response of contrition from the king, but alas none is forthcoming.[20] The king responds to Jehoshaphat to take note that Micaiah does not prophesy 'good,' but only 'trouble' (רע) concerning him (22.18). The king has been right about Micaiah all along. However, the reader is left wondering how it is that Micaiah could earlier prophesy success and only now prophesy disaster for the king.

Testing Spirits (1 Kings 22.19-28)

While the king of Israel seems to brush aside Micaiah and only ad-dress Jehoshaphat, Micaiah addresses the gathered royal council with a second vision declared to be the דבר־יהוה 'word of Yahweh' (22.19). It is Yahweh who sits enthroned and holds council with the gathered hosts of heaven. It is Yahweh who inquires for direction concerning Ramoth Gilead. Yet it is Yahweh seeking for a plot to provoke the king of Israel to attack Ramoth Gilead in order for the king to die.

The heavenly court of Yahweh is not intended to portray a place elsewhere, but the reality 'both *now* and *here*' in the narrative suggest-ing King Yahweh has been holding court even as the kings of Israel

---

[19] Miller, 'The Wiles of the Lord', p. 52.
[20] Miller, 'The Wiles of the Lord', p. 48.

and Judah have held court.[21] Three primary levels for understanding Micaiah's words to Ahab might be offered: (1) 'the communicative dynamics of Micaiah's trying to get through to Ahab' by telling him he is being deceived to provoke a right response, (2) Ahab is morally challenged not to be self-seeking and listen to deceitful self-seeking prophetic words, and, finally, (3) Ahab is confronted by Yahweh, the God of Israel, in order to seek mercy and do what is right, or be judged by rejecting this word and this God.[22]

It is here for the first time in the immediate narrative we hear the name of the king of Israel: *Ahab* (22.20). The name of the king that might have been suspected throughout the narrative only now is confirmed and only now in the mouth of Yahweh![23] The result of this would not be missed by the readers who have suspected Ahab but are now confirmed in their assumptions, even as they might have wondered which word – victory or defeat – would hold true. Ahab has averted disaster before in the narrative (21.29). Will he once again?

In the council of Yahweh multiple suggestions of how to destroy Ahab are offered until finally 'the Spirit' (הרוח) approaches and offers the enticement of 'a lying spirit (רוח שקר) in the mouths of all his prophets' to which Yahweh agrees (22.21-22). Micaiah continues by affirming that Yahweh in fact 'has put a lying spirit in the mouths of all these prophets of yours' (22.23). 'Trouble' (רעה; or better here: 'disaster') has been pronounced by Yahweh for Ahab.

How should the readers hear that Yahweh, by his Spirit, indulges in deception? If deceit were really the endgame for Yahweh, then

---

[21] Moberly, 'Does God Lie to His Prophets?', p. 9, original emphasis.

[22] Moberly, 'Does God Lie to His Prophets?', pp. 10-11.

[23] This ambiguity of victory pronounced for 'the king' in v. 15 is used to argue for its referring to the Aramean king by H. Gressmann, *Die älteste Geschichtsschreibung und Prophetie Israels: von Samuel bis Amos und Hosea* (Die Schriften des Alten Testaments 2.1; Göttingen: Vandenhoeck & Ruprecht, 1921), p. 280; however, G. Miller contends this could not be the appropriate reading because Ramoth Gilead would already belong to the king of Aram and also because this suggests to him that the 400 prophets would be speaking the truth instead of lying, 'The Wiles of the Lord', p. 50 n. 20. The LXX and Vulgate both add 'king of Israel' after 'Ahab'. This would potentially make the naming of Ahab even more emphatic and draw out further the community implications for his decision to resist the word of Yahweh.

Yahweh undermines that plan by exposing the plot to deceive.[24] If anything, the revelation of the deceit functions to call Ahab to respond appropriately. This is made all the more emphatic by Ahab's name being used first in the account at this very point. Some readers might seek to guard any sense of culpability for deceit with regard to Yahweh even going so far as to attribute the deception to Satan against the text.[25] However, it 'is difficult, if not impossible, to deny that the Lord was the source of this deception'.[26] In fact, 'the false message of victory was ... the Lord's word'.[27] Not only is the effect of the message that the king should be deceived, but the messengers deceive: Micaiah and the Spirit of Yahweh.[28] Micaiah (and his claim of only speaking what Yahweh tells him) either lies in affirming Ahab to go to battle and be victorious, or he lies in declaring this is the Spirit of Yahweh that is deceiving the 400 prophets and ultimately Ahab.[29] The more observant reader would possibly hear not an issue of deceit as to the words themselves, but as to the interpretations of *what* might be given into the hand of *which* king?[30] The deceit is latent in the ambiguities of the revelation.

The article prefixed to רוח indicates either that the רוח is 'vivid and definite in the mind of Micaiah' or more likely is the Spirit of Yahweh that is also sent to deceive.[31] While the reader might be discomfited by the text, the context seems to indicate this is *the* Spirit of Yahweh who has offered to put רוח שקר 'a spirit of deception' into

---

[24] Miller, 'The Wiles of the Lord', p. 53.

[25] R.L. Mayhue, 'False Prophets and the Deceiving Spirit', *TMSJ* 4 (1993), pp. 135-63. Mayhue cites the early and extensive evidence for this reading, p. 147 n. 32. He also cites numerous witnesses to a 'Demonic View' of this passage, pp. 142-43 n. 20, and a 'Personified View', p. 144 n. 25.

[26] R.B. Chisholm Jr., 'Does God Deceive?' *BSac* 155 (1998), pp. 11-28 (13). Similarly, S.J. De Vries notes, 'Yahweh ... not only superintends historical event but actually instigates the revelatory incitement to such event', *Prophet against Prophet: The Role of Micaiah (1 Kings 22) in the Development of Early Prophetic Tradition* (Grand Rapids, MI: Eerdmans, 1978), p. 44.

[27] Chisholm, 'Does God Deceive?' p. 14.

[28] Against Konkel, *1 & 2 Kings*, p. 353.

[29] Provan, *1 and 2 Kings*, p. 163.

[30] Block, 'Empowered by the Spirit of God', pp. 49-50.

[31] Chisholm, 'Does God Deceive?', pp. 15-16.

the mouths of the prophets.[32] Indeed, this is Yahweh who agrees to the subterfuge. Was such shrewdness necessary? 'Ahab is a shrewd king, and so Yahweh deals with him shrewdly, revealing the truth to him in a creative and roundabout way. Far from luring an unsuspecting monarch to his death, Yahweh graciously provides him with a way out of his predicament'.[33] Arguably, though troubling, 'divine truth-telling will sometimes entail divine deceit, especially if a person has been acting deceptively himself'.[34]

Zedekiah's response to Micaiah's visionary word of the deceitful plans of Yahweh's Spirit (and thus Yahweh) is to slap Micaiah and inquire, אי־זה עבר רוח־יהוה מאתי לדבר אותך 'Which way did the Spirit of Yahweh go when he passed from me to speak to you?' (22.24).[35] Micaiah retorts with a prophetic pronouncement of judgment on Zedekiah intended to reveal that Micaiah has spoken truthfully (22.25). The reader waits in vain for the fulfillment of this word in the text, but 'suspects that it is Micaiah who is speaking the truth'.[36] The king has Micaiah imprisoned and fed siege rations. The king offers a כה אמר המלך 'Thus says the king' that he should be kept this way until the king returns בשלום 'in peace' (22.27). Micaiah offers one parting word: אם־שוב תשוב בשלום לא־דבר יהוה בי 'If you really return in peace, [then] Yahweh has not spoken by me' (22.28a). The

---

[32] Contra D.I. Block who argues this 'is obviously not the Holy Spirit … Though he operates on Yahweh's behalf, he has independent identity', 'Empowered by the Spirit of God', p. 49. In support of reading the text as indicating the Spirit of Yahweh, see Hildebrandt, *An Old Testament Theology*, p. 181.

[33] Miller, 'The Wiles of the Lord', p. 57.

[34] Miller, 'The Wiles of the Lord', p. 57. See also the extended defense, specifically for 1-2 Samuel but inclusive of the entire OT, of a distinction between deceit and lying in M. Newkirk, *Just Deceivers: An Exploration of the Motif of Deception in the Books of Samuel* (Eugene, OR: Pickwick, 2015).

[35] The LXX offers a reading where Zedekiah asks, '*What sort of* [ποῖον] Spirit of Yahweh' spoke to Micaiah (my translation). According to E.G. Dafni, this reading suggests there are 'several spirits' involved who remain 'under the power of God': one 'is a spirit of prophecy' and 'trustworthiness' and another is 'a spirit of pseudo-prophecy' or 'lies'. E.G. Dafni, 'רוח שקר und falsche Prophetie in I Reg 22', *ZAW* 112.3 (2000), pp. 365-85 (373), translations of this article are mine. The MT reading is to be preferred, though my proposal is that the LXX demonstrates that the translator read this ambiguously and determined to clarify theologically in order to distinguish spirits in the text emphatically.

[36] Provan, *1 and 2 Kings*, p. 164.

closing words in answer to this statement, שמעו עמים כלם, 'Listen all you peoples' (22.28b), are read variously as the words of Micaiah or as the words of Ahab.[37] In either reading, there a clear call for the wider community to test the words of the prophet/s and verify who it is that speaks for Yahweh.

This becomes Ahab's vain attempt 'to evade the prophetic word by incarcerating the prophet and avert the forecast of judgment by surviving the battle'.[38] Neither succeeds. Ahab dies and as such fulfills prophecy. The end of the prophet Micaiah is never mentioned. Further, there is no fulfillment word for Zedekiah hiding himself (22.25), which is left as a word hanging on the mouth of Micaiah who ends with himself being forcibly hidden away in prison (22.27).[39] If the readers were to attempt to discern whether Micaiah is a true prophet, the text only hints at such in the fulfillment against Ahab which even here offers twists.[40]

---

[37] Bodner makes a compelling case for his literary reading of 1 Kgs 22.28b that hears the words 'Listen, all you people' as the response of Ahab to Micaiah rather than a resumptive statement by Micaiah. Following his proposed reading, Micaiah speaks an 'if … then' statement in v. 28a and is answered by Ahab in v. 28b via a circumlocution addressing all people to hear what has been spoken. Several ironic twists follow: (1) Ahab apparently believes the word of Yahweh sufficiently to attempt a disguise to subvert the fulfillment of the word, but this leads to a 'random' arrow killing him, (2) the crafty Ahab meets his end, while the apparently gullible Jehoshaphat is spared, and (3) 'all Israel' (22.17) are scattered by Ahab's death as they return home (22.36) as testimony to Ahab's call to 'all people' to take notice. K. Bodner, 'Critical Notes: The Locutions of 1 Kings 22:28: A New Proposal', *JBL* 122.3 (2003), pp. 533-46; L.M. Wray-Beal, *1 & 2 Kings* (AOTC 9; Downers Grove, IL: InterVarsity, 2014), p. 285. V.P. Hamilton implies as much by referring to 'Micaiah's last words recorded in Scripture' and quoting only 22.28a, *Handbook on the Historical Books*, p. 443. This second half of the verse is lacking in the LXX and Vulgate, and thus is lacking in one English translation: NJB. Many ETT have read this portion as explicitly the continuing words of Micaiah: CEB, CEV, NAB, NET, NIV, and NLT. Further, it is missing from the LXX[BL] and is identical to Mic. 1.2.

[38] Bodner, 'Critical Notes', p. 542 n. 35.

[39] R.D. Patterson and H.J. Austel contend, 'The fulfillment of Micaiah's prophecy regarding Zedekiah is not recorded but likely took place when Jehu seized the palace (2 Kings 10:17-27)', '1, 2 Kings', in F.E. Gaebelein (ed.), *1 Kings-Job* (EBC 4; Grand Rapids, MI: Zondervan, 1988), p. 165. This is speculative given the very specific fulfillment language used in this passage for other prophetic words.

[40] Knoll argues on several literary grounds that Micaiah is in fact to be regarded as a false prophet whose words end up being true with regard to Ahab and that the 400 prophets and Zedekiah are in fact regarded as true prophets who get it wrong

(Un)Believing the Truth All the Way to the End (1 Kings 22.29-40)

Ahab appears to disbelieve the words of Micaiah by still persisting in his attack on Ramoth Gilead (22.29). Jehoshaphat seems even to join him in this disbelief. At another level Ahab believes the words of Micaiah and chooses a disguise for himself and instructs Jehoshaphat to wear his royal accoutrements. Even the character of Ahab seems to waffle as to whom he believes. Or if he does believe Micaiah, he is attempting to avert the 'trouble' pronounced against him through his own subterfuge. A careful reading suggests 'God is not manipulating a simple-minded man or wasting his time with an inexorable monarch. Rather, Yahweh is dealing with a man willing to ruminate over his decision and who can be gotten through to'.[41]

As it happens, a 'random'[42] arrow strikes the king of Israel. He pretends his strength longer by being propped up in his chariot until he bled out sufficiently to die in his chariot. The armies withdraw from the conflict. It is striking that the security of returning home for Israel from the battle is only found once Ahab is dead and thus

---

for Ahab. That the king of Israel complains about Micaiah only speaking 'evil' (רע) about him despite that 'evil' has not in fact come upon him and that mercy was granted previously when Ahab responded well to a true prophet (1 Kgs 21.27-29). Noll notes that 'any evil [predicted by Micaiah] has been, at best, slow to arrive'. Noll goes on to point to Ahab reminding Micaiah to speak only the truth suggesting Micaiah has been false to this point, which Micaiah does not counter. Further, Micaiah speaks a prophetic oracle against Zedekiah, and the city Zedekiah lives in, which fails to come to fulfillment in the narrative, as the battle does not appear to 'ever ... escalate to that level'. Thus, Noll contends it is in fact Micaiah who is regarded by the narrator as a 'false prophet'. While Micaiah seems to speak the truth in 22.17 (cf. 22.36), 22.25 suggests Micaiah prophesies falsely (according to Deut. 18.22). Noll extrapolates from this reading that at issue is a story of an 'incompetent' God who was manufactured and was nothing more than 'a repulsive, fictional thought experiment'. This does not seem to be the intent of the text, which instead seems to indicate that the God of Israel is thoughtful and merciful even in carrying out justice and judgment. It also functions to call for discernment at every level. K.L. Noll, 'Presumptuous Prophets in a Deuteronomic Debate', in Boda and Beal (eds.), *Prophets, Prophecy, and Ancient Israelite Historiography*, pp. 137-41.

[41] Miller, 'The Wiles of the Lord', p. 56.

[42] This is reading לתמו as meaning something like he fired without intent of a specific target (see ESV, NAB, NAS, NET, NIV, NKJV, NLT, NRSV) though it could possibly be read as 'well [aimed]' following the LXX εὐστόχως.

without an earthly king. The king's body is returned to Samaria to be buried as might befit a king. However, there the blood from his chariot is washed in the pool of Samaria where 'dogs licked up his blood and the prostitutes bathed' (22.38).

The word of Yahweh finds specified fulfillment in the words of the narrator (22.38) concerning how 'dogs licked [Ahab's] blood' after his death. This word had been earlier spoken by Elijah (1 Kgs 21.19). The prophetic word in 21.19 specifies this would happen 'in the place where dogs licked up Naboth's blood' which presumably would be in the Valley of Jezreel, but Ahab's blood is licked up in Samaria. Perhaps the later description of his son's blood being licked by dogs in the Valley of Jezreel is yet a further fulfillment of this word (2 Kgs 9.24-26). This fulfillment should be heard as 'not quite straightforward' and thus to call for yet greater discernment among the readers apart from an overly literalistic fulfillment.[43] This reading suggests readers search in vain to find direct fulfilment in the narrative even as there is certainty of fulfillment. Is it possible this is yet another way for the narrative to call for discernment from the readers rather than a mathematical precision to prophetic words, testing of those words, and their fulfillment?[44]

Conclusion

Several of the functions and intents of this narrative might be proposed. First, this 'is a story meant to be understood as tragic' or more specifically 'a human tragedy in the classic mold' that is 'a tragedy of flaw rather than of fate'.[45] It was not inevitable that Ahab would find his demise in this account. He rushes headlong over a cliff into what seems a road beset with cautionary signs along the way all sent from the Spirit. Does land that had once been pronounced as a given by Yahweh mean a guaranteed victory? Do prophets speaking in the name of Yahweh together mean victory? Does a lone troublemaking prophet deserve to be listened to when he switches between

---

[43] Moberly, 'Does God Lie to His Prophets?', pp. 18-19.
[44] Wray Beal, *1 & 2 Kings*, pp. 286, 287.
[45] Hamilton, 'Caught in the Nets of Prophecy?', p. 662, and 662 n. 25.

seemingly antithetical messages from Yahweh? Has the Spirit indeed spoken by the mouths of Zedekiah in light of Micaiah's word?

Second, this story 'warns us against questioning the priority of grace' by taking advantage of the generosity of Yahweh.[46] The Spirit does not remain patient with the unfaithful forever. Among the emphases of the chapter is the well-being of the people of God which is not necessarily to be identified with the well-being of the leader who is replaceable.[47] The greater issue for Micaiah is not that Ahab be spared, but that Israel is spared.[48] It was for the sake of Israel that Ahab should be judged and removed from kingship. That Yahweh could deal in such a fashion with the king of Israel meant that Israel itself could be dealt with similarly and must not presume upon the goodness of Yahweh. The Spirit would not abide with 'man' forever but working as (and at) the right hand of Yahweh will not be presumed upon.

Third, the Spirit allows for ambiguities and demands (and facilitates) discernment. The readers hear this as a story of a single prophet that faithfully delivers the word of Yahweh against a majority who serve the king's interests which later would serve Judah as a witness to faithfulness in discerning prophetic witnesses.[49] Ambiguities abound in the text. Even some of the characters are portrayed in ways that suggest they could not see the end from the beginning clearly. This should cause readers pause. Conflicting words from Yahweh provoke responses of careful attentiveness to the Spirit and ultimate obedience in faith.

Fourth, the function of this narrative introducing Micaiah in the midst of the accounts of Elijah and Elisha testifies to the 'certainty that God did not leave Himself without a true witness in Israel!'[50] The Spirit speaks through the various prophets as self-witness to the continuing witness apart from individual persons. Readers might hear

---

[46] Hamilton, 'Caught in the Nets of Prophecy?', p. 662.

[47] Hamilton, *Handbook on the Historical Books*, p. 441. See also, De Vries, *Prophet Against Prophet*, p. 38.

[48] Miller, 'The Wiles of the Lord', p. 52; and Moberly, 'Does God Lie to His Prophets?', pp. 7-8.

[49] J. Blenkinsopp, *A History of Prophecy in Israel: From the Settlement in the Land to the Hellenistic Period* (Philadelphia, PA: The Westminster Press, 1983), p. 187.

[50] Mayhue, 'False Prophets and the Deceiving Spirit', p. 138.

in this account a 'truly suspenseful' story unfolding without a predetermined end.[51] From the narrative flow, the future is an open one.
The Spirit speaks not as *fait accompli* but as an invitation to respond.
The possibility of Ahab once again repenting (following the literary
placement of the account of chapter 21 just prior to this account)
and receiving mercy seems a *real* possibility all the way to the very
end.[52] The readers would not miss the possibility before them.

Fifth, this account is not primarily about distinguishing between
true and false prophets,[53] but about revealing the nature of Yahweh
(and Yahweh's Spirit) however disturbing that nature may seem to
human discernment.[54] 'God's needy and faithful people will always
find Him reliable and truthful, but His enemies may discover He is
willing and able to use deception and enticement to evil to hasten
their journey down the pathway of destruction they have chosen to
travel'.[55] The Spirit speaks, but the Spirit also discerns. Prophets may
hear from the Spirit, but have they discerned rightly the intent of the
Spirit's words?

Finally, readers would note the ways in which the Spirit bears witness to Yahweh as sovereign. It is the court of Yahweh that is ultimate. The court of Ahab and Jehoshaphat is only to serve the larger
purposes of the court of Yahweh. The Spirit testifies to the sovereignty of Yahweh over this court through the prophetic revelation to
Micaiah that is implicitly the work of the Spirit and accepted as such,
even if not truthfully, by the words of Zedekiah concerning the passing of the Spirit. The Spirit also bears witness to Yahweh's sovereignty in offering the plan to overcome Ahab that was requested, and
finally is approved, by Yahweh.

---

[51] Hamilton, 'Caught in the Nets of Prophecy?', pp. 653, 656, 662.

[52] Hamilton, 'Caught in the Nets of Prophecy?', pp. 656-57.

[53] Against Möller who refers to two ways of interpreting the account of Micaiah: first, as an 'interprophetic conflict' entailing 'verification or falsification' of
the prophecies given, or, second, 'in terms of the opposition between central and
peripheral prophets'. K. Möller, 'Prophets and Prophecy', in Arnold and Williamson (eds.), *DOT: HB*, pp. 825-29 (828-29).

[54] Hamilton, 'Caught in the Nets of Prophecy?', p. 656.

[55] Chisholm, 'Does God Deceive?', p. 28.

7

THE DOUBLE PORTION SPIRIT: SIGN OF THE TRUE SON (2 KINGS 2-9, 13)

Introduction

Elijah was a prophet 'like Moses' and becomes one of the leading figures of the book of First Kings. He is a prophet unlike the other prophets of Israel in the days of Ahab (even Micaiah who gets mentioned in 1 Kings 22). He is a prophet of Yahweh who calls for a return to the singularity of Yahwistic worship against the hundreds of prophets of Baal and Asherah. However, despite the attempts to take his life by the royal family, he successfully passes his prophetic endowment on to another: Elisha. As Elijah passes from the scene there appears a sort of prophetic family which forms around the leadership of Elisha, though it is already present in the time of Elijah and always in a form of distinction from the role of Elijah and Elisha in the life of Israel.

This 'family' in the Hebrew text is called בני הנביאים which has been variously translated 'guild' (NAB, NET), 'company' (NRSV), and 'group' (NLT), but most literally is translated 'sons of the prophets'. The translation 'sons of the prophets' is not simply a moniker for formal affiliation in the sense of 'guild',[1] but instead seems to

---

[1] Contra those who argue beyond the text that such a group was a formal organization of sorts that supposedly gathered around their guild leaders to be taught how to prophesy via means of meditation leading to mantic ecstatic states. For example, K. Koch, *The Prophets: The Assyrian Period* (Vol.1; Philadelphia, PA:

belong to the very specific literary and theological function discerned by the readers concerning the passing of the prophetic *pater familias* of the prophets and of Israel from Elijah to Elisha.[2]

Thus, the Elijah/Elisha cycles[3] in the books of Kings are read to portray Elisha as the true son of the prophet Elijah in his inheriting the 'double portion' of the רוח ('S/spirit') of Elijah (and thus to become yet further a prophet 'like Moses').[4] The narrative functions at one level as a legitimation of Elisha's prophethood in distinction to other prophets.[5] Yet perhaps prophetic legitimation is not simply a

---

Fortress, 1983), pp. 24-25; and G. Rice, 'Elijah's Requirement for Prophetic Leadership (2 Kings 2:1-18)', *JRT* 59-60.1 (2006), pp. 1-12 (3), who refers to them as 'prophetic orders'.

[2] It is of note that בני הנביאים only occurs in 2 Kings (2.3, 5, 7, 15; 4.1, 38 twice; 5.22; 6.1; 9.1) with the singular exception of 1 Kgs 20.35. There are similar phrases elsewhere in the OT (in 1 Sam. 10.5, 10; Amos 7.14), but none which duplicate this construct chain. W. Bergen argues that groups of prophets are consistently portrayed in the texts of Samuel and Kings in a negative light in contrast to prophets acting as individuals who may or may not be positive. See W.J. Bergen, *Elisha and the End of Prophetism*, pp. 172-74. While many argue that it is this very group which preserved the Elisha cycle, this lay beyond the text as a matter of historical inquest and is not properly a literary matter in the text as preserved, on this notion see as examples: Gray, *I & II Kings*, pp. 29-30; and K.W. Whitelam, 'Elisha', in D.N. Freedman (ed.), *ABD* (New York: Doubleday, 1992), II, pp. 472-73. T.R. Hobbs provides an extended excursus on the בני הנביאים which he finally argues is a unique feature associated with the Elisha stories and that one should not offer wider notions of historical recreation of Israel (or the wider region) in the mid ninth century, *2 Kings*, WBC 13 (Waco, TX: Word, 1987), pp. 25-27.

[3] The use of 'cycle' with regard to Elijah and Elisha is not here intended to indicate a prehistory to the canonical text, but only a literary unit that deals primarily with each respective prophet contra such over-developed attempts at parsing the historical origins of each account in the likes of DeVries, *Prophet Against Prophet*, pp. 116-20.

[4] Konkel, *1 & 2 Kings*, p. 381. J. Blenkinsopp states, 'The metaphor of fatherhood and sonship current in prophetic groups lies behind the conferring of the double share of Elijah's spirit on Elisha', citing the Deuteronomic law of the first born son, *A History of Prophecy in Israel*, pp. 75-76. As such, DeVries, *Prophet Against Prophet*, pp. 54, 56, locates this text as a 'prophetic legitimation' text. E.B. Gertel, 'Moses, Elisha and Transferred Spirit: The Height of Biblical Prophecy? Part II', *JBQ* 30.3 (2002), pp. 171-77, specifically regards the Elisha account as demonstrating the failure of Elisha as prophet because of an attempted manipulation and control of the Spirit of Elijah.

[5] R.D. Moore lays out a strong case for this reading, *God Saves: Lessons from the Elisha Stories* (JSOTSup 95; Sheffield Academic, 1990), pp. 111-17.

matter of contrasting Elisha with other prophets (including the 'sons of the prophets'), but also affirming his role as leading inheritor of the prophetic mantle of Elijah's רוח.[6] In fact, this רוח seems to play the most significant role in the ministry of Elisha as distinguishing him from all others and carrying forward the work of Yahweh on Israel's behalf.

There is some ambiguity in the text concerning this double portion רוח.[7] Is this the רוח of Elijah or the רוח of Yahweh (2 Kgs 2.9, 15-16)? The fifty sons of the prophets from Jericho who saw the miraculous return of Elisha across the Jordan admit that Elisha has received the רוח *of Elijah*, but immediately follow this with a statement that the רוח *of Yahweh* must have placed Elijah somewhere else that they could go and find him. While this may not be a direct challenge to Elisha as endowed with the fullest authority and power of Elijah, it seems subtly to undermine it. Are the readers to understand the text itself to distinguish whose רוח Elisha has received? Must there be a choice? The רוח of Yahweh is intended to be signified throughout the text by the words Elisha speaks being fulfilled, as earlier the word of Yahweh through Elijah was fulfilled. The signs of this double portion רוח on Elisha therefore are intended to indicate it is also (and more properly) the רוח or Spirit of Yahweh.

The specificity within the text of this רוח being 'of Elijah' points to the mission and ministry of this particular prophet 'like Moses' rather than being a literary point of the writer to separate Elisha as somehow only having the רוח of Elijah and not Yahweh. This 'double portion' רוח of Elijah concerns Elisha's prophetic (Spirit-empowered) ministry as the new father and judge of the prophets and Israel. This is drawn in contrast to the sons of the prophets who seem to

---

[6] C. Coulot, 'L'investiture d'Elisee par Elie (1 R 19.19-21)', *RSR* 57 (1983), pp. 87-92; Hildebrandt, *An Old Testament Theology*, pp. 176-79; Whitelam, 'Elisha', p. 472.

[7] D.I. Block suggests a 'surface' reading might only indicate he desires 'twice the heart, twice the vitality, or twice the spiritual fortitude' of Elijah, but concludes that a more robust reading clarifies it is 'the Spirit of Yahweh which resides upon Elijah' which Elisha is seeking and receives, 'Empowered by the Spirit of God', p. 46.

falter at every turn to produce evidence of their own proper sonship with regard to Elijah, in contrast to the successful ministry of Elisha.[8]

Why the Request for the 'Double Portion'?

Elijah has already anointed Elisha to the task of completing the judgment against Israel and the house of Ahab (1 Kgs 19.19-21), but after they have miraculously crossed the Jordan River Elijah asks Elisha what he might give him. Elisha's response is to receive a 'double portion of your spirit' (2 Kgs 2.9). This 'double portion' is Elisha invoking the Deuteronomic command to give the 'double portion' (פי־שנים literally 'mouth of two') to the eldest son even if he is not the most beloved (Deut. 21.17).[9]

The 'double portion' might have been read as referring to Elisha demonstrating twice the power of Elijah via twice the number of miracles attributable in the book of Kings to Elisha.[10] However,

---

[8] A. Phillips discusses the terms אב and בני הנביאים at length and concludes that the אב functions as a technical term emphasizing a prophetic interpretive ability. He further connects these terms to 'speaking in tongues' and 'interpreting' tongues respectively. Thus, he argues that the אב was necessary for understanding the words of the בני הנביאים. See his 'The Ecstatics' Father', pp. 183-94 in Ackroyd and Lindars (eds.), *Words and Meanings*, p. 190.

[9] E. Davies, 'The Meaning of *pî š^enayim* in Deuteronomy xxi 17', *VT* 36, 3 (1986), pp. 341-47, argues that the reading of 'double portion' is to be preferred instead of 'two-thirds' as proposed by M. Noth and H. Gunkel. Davies makes an exegetical case for the reading 'double portion' by noting the fractional nature of פי־שנים in Biblical Hebrew when another fraction is present as is the case in Zech. 13.8. However, P. Watson works to demonstrate that 'two-thirds' is the likeliest translation based on his analysis of cognate literature (Akkadian, Middle Assyrian and Nuzi) along with a question of why the writer of Deut. 21.17 and 2 Kgs 2.9 (followed by Sir. 12.5, 18.32, 48.12 and the Mishna and Talmud) did not choose one of the terms most readily meaning 'double' (*mišneh* or *šenayim*). See his article 'A Note on the "Double Portion" of Deuteronomy 21:17 and II Kings 2:9', *RQ* 8.1 (1965), pp. 70-75.

[10] V.P. Hamilton mentions an early Jewish tradition 'that Elisha actually outdid his famous predecessor in working signs and wonders ("Elisha performed sixteen miracles and eight was all his master performed")' as indicating an early notion of the 'double portion' referring to twice as many miracles. However, he finds only thirteen miracles enumerated by his count (1) parting the waters of the Jordan with Elijah's cloak, (2) turning bad water to good, (3) the miracle of water in the assault on Moab, (4) provision of oil for the widow, (5) prophetic promise and fulfillment of a son to a barren woman, (6) resurrection of that same son who died, (7) curing

careful readers would not understand this to refer to twice the number.[11] Such a reading fails to grasp the sense of the term 'double portion' which instead refers not to a numeric quantity so much as, following the Deuteronomic code, to the firstborn's share in contrast to the other sons of that same father.[12] In other words, Elisha is requesting that he receive the eldest son's inheritance of the רוח which was upon Elijah. Thus, the sons of the prophets might be read to 'function' in the Elisha cycle 'as other "sons" of Elijah. [Where] Elisha wishes to be recognized as the firstborn of these "sons," with all the rights and privileges of the firstborn duly accorded to him.'[13]

This 'double portion' functions in the narrative as a sign of authority within the family or clan wherein the double portioned (eldest) son stands as the intended patriarch upon the passing of the father.[14] As the 'double portion' son he would be immediately placed

---

a poisoned stew, (8) feeding a large group with a little food, (9) cleansing Naaman's leprosy, (10) floating an axe head to recover it, (11) the opening/closing of eyes, (12) prophecy of an end to the famine, and (13) raising of a dead man who was thrown onto Elisha's bones, in his *Handbook on the Historical Books*, pp. 444-45. See also N. Levine, 'Twice as Much of Your Spirit: Patter, Parallel and Paronomasia in the Miracles of Elijah and Elisha', *JSOT* 85 (1999), p. 25, for the citations in the various Midrashim concerning this reading of the 'double portion' in the rabbinic literature. Extending this logic to the multiplying of 'complexity' in the narrative of Elisha, Levine argues specifically that 'Elisha's miracles not only double Elijah's but seem to parallel and multiply them in their themes, elements and language', pp. 25-26.

[11] Understanding this 'double portion' to refer to twice as many miracles is earliest noted in the Cairo Geniza text of Sir. 48.12 which reads: 'Elijah was enveloped in the whirlwind; Elisha was filled with his spirit / a doubled portion [פי שנים] of the many signs, and wonders with every word of his mouth'. The LXX and Vulgate versions do not include the second bicolon of verse 12 as found in the Geniza fragment, 'a double portion of the many signs'. Despite this interpretation being widely held at a more popular level and also enjoying the favor of the author of Ben Sira, it is not supported by numerous critical commentators and scholars (and for good reason). On which see, H.L. Ellison, *The Prophets of Israel: From Ahijah to Hosea* (Grand Rapids, MI: Eerdmans, 1969), p. 44; Hobbs, *2 Kings*, p. 21; House, *1, 2 Kings*, p. 258; and Konkel, *1 & 2 Kings*, p. 380.

[12] Contra R.D. Patterson, '1-2 Kings' (*EBC* 4; F. Gaebelein (ed.); Grand Rapids, MI: Zondervan, 1988), pp. 177-78.

[13] Watson, 'A Note', pp. 74-75.

[14] Rice, 'Elijah's Requirement', pp. 5-6.

'second in rank to the *pater familias*'.[15] In this sense, then the readers would understand Elisha to be asking Elijah that he might be the inheritor of the full authority of the father (Elijah) to carry forward all that the father had planned and been called by Yahweh to accomplish.[16] In this particular case, Elisha is tasked and equipped to carry out the anointing of Jehu as king of Israel and Hazael as king of Syria in order to bring about the judgment of Israel and specifically the house of Ahab. The narrative moves forward offering '[n]umerous literary echoes [that] clearly portray him as Elijah's rightful successor'.[17] Elisha, as double portioned son of Elijah, will carry forward the work of his 'father' in Israel in the Spirit of Elijah. Twenty literary connections are indicated as evidence of this genuine eldest sonship of Elisha as new head of the prophetic family and ultimately of Israel.[18]

(Twenty) Signs of the Double Portion Spirit

The most obvious sign of the double portion Spirit is the initial sign of Elisha seeing Elijah as he was taken up into the heavens (2 Kgs 2.10). Elijah initially seems reticent or perhaps even incapable of granting Elisha's request for the double portion and yet the sign is given as confirmation of the Spirit endowment to enable Elisha to carry on in the power and authority of Elijah. Yet this initial most basic sign serves only to confirm the inheritance to Elisha himself. The other signs that would be given would serve to confirm the double portion to those numbered among the prophets, kings, and all Israel.

---

[15] I. Mendelsohn, 'On the Preferential Status of the Eldest Son', *BASOR* 156 (Dec.1959), pp. 38-40.

[16] M. Cogan and H. Tadmor, *II Kings: A New Translation* (Garden City, NY: Doubleday, 1988), p. 39; Gray, *I & II Kings*, p. 474; Hildebrandt, *An Old Testament Theology*, pp. 176-79; Hobbs, *2 Kings*, p. 21.

[17] J.K. Mead, 'Elisha', pp. 254-58 in *DOT:HB*, p. 257.

[18] K. Möller writes that this request for the 'double portion' means 'his prophetic succession is conceptualized in terms of sonship', 'Prophets and Prophecy', pp. 825-29 in *DOT: HB*, p. 827.

The second sign followed quickly after this first sign. Elisha tore his own clothing in two as he mourned Israel's loss and cried[19] aloud, 'My father! My father! The chariots and horsemen of Israel' (2 Kgs 2.12)! He then took up the prophetic hairy cloak of Elijah which had fallen to the ground upon the catching up of Elijah (v. 13). With the cloak in hand he returned to the Jordan River in full sight of the sons of the prophets and hit the water with the cloak (2 Kgs 2.14). At this, the waters of the Jordan divided as they had when Elijah had done likewise at the first crossing with the sons of the prophets looking on. The sons of the prophets had watched Elijah divide the waters with his hairy cloak and now watch Elisha do the same with the cloak of Elijah. That Elisha should receive and use the cloak of Elijah would serve as a testimony of his filling the role of Elijah to Israel. In fact, Elijah had already covered Elisha with his hairy cloak immediately after his encounter with Yahweh on Horeb when Elijah had been instructed to anoint Elisha to replace him and carry out the judgment against Ahab and Israel (1 Kgs 19.16-21).[20] Now Elisha permanently bears the mantle.

The third sign occurs when the sons of the prophets near Jericho who await Elijah and Elisha's return on the west bank of the Jordan refuse to believe that Elijah has truly been taken away *permanently* and *replaced* by Elisha (2 Kgs 2.15-18).[21] They stood and watched the same miraculous crossing by Elisha,[22] see him with Elijah's all-too-familiar cloak and yet seem to fail to discern the presence of the רוח that had been on Elijah that is now on Elisha (despite their words indicating otherwise). In their refusal to accept Elisha as proper heir to Elijah, the sons of the prophets propose to go on a search for Elijah (2 Kgs

---

[19] Levine, 'Twice', pp. 29-30, notes the pervasive use of יצק 'to pour' (and the similar sounding צעק 'to cry') in the Elisha cycle and connects this high usage to the similarly high usage in the building of Solomon's temple (1 Kings 7).

[20] Levine, 'Twice', pp. 45-46, makes an observation that Elijah at Horeb (חרב) had been shown the 'sword' (חרב) in the hand of both Hazael and Jehu against the house of Ahab, but Elisha is never described as having a 'sword'. Instead, he proposes that Elijah bequeaths the mantle to carry out his calling of judgment.

[21] P.H. House, however, believes that 'Elisha's repetition of the act [of using the cloak to separate the waters of the Jordan and cross over] ... confirm in their minds that Elisha is truly Elijah's successor', *1, 2 Kings*, p. 258.

[22] This is assumed by their proximity to Elisha returning, see Rice, 'Elijah's Requirement', p. 9.

2.16), whom they wrongly believe has been taken by the Spirit of Yahweh and set down somewhere else.

Though Elisha initially dismisses their proposal, he eventually relents (2 Kgs 2.15-17). They return after three days without finding him. Their deference to his authority suggests a fourth sign. In line with Deut. 21.17 the readers might surmise such a reading because the one with the Spirit of Elijah (and thus Elijah himself) is among them. Better yet, the Spirit which had been upon Elijah is among them. They should have no need to look elsewhere. And though they initially recognize this endowment of the Spirit, they just as quickly seem to reject it as conclusive as indicated by their oppositional request. Their search should have led them to conclude otherwise. It did not. Yet even in their seeming rejection of Elisha in the place of Elijah as 'father' they still defer to his authority for their errant quest as the fourth sign.[23]

As Elisha carries on his prophetic patriarchal ministry, the sons of the prophets of Jericho who had just witnessed the miraculous return of Elisha apparently lack the ability to care for the inhabitants of their city (2 Kgs 2.19). The water of Jericho is described as 'bitter' and thus making the inhabitants sick and the land 'unfruitful' (2 Kgs 2.19-20). Elisha arrives in the power of the Spirit of Elijah to 'heal' (רפא; 2 Kgs 2.21) the water of Jericho with a dash of salt thrown into the water and the word of Yahweh spoken and thus to end the sicknesses and miscarriages it was causing as a permanent healing of the water of the land (2 Kgs 2.21-22). This fifth sign in the narrative comes when the word of Yahweh was with Elisha to heal water. The readers would remember that Elijah before him (cf. 2 Kgs 1.17) had 'healed' (רפא) the altar on Mount Carmel (1 Kgs 18.30) and restored life to the land by the returning waters that followed.[24]

The sixth sign unfolds bearing disturbing testimony (2 Kgs 2.23-25). As Elisha continued in the retracing of his earlier journey with Elijah, he came up toward Bethel and was encountered by a band of young lads[25] on the road. This motley crew of youth takes to mocking

---

[23] Bergen, *Elisha*, pp. 60-61.

[24] Levine, 'Twice', p. 34.

[25] 'Young lads' seems a preferable translation of the Hebrew which occurs in several other places (1 Sam. 20.35: the lad is sufficiently old enough to run and fetch arrows in a field; 1 Kgs 3.7: Solomon considers himself such; Isa. 11.6: still

the prophet, yelling: 'Go up, baldy! Go up, baldy' (2 Kgs 2.23)! One might assume they are referring to his head (and many translations have added such a reference: ESV, JPS, KJV, NAB, NAS, NIV84, NKJV, and NRSV). However, the text seems to indicate something besides the numbering of hairs on his head. 'Baldy' (NET, NIV11, NJB, and TNIV) follows the Hebrew more closely and allows for the literary connection back to Elijah in 1 Kings 1 who is immediately known by King Ahaziah for being 'hairy' when the king questions his servants who the man was that prophetically confronted them on the road to seek other gods (v. 8). The literary connection is striking: Elijah is recognized for being 'hairy' and Elijah's 'double portion' son is mocked as 'baldy'. Could it be that these youths of Bethel (another city known to be home to sons of the prophets) are specifically rejecting Elisha as the prophetic son of Elijah rather than offering commentary on his receding hairline?[26] This story ends with a sixth sign of Elisha cursing them 'in the name of Yahweh' and two bears coming out from the woods[27] to maul 42 of them. This offers another link to Elijah, the 'man of God', calling down the 'fire of God'[28] from heaven on the two captains with their 50 soldiers sent up the hill to reject his status as prophet in 2 Kgs 1.9-14. A significant contrast is that Elijah is told to 'come down' while Elisha is told 'go up', yet in both cases each is in turn being rejected as the prophet of Yahweh and each answers the bands of antagonists with a divine sign of judgment.

The seventh sign of Elisha's special sonship came in the form of unexpected watering of the land in 2 Kings 3. Elijah had earlier played his role in halting the rain on Israel until the time that Yahweh

---

old enough to shepherd; 2 Kgs 5.14: to describe the restored skin of Naaman) which similarly do not seem to suggest 'little children' as some have read this text (with the possible exception of Hadad in 1 Kgs 11.17). On this reading see Ellison, *The Prophets*, p. 47.

[26] Gray, *I & II Kings*, p. 480; Konkel, *1 & 2 Kings*, p. 381-82. Though Hobbs, *2 Kings*, p. 24, believes this refers to a natural baldness which seems far less likely despite the preference for such a reading in the English translations noted.

[27] The Hebrew for 'from the woods' (מן־היער) in 2 Kgs 2.24 offers a wordplay with the young lads coming 'from the city' (מן־העיר) in the previous verse.

[28] A wordplay occurs in this passage (2 Kgs 1.12) where Elijah is called the 'man of God' (איש האלהים) and declares that the defense of his prophethood is 'fire from God' (אש־אלהים).

declared it would rain (1 Kgs 17.1). Elisha is called upon to inquire if Yahweh will grant water (as a true prophet of Yahweh) just like Elijah, and his relationship to Elijah even receives mention explicitly (2 Kgs 3.11-12). In both cases the word of Yahweh declares the unseen water is coming (1 Kgs 18.1, 41; 2 Kgs 3.12, 16) as the prophets patiently await the provision of the word (Elijah by praying seven times: 1 Kgs 18.42-44; Elisha by calling for a harpist: 2 Kgs 3.15). Elisha proves himself to be the true prophet of Yahweh and inheritor of the Spirit of Elijah.[29] That Elisha has asked for a minstrel in order to prophesy offers literary echoes of the Spirit-ed prophetic band finding Saul overwhelmed and counted among them (1 Sam. 9.5-6, 10-11) and David playing his prophetic salvific tunes of victory (1 Sam. 16.14-23). The reader likewise notes that it is Jehoshaphat, king of Judah, who becomes the character voice inquiring for a prophet of Yahweh to which Elisha is the one indicated in similar fashion as Micaiah in 1 Kings 22.[30]

In 2 Kings 4, a widow of one of the sons of the prophets receives miraculous provision of oil until the immediate need of paying debtors is met with sufficient provision for her and her two sons (vv. 1-7). Similarly, Elijah had earlier met the needs of a widow (this one at Zarephath of Sidon) and her son by the provision of ceaseless oil and flour until the need was no longer present (1 Kgs 17.7-16). While Elijah performs his miracle in the home of a widow in Baal's territory, Elisha performs his miracle in the home of a son of the prophets of Yahweh. Elijah's miracle proves Yahweh's ability to provide for a widow and an orphan in the place of Baal's failing. Elisha's miracle (and the eighth sign) proves he is the double portion son of the prophet Elijah in contrast to the sons of the prophets who apparently cannot provide for one of their own.

---

[29] The motif of 'firstborn' as primary inheritor of the father is actually continued in the account of the king of Moab in 2 Kgs 3.27. King Mesha offers his 'firstborn son who was to succeed him as king' as a sacrifice which ends the siege.

[30] L.M. Wray Beal helpfully notes that messages by the prophets to Israelite kings in 1 Kings are given primarily when a Judahite king is present, 'Jeroboam and the Prophets in 1 Kings 11-14: Prophetic Word for Two Kingdoms' in Boda and Wray Beal (eds.), *Prophets, Prophecy, and Ancient Israelite Historiography*, pp. 105-24 (121-22).

The raising of a dead boy serves as a ninth sign (2 Kgs 4.8-37). Elisha goes to Shunem and is cared for by a wealthy woman who has no son. The man of God prophesies the birth of a son that finds fulfillment only to be met by the boy's untimely death (2 Kgs 4.17-20). Elisha is on Mount Carmel[31] when he hears of the death and finally arrives at the home, he finds the boy in the prophet's bed. He offers prayers to Yahweh and 'stretched himself out' (יגהר vv. 34, 35) on the boy two times: the first time the boy's body warmed, the second time the boy sneezed seven times and opened his eyes (2 Kgs 4.32-37). Elijah before him had similarly raised a dead boy. In the case of Elijah, he 'stretched out' (יתמדד 1 Kgs 17.21)[32] on the boy (who also had been laid on the prophet's bed) three times as he called on Yahweh before the boy was finally raised (1 Kgs 17.17-23). In the Elisha account, Gehazi (the servant of Elisha) cannot raise the dead boy despite being sent by Elisha but is raised by Elisha himself in the same manner as Elijah raising the widow's son. Gehazi is never named a 'son of the prophets', yet he is certainly a servant of a prophet who fails to carry out the task which only Elisha as double portion son of Elijah apparently can.

A tenth sign is provided in the narrative when Elisha returns to Gilgal in a time of famine and there meets with sons of the prophets (2 Kgs 4.38-41). One of the sons of the prophets sent to gather ingredients for a stew ends up picking a poisonous gourd and adding it to the stew. Unaware, the sons of the prophets begin eating the stew only to realize too late that 'there is death in the pot' (2 Kgs 4.40). The sons of the prophets call Elisha 'man of God' an epithet regularly used for Elijah and somehow conceived as distinguishing themselves from him. Elisha has flour added to the pot as a miraculous elixir against the poison. Should the readers not surmise that sons of the prophets should have been able to distinguish safe foods from poisonous or at least to cure the poison as Elisha does? Instead the sons of the prophets falter where Elisha succeeds.

---

[31] Levine, 'Twice', p. 32, points to a couple of literary affinities between this account and the Elijah cycle. First, the Hebrew phrase חי־יהוה וחי־נפשך אם־אעזבך as the affirmation of Elisha to Elijah (2 Kgs 2.6) and as the verbatim affirmation of the Shunnamite to Elisha (2 Kgs 4.30); and, second, both include the location of the respective prophet at 'Mount Carmel' (1 Kgs 18.19, 20; 2 Kgs 4.25).

[32] Elijah had earlier 'bowed down' (יגהר) on Mount Carmel to pray for rain (1 Kgs 18.42).

An eleventh sign: not only can Elisha cure the poisoned food of the sons of the prophets of Gilgal, but he also miraculously multiplies food in the same location (2 Kgs 4.42-44). Elisha commands the man from 'Baal Shalishah' (בעל שלשה) donating the twenty loaves of 'freshly ripe grain' (כרמל) to give it to the people gathered to eat. The man refuses on the grounds that there are a hundred men present. Elisha persists even noting that there would be left-overs after all had eaten. Exactly as Elisha predicts, the food multiplies to exceed even the feeding of the hundred 'according to the word of Yahweh' (v. 44).[33] The sons of the prophets at Gilgal stand by as Elisha provides for members of the house of Israel. The text offers literary echoes of the work of Elijah on 'Carmel' (כרמל) confronting the prophets of 'Baal' (בעל) with the 'three' (שלש) times of pouring the water over the sacrifices and expecting the miraculous provision of fire from heaven which fulfills the call by exceeding all expectations (1 Kgs 18.20-38).[34] Thus the readers have now witnessed Elisha caring for the food needs of the sons of the Prophets on two separate occasions in Gilgal.

The twelfth sign finds Elisha altering the future course of Aram (2 Kings 5) apparently as a precursor to the judgment of the house of Ahab entrusted to Elijah at Horeb (1 Kgs 19.17). The commander of Aram's armies, Naaman, reticently receives healing from leprosy in the Jordan River at the instruction of his Israelite servant girl's advice to seek the prophet of Israel, Elisha. In fact, Elisha performs this healing in order that Naaman the Aramean might 'know that there is a prophet in Israel' (2 Kgs 5.8). Not only does Naaman become convinced of the genuine prophethood of Elisha, but he also commits to the singular worship of the God of Israel, Yahweh. This would serve as a precursor that indeed Yahweh would fulfill His plans given to Elijah to judge Israel and the house of Ahab.

---

[33] Bergen, *Elisha*, p. 67, argues that the 'word of the LORD' spoken by Elisha is never affirmed as Yahweh's, but negatively is fulfilled as 'according to the word of Elisha'. This seems to miss the point being made in this chapter that Elisha is being affirmed and thus the fulfillment 'according to the word of Elisha' is not a denigration of Elisha in distinction to Elijah, but instead an affirmation that just as Elijah before him, so now Elisha speaks for Yahweh and it is accomplished.

[34] As noted in Levine, 'Twice', p.34.

As a thirteenth sign, Elisha is again with the sons of the prophets near the Jordan River (2 Kgs 6.1-7) which some might read as a return by the sons of the prophets to the very location of Elijah's depar-ture.[35] In this account, the sons of the prophets function as lesser equals of Elisha with regard to saying they gather to meet with *him* (v. 1), desiring *his* permission to go and gather materials to build a larger facility (v. 2), and finally requesting *him* also to join them (v. 3). As it happened, one of the sons of the prophets lost his axe head in the river while chopping a tree. Instead of functioning with the power of a prophet and retrieving the lost axe head, he calls to Elisha, his 'lord', for help (v. 5). Elisha recovers the head by casting a stick onto the water over where it had fallen, and the axe head floated to the surface for the son of the prophets to fetch it. Again, Elisha demon-strates his headship over the family of prophets.

In the fourteenth sign, the Kings narrative is suddenly shifted to an undisclosed time when Aram has taken to attacking Israel and Is-rael's unnamed king (2 Kgs 6.8-23). Yahweh reveals the maneuvers of Aram to Elisha who informs the king of Israel. This sign describes Elisha's ability to give sight to see what would not be apparent to the natural eyes. At every turn Elisha knows what is coming and keeps Israel from destruction. The king of Aram attempts to capture Elisha at Dothan by night with a large force of horses and chariots, yet 'horses and chariots of fire' create an overwhelming guard for Elisha (2 Kgs 6.17). Initially Elisha's servant could not see these. In a similar manner, it seems the sons of the prophets could not see the 'chariot of fire and horse of fire' that passed between Elijah and Elisha near the Jordan (2 Kgs 2.12).[36] Readers would encounter this as the very same phenomenon noted as passing between Elijah and Elisha as the whirlwind snatched Elijah away. The servant of Elisha requires divine enablement to see this. 'Noticeably lacking among the parallels of the servant's heavenly vision … is any mention of an army. Can it be that Elisha himself is filling this role?'[37]

In the very next moment divine blindness comes over the Ara-mean army by the prayers of Elisha (as a fifteenth sign) where he is able to lead them right into the capital city of Samaria. In the previous sign Elisha opens eyes to see; but in this sign, he closes eyes not to

---

[35] Levine, 'Twice', p. 36 n. 20, citing 'Abravanel to 6.2'.
[36] Levine, 'Twice', p. 41.
[37] Moore, *God Saves*, p. 89.

see until the appropriate moment. The Aramean eyes are opened by the prayers of Elisha and the Arameans realize where they have been taken. The king of Israel eagerly asks of Elisha, 'Shall I kill them, father? Shall I kill them' (v. 22), whereupon Elisha replies that they should not kill them, but instead prepare a feast for them and return them home. This led to a temporary hiatus in the attacks on Israel (v. 23). It is striking that the king of Israel should defer so distinctly to the authority of Elisha and even call him 'father' given the ever tense relations of Elisha toward the Omride dynasty.[38] In the extended account of the Former Prophets there has already been a link between questioning who the 'father' of a 'prophet' was in the proverbial saying about Saul as he prophesied in the company of prophets (1 Sam. 10.11-12). Perhaps this question might also be asked of Elisha.

In the course of time a sixteenth sign is given. Elisha prophesies famine for Israel that would last seven years, though this famine would apparently not affect the land of the Philistines (2 Kgs 8.1-2). The Shunammite woman whose son was raised was protected from this famine by the word of Elisha to her. In similar fashion, the widow of Zarephath was protected from the drought in the days of Elijah by obeying the word of Yahweh through His prophet.

As the seventeenth sign and in direct fulfillment of the charge to Elijah at Horeb (1 Kgs 19.15), Elisha carries on the calling to anoint the next king of Aram (2 Kgs 8.7-15). Although Elijah had been commanded to 'go back the direction he had come and go to the Desert of Damascus … to anoint Hazael king over Aram', readers encounter Elisha doing exactly this in the place of Elijah. Readers likely would have expected Elijah immediately to carry this task out, but in the provenience of time, Elisha acts in Elijah's stead when years later Ben-Hadad inquired, via his servant Hazael, of Elisha (who had travelled to Damascus) if he would recover from his illness. Hazael's address to Elisha calls Ben-Hadad Elisha's 'son' (v. 9). Could it be that Elisha was counted the 'father' even of Aram? By word of Yahweh Elisha tells Hazael that the king would recover from his illness, but would die and Hazael would replace him as king of Aram and become the one who would bring judgment upon Israel (vv. 10-13)? As double portion son of Elijah, Elisha continued to father his

---

[38] Perhaps such a literary feature might suggest this account is out of sequence with the surrounding text and speaks of some other king who was not Omride but belonged to the house of Jehu.

people Israel as kingmaker and national judge. The readers could not miss that Elisha is indeed Elijah's direct heir.

The eighteenth sign: Elisha anoints the next king of Israel, Jehu son of Nimshi (2 Kgs 9.1-13), who also had been included by name in the instructions to Elijah at Horeb (1 Kgs 19.16). Elisha sends one of the sons of the prophets to anoint Jehu the next king that he might be the hand of judgment upon the house of Ahab. Though carried out by a prophet, a son of the prophets, the work of Elisha is recognized by those with Jehu (2 Kgs 9.11). Elisha's words to Jehu concerning the judgment of Ahab's house and Jezebel (2 Kgs 9.8-10) are the very words of Elijah to Ahab and Jezebel following their murder and robbing of Naboth (1 Kgs 21.19; see also, 1 Kgs 22.21-23): the whole house of Ahab will perish as the houses of Jeroboam son of Nebat and Baasha son of Ahijah before him and Jezebel would be devoured by dogs at Jezreel.[39]

As a nineteenth sign, in the deliverance of Israel from Aram the 'horses and chariots of fire' are noted as protectors of Elisha. Some years later in his final days, Elisha has been so associated with these 'horses' and 'chariots' that *he* even becomes known as רכב ישראל ופרשיו 'the chariots and horses of Israel' according to Jehoash, king of Israel (2 Kgs 13.14). Not only does the king of Israel pronounce Elisha as the 'chariot and horses of Israel', but now emphatically calls him, אבי אבי 'My father! my father!'. In fact, these words at Elisha's death bed are the very ones he had cried all those years before at the taking of Elijah in the whirlwind, אבי אבי רכב ישראל ופרשיו 'My father! My father! The chariot and horses of Israel!' (cf. 2 Kgs 2.12).

Now at the end of his life, the twentieth sign is given as Elisha is the confessed father and judge of Israel. Elisha has died. The readers wonder what this might mean for Israel, but Elisha has carried out the commands given to Elijah at Horeb in 1 Kings 19. With his passing no successor is found even while the double-portion functions post mortem to raise the dead.[40] Even in his passing from life he

---

[39] Minor variants occur between the two passages with one example being Elijah's referring to Jezebel being devoured by dogs 'by the wall of Jezreel' (1 Kgs 21.23) while Elisha states it will be 'on the plot of ground at Jezreel' (2 Kgs 9.10).

[40] Bergen, *Elisha*, p. 56; and Levine, 'Twice', pp. 41, 45. Gray picks up on this idea and notes that 'whereas the authority of Elisha gave the stamp of final authenticity to the traditions of his older contemporary Elijah, no single great figure

guarantees the life of others to continue the life-giving work of the רוח on behalf of Israel.

Conclusion

What might be discovered about the Spirit in these texts? First, the Spirit is not limited by the life of the prophet. Elijah passes from the narrative, but the Spirit remains. The Spirit has chosen another in Elisha (and one might surmise the lesser 'portion' for the sons of the prophets). Even with the passing of Elisha, the Spirit persists. The dead are raised. The Spirit of life reigns. The Spirit goes wherever the Spirit desires.

Second, the Spirit will carry forward the work of Yahweh with another. While Elijah bemoans his singularity on Horeb (1 Kings 19), Yahweh is clear that others have been set aside for divine purposes. Yahweh has provided a replacement for Elijah's ministry and has even managed to preserve a remnant of faithful worshipers numbering in the thousands. The only thing Elijah is instructed to do once leaving Horeb is to anoint Hazael king of Aram, Jehu king of Israel, and Elisha prophet of Yahweh. Elijah only does the last of these and, in the flow of the narrative, does it immediately after leaving Horeb. The readers would notice that Elijah has inverted the instructions of Yahweh at Horeb. Further, the readers would note that there is no fulfillment of the first of the two commanded anointings Elijah was to carry out. Some could read this as a narrative demonstration of Elijah's failure. However, it might also be read as trusting to the Spirit to carry on the work via another as the narrative immediately moves to Elijah seeking out Elisha and passing his mantle on to him. This leaves room for Elisha later in the narrative to anoint Hazael and Jehu to finalize the judgment against Ahab that Yahweh had determined. The Spirit passes to Elisha to assure Israel of at least one commissioned to father Israel in bodily form. The one anointed is the one Spirit empowered.

---

did the same for him, but in their very zeal to enhance the reputation of Elisha the dervish fellowships actually impaired it by their emphasis on miracles for its own sake', *I & II Kings*, p. 466.

Third, the Spirit empowers for witness to the God of Israel as Yahweh. Elisha satisfied 'Elijah's requirement for prophetic leadership' and thus was 'fortified' with the power of the one commanding the [fiery] chariots and horses of Israel.[41] The horses and chariots were a testimony of the power of Yahweh present with Israel to defend and to judge as need be. The God of Israel afforded Israel Spirit empowered witnesses to protect, to heal, to defend, to rebuke, and to restore. This witness of the Spirit functioned as a testimony that Yahweh had not abandoned Israel even if Israel persisted in wavering in full admonition of the God of Israel.

Fourth, the Spirit enables supernatural insight. The eyes of enemies are closed by the work of the Spirit. Their eyes (and the eyes of others) are opened by the Spirit. This insight is demonstrated further in the ways that Elisha discerns how to respond to various situations whether with prophetic words, providing cures, or instructing kings. He can see the movements of the enemy and the armies of Yahweh.

Fifth, the Spirit gives supernatural signs as affirming testimony of Yahweh's choice of leadership for Israel. It would not be enough that Elisha wore the hairy cloak of Elijah. He had, after all, been previously clothed with it (1 Kgs 19.19). It would not be enough that he simply is known to be aligned with Elijah in following him faithfully (2 Kgs 2.1-8). Testimony is given through the supernatural signs that the Spirit of Elijah is indeed upon Elisha to part rivers, provide water and fruitfulness, cause iron to float, provoke the prophetic via music, multiply oil, raise the dead, heal the sick, and overcome enemies. All of these served as signs of the son with the double portioned Spirit.

---

[41] Rice, 'Elijah's Requirement', p. 12.

8

TOWARD A CONSTRUCTIVE PENTECOSTAL THEOLOGY OF THE SPIRIT IN THE FORMER PROPHETS

Introduction

The first move in the constructive Pentecostal theology of the Spirit in the Former Prophets consists of a summation of the numerous functions of the Spirit within the Former Prophets. This summation is drawn from the Pentecostal narratological readings of chapters four through seven and the conclusions offered for each respective chapter.

The Liberating Spirit

The liberating Spirit of Judges offers at least six functions of the Spirit toward a theology of the Spirit in the Former Prophets. First, the Spirit is intimately connected to Yahweh as carrying out the work of Yahweh. That language of the preparatory materials in Judg. 2.16-19, and specifically verse 18, which reads that 'Yahweh raised up judges, and Yahweh was with the judge'. This is dramatically played out in the text through the naming of the Spirit of Yahweh explicitly enabling Othniel (Judg. 3.10), Gideon (Judg. 6.34), Jephthah (Judg. 11.29), and Samson (Judg. 13.25; 14.6, 19; 15.14). This explicit mentioning of the Spirit of Yahweh is the way in which the narrative demonstrates that Judg. 2.18 finds fulfillment for Yahweh being present with the judges. This demonstrates that Yahweh saves his people by sending his Spirit to enact the deliverance.

Second, the Spirit preserves Israel. The preservation of Israel as a people functions as part of the plan of Yahweh for redemption. The Spirit coming upon and clothing judges is the manner in which this preservation is enacted in Judges. The preservation of Israel is carried out again and again in Judges despite the unfaithfulness of Israel after the passing of each judge. Further, the Spirit seems to preserve Israel in the life of each Spirit-ed judge by bringing some form of peace to Israel and rest from the hands of enemies for extended periods. This leads to the next point.

Third, the Spirit empowers leaders. One function of the Spirit in Judges (and the Former Prophets overall) is to empower leaders to call Israel to action. Othniel, Gideon, and Jephthah all fulfill such a function by the Spirit. However, Samson acts as an individual throughout and never calls Israel to action, but only provokes the Philistines to engage Israel. While Samson might lead the way for a later generation of the Spirit endowed (Saul and later David) to lead Israel in overcoming the Philistines, he does not lead any individuals in this function in Judges. As relates to the empowerment for leading, the text is not clear how others might know that the Spirit had come upon, clothed, or stirred these individuals other than to note the supernatural provisions given in each case. Further, the empowerment of leaders is not a temporary matter as the judges 'judged' Israel for years. The note of the Spirit's empowerment would be highlighted to emphasize the specific points of noteworthy empowerment, but not to suggest to the readers that the Spirit of Yahweh was then suddenly absent from the judges in their acts of guaranteeing peace for Israel for years to come. This enablement is suggestive that they actually were enabled in order to keep Israel in faithfulness toward Yahweh.

Fourth, the Spirit transforms individuals. Othniel defeats a greater enemy threat after the text says the Spirit of Yahweh came upon him. Gideon takes actions that might be considered courageous by the readers after being clothed by the Spirit even if he persists in testing Yahweh to receive confirmations. Jephthah goes from leading a nomadic band of raiders to leading several of the tribes of Israel to victory by the Spirit's empowerment. Samson is stirred and empowered by the Spirit to tear a lion, kills thirty Philistines in the city, and slaughters a thousand Philistines in the countryside. Further, the transformation of the first two of these judges is implied both by the comment of Judg. 2.18 and the notes concerning 'peace' for all of the days of their judging Israel (Judg. 3.11; 8.28). For the latter two judges, there is no note of 'peace'.

Fifth, the Spirit does not override individuals. Though there is a noted transformation of the judges when the Spirit empowers them, this does not mean that their will is somehow lost in the empowerment. Gideon can assault Israelites and make an ephod that leads Israel into 'prostituting themselves by worshiping there' (Judg. 8.16, 17, 27). Immediately after the texts says Jephthah experiences the Spirit, it says he made a rash vow to make a sacrifice as if further to procure victory and then carried it out against his own daughter (Judg. 11.30-40). He even leads Israel into an inter-tribal conflict. Samson can take up with prostitutes (Judg. 16.1) and abandon his Nazirite vows (Judg. 14.9; 15.16; and 16.17) all the while enjoying multiple notable moments of the Spirit's enablement. These individuals might have been transformed, but this was not a transformation making them into faithful automatons. They might have been liberated by the Spirit to work wonders, but this liberation did not guarantee they would do everything in faithfulness to Yahweh. The Spirit only makes the liberated life possible. The Spirit does not negate participation but invites such.

Sixth, the Spirit empowers even those not explicated as endowed. Again, following the narrative indicator of Judg. 2.18 would lead the readers to understand (in light of the explicit mentions of the Spirit upon Othniel, Gideon, Jephthah, and Samson) that the Spirit was upon all of the judges to carry out the plans of Yahweh to deliver Israel. As a prime example, readers could not possibly encounter Deborah as a *prophetess* who leads Israel in *supernatural victory* over Sisera and his army without hearing this as the work of the Spirit of Yahweh in and through Deborah. The other exploits of the judges would likewise not be understood as owing to the natural abilities of the judges, but attributable to the Spirit of Yahweh.

Strings of the Spirit

The Spirit in relation to both Saul and David offers at least six functions of the Spirit toward a theology of the Spirit in the Former Prophets. First, the Spirit endows the prophetic and inspires prophecy. The Spirit is directly connected to the prophetic throughout these narratives. Samuel, the 'seer' (which the text even clarifies as older language for a prophet: 1 Sam. 9.10), is prophetically empowered to anoint Saul as king of Israel. He predicts signs for Saul that the Spirit of Yahweh would come upon him to aid him as king to bring about the redemption of Israel. As such, Saul would find himself joining the prophetic band and becoming known in Israel as one of the prophets (even if by derision). Saul later prophesies (under the impulsion of the 'troubling spirit'?) in his house while David minstrels (1 Sam. 18.10). Later, when Saul seeks the life of David, he and his messengers encounter those prophesying and find themselves joining in the prophesying by the Spirit of God (1 Sam. 19.18-24). Finally, David, at the end of his own life, attributes his prophetic psalmistry to the Spirit of Yahweh (2 Sam. 23.2). This all indicates for the readers that it is the Spirit that speaks the words of Yahweh through people. The nature of the prophetic words of the Spirit is only delineated in the songs of David in these texts. Thus, the readers would likely hear the undefined prophetic words to be of a similar nature to David's Spirit-ed singing.

Second, the Spirit transforms. The text explicitly states that when the Spirit of Yahweh would come upon Saul he would be made 'a new man' (1 Sam. 10.6) and the fulfillment note that God had given him 'a new heart' (1 Sam. 10.9). Saul was a changed man with a changed heart. The evidence for those who witnessed Saul's transformation was given in his joining the prophets in also prophesying. Israel may not have understood his place among the prophets, but they could not help but include him among them by the Spirit. Later, Saul is transformed in his anger by the Spirit of God to call Israel to take up arms against Nahash the Ammonite and deliver Israel (1 Sam. 11.6). Saul has been transformed in the text into one who would deliver Israel from enemies like the judges before him. Saul experiences other transforming encounters with the S/spirit of Yahweh, but these several notable occasions are troubling (1 Sam. 16.14; 18.10; and 19.9). He has now been changed from a delivering king to a troubled despot. Finally, he is transformed by the Spirit of God in the presence of Samuel and the prophets at Naioth in Ramah (1 Sam. 19.23-24). He is transformed from troubled despot to humbled and stripped prophet while David is exalted in the garb of royalty. The Spirit may transform, but the one being transformed was not guaranteed a positive personal outcome. The transformations pertained to the continued orientation of the recipient in faithfulness or unfaithfulness.

Third, the Spirit is en-joined by Spirit-ed music. The Spirit impartations and transformations are notably connected to musical elements in these narratives. Saul enters into the musical prophesying as they come down from the high place at Gibeah (1 Sam. 10.5). The narrative even lists the prophets as armed with 'harp, tambourine, flute, and lyre'. After the Spirit of Yahweh has departed and the troubling spirit of Yahweh has come upon Saul, he finds himself provoked by music. The troubling spirit of Yahweh seems provoked by the Spirit-ed tunes of David either for Saul to be given 'relief' (1 Sam. 16.23) or to make attempts on David's life (1 Sam. 18.10; 19.9). While no explicit mention is made of any music associated with the prophesying of 1 Sam. 19.20-24, readers would perhaps fill in such a connection in light of each of the previous occasions of the Spirit coming upon Saul associated with prophesying.

Fourth, the Spirit confirms and enables leadership. As the Spirit had confirmed and enabled the leadership of the judges, so the Spirit does likewise explicitly for the first two kings of Israel: Saul and David. Thus, similar to the function of Othniel in Judges, readers may hear these first two kings as demonstrating that all future kings would (or at least should) be enabled by the Spirit to lead even without the text explicating this information. The anointing with oil and the Spirit endowment functioned to confirm Saul and David as kings of Israel. Further, the readers would consider the responsibilities of kings with regard to such things as wisdom, wars, and management to require divine aid in order to do well.

Fifth, the Spirit empowers for victory over enemies. 1 Samuel 11.6 explicitly indicates it was the Spirit of God which 'came powerfully upon Saul' to call Israel to respond against Ammonite aggressions. The provocation of enemies and the cries of afflicted Israelites had previously led to explicit Spirit enablements in Judges. In fact, Saul appears to summon the entirety of Israel in his Spirit-ed anger in contrast to the tribal work of Gideon and Jephthah by the Spirit of Yahweh upon them. While David is said to have the Spirit of Yahweh 'come powerfully' upon him from the day he was anointed king in the presence of his family (1 Sam. 16.13), he does not specifically take any action at this point. The narrative then finds him immediately being summoned to the aid of Saul as Spirit-ed minstrel and armor bearer (1 Sam. 16.14-23). This leads into David's victorious encounter with Goliath that provokes Israel to defeat the Philistines (1 Samuel 17). The readers could not help but hear this victory in light of the previous claim of the Spirit of Yahweh coming upon David despite lack of explicit Spirit statements in chapter seventeen. Thus, the Spirit would not always be explicated in texts of victory over enemies, even while carried forward from leading texts.

Sixth, the Spirit troubles the unfaithful. Saul discovers that unfaithfulness on his part results in a troubling spirit from Yahweh/God replacing the (comforting?) Spirit of Yahweh (1 Sam. 16.14). Chapters 13 and 15 of 1 Samuel find Saul confronted and rejected by Samuel on behalf of Yahweh because of Saul's failure to remain faithful to the instructions of Yahweh given by Samuel. Saul is regularly harassed by the troubling spirit of Yahweh/God yet persists in his unfaithfulness and becomes hatefully obsessed and murderous. If the Spirit of Yahweh is not yielded to in faithfulness, then the troubling spirit of Yahweh is given room to wreak havoc.

Discerning the Spirit

The Spirit in 1 Kings 22 offers at least six functions of the Spirit toward a theology of the Spirit in the Former Prophets. First, the Spirit inspires prophecy. According to the words of Micaiah, the 400 prophets and Zedekiah have spoken their prophetic words of affirmation to the plans of Ahab by the Spirit (1 Kgs 22.21-23). Zedekiah has believed that his prophetic words were those of the Spirit of Yahweh all along (1 Kgs 22.24). By Micaiah delivering his first prophetic oracle that sounds like the words of Zedekiah and the 400 prophets, he also speaks by the Spirit. Further, in the vision of Micaiah it is the Spirit that offers to be 'a deceiving spirit' in the mouths of Ahab's prophets (1 Kgs 22.21-22). Micaiah's prophetic words are confirmed in the fulfillment account that also affirms the earlier prophetic words of Elijah concerning the death of Ahab (1 Kgs 22.38). Ahab might challenge the words as being true (1 Kgs 22.28b), but he finds it so despite his best attempts to evade what the Spirit has revealed (1 Kgs 22.30).

Second, the Spirit does not abide forever for the unfaithful. Ironically, readers discover that the words of Zedekiah (1 Kgs 22.11) were the words of the Spirit to Ahab as Micaiah discloses their intent to deceive Ahab (1 Kgs 22.19-23). The Spirit has thus inspired words to provoke Ahab implicitly to repentance, but explicitly to destruction. Zedekiah furthers the irony when he slaps Micaiah with words of the movement of the Spirit of Yahweh from himself to Micaiah (1 Kgs 22.24). Ahab's end is pronounced by the Spirit's words of victory and revelation of defeat. He has persisted in unfaithfulness despite previously averting immediate judgment by repentance (1 Kgs 21.27-29). Here at the end of 1 Kings 22 there is no repentance but only subterfuge on Ahab's part to attempt to skirt the revelation from the Spirit.

Third, the Spirit is essential to discerning what the Spirit has spoken. Careful readers of 1 Kings 22 note the ambiguities throughout the narrative. They further might note the ways in which the Spirit is necessary for proper interpretation of both the events and the words. Jehoshaphat requires further prophetic words perhaps due to discernment that the words of the 400 might not be as they seem on the surface (1 Kgs 22.7). Ahab questions the trustworthiness of the words of Micaiah (1 Kgs 22.16). Perhaps even for a moment the Spirit has aided Ahab in discernment of the prophetic words. The revelation of the Spirit through Micaiah functions to reveal to Ahab and his court that the words spoken by the Spirit previously were not to be interpreted as they had previously been interpreted (1 Kgs 22.19-23). The Spirit of Yahweh had given words which properly interpreted by the Spirit of Yahweh were words leading to judgment for those with an unwillingness to be faithful (1 Kgs 16.30-33).

Fourth, the Spirit persists by raising up others to carry forward the work of Yahweh. Micaiah functions as one alongside of Elijah, in the narrative flow of 1 Kings, to do the prophetic work of the Spirit of Yahweh in faithfulness. Readers discover that the Spirit finds ways of speaking to kings and even clarifying words to kings. Thus, the Spirit has not left Israel without a witness. Micaiah is known by Ahab as one who only speaks 'trouble' to him and never 'good' (1 Kgs 22.8, 18), but readers know that Ahab deserves 'trouble' because he only acts in ways that are unfaithful to Yahweh. Ahab's negative appraisal of Micaiah becomes the reader's positive appraisal.

Fifth, the Spirit brings both good and trouble. The Spirit of Yahweh is not safe nor to be taken for granted. The Spirit can speak words that bring about life or death, peace or judgment. Ahab might appraise the words of Micaiah as 'trouble', but the results mean 'peace' for Israel. The readers would discern that if the words of victory (as Ahab interpreted them) had proven true then this would only result in further trouble for Israel at the hands of Ahab. The Spirit thus spoke up in the council of Yahweh to end the troubler of Israel once and for all.

Sixth, the Spirit bears witness to Yahweh as sovereign. The kings of Israel and Judah hold court to carry out wars, but it is Yahweh who sits enthroned over all. It is the Spirit of Yahweh that gives the testimony through the revelation (even surprisingly to Yahweh) of the plans to defeat Ahab and deliver Israel (1 Kgs 22.19-23). Kings and prophets may speak with authority and demonstrations of that authority. Ahab calls for the community to hear the words spoken as witnesses (1 Kgs 22.28a) and to demand truthfulness (1 Kgs 22.16). Zedekiah both prophetically acts out the victory promised by raising the horn (1 Kgs 22.11), and he slaps Micaiah for invoking the Spirit against Ahab thus trying to give himself credibility as prophet of Yahweh (1 Kgs 22.24). Both Ahab and Zedekiah miss the point that the Spirit of Yahweh is sovereign and not attached to the throne of any human authority. The Spirit speaks and makes plans that come to fulfillment (1 Kgs 22.21-22, 34).

The Double Portion Spirit

The Spirit in relation to the double portion of the Spirit of Elijah upon Elisha offers at least five functions of the Spirit toward a theology of the Spirit in the Former Prophets. First, the Spirit persists in raising up others. Elijah bemoans his isolation as a prophet of Yahweh, but the Spirit is poured out on Elisha in the passing of the mantle from father to true son by the Spirit (1 Kgs 19.10, 14, 17, 19-21; 2 Kgs 2.9-15). Yahweh will not be left without a witness in Israel. Careful readers would consider the impartation of the Spirit upon Elisha from Elijah not to be Elisha's first experience of the Spirit. The Spirit had not been mentioned previously in the Elijah and Elisha narratives. What Elisha requests is not that he have the Spirit as if he had not had the Spirit, but that he have the double portion of the Spirit suggesting he become the prophetic father in place of Elijah. If Elisha was already a part of the prophetic company of Elijah

(1 Kgs 19.21) then careful readers would consider him already to enjoy the Spirit prior to this endowment to fulfill Elijah's commission. Second, the Spirit will carry forward the work of Yahweh. The Spirit empowers Elisha to carry out the tasks given to Elijah at Horeb (1 Kgs 19.16-17). The plans of Yahweh will not be thwarted by the passing of the prophet of Yahweh. The Spirit will enable another to continue to protect and provide for Israel as Israel is called to faithfulness to Yahweh. The Spirit will provide water and food to sustain and give life (2 Kgs 2.19-22; 3.17; 4.1-7, 38-44). The Spirit will heal the sick and raise the dead (2 Kgs 4.34; 5.14; 13.21). The Spirit will deter antagonists (2 Kgs 2.23-24) and enemies alike (2 Kgs 6.8-23). The Spirit will blind and open eyes to see that Yahweh is at work in caring for his people (2 Kgs 6.8-23).

Third, the Spirit empowers for witness to Yahweh. The testimonial function of the double portion of the Spirit of Elijah upon Elisha served to point Israel to Yahweh as the God of Israel. The Spirit testifies through the words and deeds of Elisha to point to Yahweh as provider and sustainer of Israel. That the instructions to Elijah for Elisha were given at Horeb (known to be the mountain that Yahweh spoke to Moses upon) memorializes the work of Elisha as flowing from the commands given at the foot of Horeb after being delivered from the bondage of Egypt. Yahweh had been a father to Israel and was still sending his Spirit-ed witnesses to call Israel to know and love the God who was true Father and King.

Fourth, the Spirit enables supernatural insight. Elisha discerns the plans of the king of Aram so that the king of Israel is spared destruction (2 Kgs 6.8-12). The armies of Aram locate Elisha and seek to capture him. The servant of Elisha needs his eyes opened by Yahweh to see what Elisha sees by the Spirit concerning their protection from Aram: the 'horses and chariots of fire' guarding Elisha (2 Kgs 6.15-17). However, these divine armies never engage. Instead, Elisha prays and the eyes of the army of Aram are blinded. Elisha leads the blinded enemy army into the capital of Samaria and there prays and witnesses their eyes suddenly opened by Yahweh to discover themselves surrounded (2 Kgs 6.18-20). The readers would see this as the continuing work of the Spirit through Elisha even without having to mention the Spirit explicitly where Yahweh is named.

Fifth, the Spirit confirms and enables leadership. Israel needs Spirit-ed leadership through the troubling days of King Ahab. The

Spirit is confirmed in the passing of the physical mantle of Elijah to Elisha when Elijah is taken (2 Kgs 2.9-13). Elisha then takes up the task of re-crossing the Jordan as Elijah had previously. The Spirit is upon him bearing witness with the supernatural crossing in the eyesight of sons of the prophets (2 Kgs 2.15). From the time of Elisha's taking up the mantle and bearing the Spirit of Elijah, he functions as the 'father' and 'master' both to the sons of the prophets and to the kings of Israel (2 Kgs 2.16, 19; 4.1; 6.21; 13.14). He functions by the Spirit of Yahweh as the hands and mouth of Yahweh for Israel.

Toward a *Pentecostal* Theology of the Spirit in the Former Prophets

Through an engagement with the foregoing descriptions of various theological functions of the Spirit in the Former Prophets, what follows is a move toward a constructive Pentecostal theology of the Spirit in the Former Prophets.[1] This is carried forward with two admissions: (1) there is no singular *Pentecostal* theology, but a multiplicity; and (2) *Pentecostal* is only intended to locate this theology within a particular stream of the larger Church. As such, this is offered from a particular orientation and experience of the life of the Spirit in the life of the Church as a potential witness both to those sharing that orientation and experience and to all others within the broader Church. Further, this work is not intended to develop a full pneumatology from the Former Prophets, but only to offer overtures toward a constructive Pentecostal theology of the Spirit from the Former Prophets. This is accomplished by drawing upon functions of the Spirit discerned in the *Wirkungsgeschichte* (chapter three) and the narratological readings of the Spirit in the Former Prophets that followed (chapters four through seven). As such, the following categories have emerged from a Pentecostal theological side engaging toward a constructive Pentecostal theology of the Spirit in the Former Prophets: abiding, purity, baptism, power, singing, and anointing.

---

[1] A careful reading of the Former Prophets might cause one to ask whether it is 'too much to say that, for the moment, we are watching an adumbration of Pentecost in which the community of faith turns toward God's newness with inexplicable power and freedom?', Brueggemann, *First and Second Samuel*, p. 78.

This all finds its culmination in a Pentecostal theology of the Spirit that is enjoined as the Spirit of the Lord Jesus Christ.

The Spirit Abides Within

The element of the Spirit abiding in the Old Testament has spurred numerous articles and dissertations (see chapter one). Pentecostals who believe in the work of the Spirit persisting in demonstrable power available to the Church are positioned to note the continuity of the Spirit abiding from the Former Prophets (and before) down to their own day.

The Spirit in the Former Prophets offers several evidences for the Spirit abiding in individuals in the Old Testament period. First, 1 Sam. 16.13 explicitly states that 'the Spirit of Yahweh came powerfully upon David *from that day on*'. Perhaps one might hear this as David being the exception and that this is stated about David because it was not the normal experience of the Old Testament saints. However, its literary placement juxtaposes immediately with the Spirit of Yahweh departing Saul and being replaced by a troubling spirit from God (v. 14). By implication, Saul had enjoyed the Spirit's presence from the time of his own anointing in 1 Samuel 10. Further, with the testimony of David at the end of his life he attributes his prophetic singing to the Spirit's presence (2 Sam. 23.2). While the exception does not make a rule, it is suggestive that one cannot simply assert that the Spirit does not abide with individuals until the New Testament era.[2] In an inversion of this argument, Pentecostal testimony claims to experience the Spirit as the saints of the New Testament era in fullness. They regard themselves (against all naysayers) as living in the 'this is that' of the Spirit poured out in fullness.

Second, as described in chapter four, the Spirit coming upon the four judges explicitly (Othniel, Gideon, Jephthah, and Samson) neither (1) excludes the other judges from experiencing the Spirit's enablement, nor (2) does it mean that was the only moment the Spirit came upon them. Their exploits throughout the book of Judges is suggestive of the Spirit's enablement with the highlighted moments of the Spirit's empowerment functioning literarily to demonstrate what would then be assumed everywhere else. Further, the explicit Spirit encounters leaders to take up certain prolonged activities (like

---

[2] Contra the theologically Dispensationalist project of Walvoord, 'The Work of the Holy Spirit in the Old Testament', pp. 289-317, 410-34.

summoning armies), suggesting that the Spirit was not only momentary, but gave guidance for an extended period of time. In this way the Spirit is said to *begin to stir* Samson to action early on (Judg. 13.25) and explicated at multiple other points in his narrative (Judg. 14.6, 19; 15.14) until at last it is reported that he did not know that 'Yahweh had departed from him' (Judg. 16.20), which is suggestive of the Spirit's abiding up until that point. By implication, the Spirit is highlighted at key points in the narrative of various judges to emphasize the purpose of the Spirit to liberate for new life. It is this highlighting function which resonates with the Pentecostal experience in the baptism in the Spirit. The Spirit is already present in the world, and active in the life of all those who call on the Lord, but at their Spirit baptism there is a unique experience of the Spirit worthy of highlighting that does not suggest the Spirit was absent prior. It points to a particular experience and moment where the Spirit gives testimony in power to witness to the promise of the Father to redeem all of creation through the Lord Jesus.

Third, it is often popularly believed that the Spirit only came 'upon' individuals in the Former Prophets, but that the Spirit dwells 'in' saints of the New Testament.[3] Such a conclusion would be an oversimplification missing the variant functions in both Testaments of prepositions, but particularly the Former Prophets, regarding the relation of the Spirit to individuals.[4] The language of 'come [powerfully] upon', 'clothe', and 'stir' highlight the evident presence of the Spirit for the immediate community and for the community that received these texts. There is a surge of empowerment that highlighted the Spirit's enablement rather than any ontological claim that the Spirit was only temporarily available to the likes of Samson (Judg.16.20) and Saul (1 Sam. 16.14). In a similar way Pentecostals

---

[3] A developed argument against this notion with detailed examination of the primary NT texts used to support this (John 7.37-39 and 14.16, 17): G. Fredricks, 'Rethinking the Role of the Holy Spirit in the Lives of Old Testament Believers', *TrinJ* 9 (1988), pp. 81-104 (91-96).

[4] S.M. Horton contends that the prepositions connecting the Spirit and Samson, Saul, and David are significant for understanding the overall relationship between Spirit and Spirit-ed. While he contends Samson and Saul only experienced the Spirit endowment as 'temporary and intermittent', he goes on to clarify, 'It was almost as if the Spirit was not present with them in between (*even though he was*)', *What the Bible Says about the Holy Spirit*, p. 46, emphasis added.

might testify to the Spirit coming upon an individual or individuals being baptized in the Spirit, but by this they do not mean to suggest the Spirit was not already present. They are highlighting what has been made evident in some transformation or demonstration deemed worthy of highlighting at that key moment. The distinction for Pentecostal experience seems to pertain more to the effusion of the Spirit to the entire community that is specifically a witness to the one who is full of the Spirit and baptizing in that fullness of the Spirit: Jesus.[5]

The Spirit of Purity

One of the primary reasons many have discounted the continuity of the Spirit between the Testaments is owing to the way in which many seem to believe purity to be more properly an emphasis of the New Testament outpouring while temporary and non-transformative power was the emphasis of the Old Testament experiences. However, this reading fails to appreciate the New Testament call for communities of believers to be sanctified. Some, like the Spirit-filled Corinthian church, speak in tongues, prophesy, and otherwise enjoy the power of the Spirit, but seem to be lacking at numerous points regarding purity, in much the same fashion as the judges and the ideal king, David.[6] In this way, these texts of the Former Prophets are an aid for Pentecostals who are called to, and for, the joining of the Spirit of power for purity as flowing from their hearing of the Word.

---

[5] While W.C. Kaiser, Jr. would not likely consider a Pentecostal appropriation of some of his language here, he has still offered a helpful article for understanding the distinctions between the Spirit in the OT and the NT, 'The Indwelling Presence of the Holy Spirit in the Old Testament', *EQ* 82.4 (2010), pp. 308-15. He contends that 'what happened at Pentecost was both climactic and effusive – words that conveyed a completion to what had been promised and an abundance of a downpour', p. 312. Several other excellent articles that conclude similarly that the nature of the distinctions between the Testaments has to do with the pervasiveness of the experience of the Spirit, include G.W. Grogan, 'The Experience of Salvation in the Old and New Testaments', *Vox Evangelica* 5 (1967), pp. 4-26; Fredricks, 'Rethinking the Role of the Holy Spirit', pp. 81-104; and J. Goldingay, 'Was the Holy Spirit Active in Old Testament Times? What Was New About the Christian Experience of God?' *Ex Auditu* 12 (1988), pp. 14-28.

[6] C. Amerding contends that Saul 'may have been a true child of God', but 'like the Corinthians … he was no longer spiritual but carnal', 'The Holy Spirit in the Old Testament', p. 287.

The Spirit comes powerfully on David from an early age (1 Sam. 16.13) until his final days (2 Sam. 23.2). While the text does not indicate Spirit enablement at any specific event of David's heroic (and at times tragic) life, the explicit statement of the Spirit abiding (1 Sam.16.13), and the literary framing of the Spirit in 1 Sam. 16.13 and 2 Sam. 23.2 justifies the Pentecostal reader in understanding the Spirit's presence throughout. David would not seem to be pure by almost any standard and yet he still becomes the ideal king for Israel according to the refrain of kingly assessment in 1-2 Kings. How could the Spirit remain upon such an impure leader whom the text explicitly states as taking another man's wife and having him murdered (2 Samuel 11)? Pentecostals have often struggled with this idea and yet must at the last recognize that the Spirit comes upon whomever the Spirit desires. The Spirit enables the endowed to be holy (and makes them holy by the endowment), but this in no way supersedes the recipient from their ability to be disobedient. The purity is not absolute for the individual, but a work underway in staying in step with the Spirit.[7] It is a work of renewal and transformation.

For Pentecostal readers, the judges also seem little transformed as to purity by the explicit statements of the onrushing Spirit. Prior to the explicit text of the Spirit coming upon Othniel, he has already shown he is faithful to observe the instructions of Yahweh in his marriage and in his commitment to take the land commanded (Judg. 1.14). Othniel seems already to be faithful prior to the Spirit coming upon him and there is no explication in the text of him now being purified. Gideon is timid both before (Judg. 6.27) and after (Judg. 7.10) the text informs us of the Spirit clothing him (Judg. 6.34), even though he still takes action. It would be too much to say that his cowardice is turned into boldness by the Spirit, since he still appeals to sign after sign for confirmations before and after (Judg. 6.17, 36-40; 7.10, 11). Jephthah appears to fulfill a prohibited vow (Lev. 20.1-4) of sacrificing his daughter (Judg. 11.34-35) after the Spirit comes upon him (Judg. 11.29). Samson the womanizer (Judg. 14.1; 16.1, 4) meanders from trouble to trouble (including sleeping with a

---

[7] This does not exclude the way in which Pentecostals of the Wesleyan-Holiness stream have understood sanctification to be a distinct experience of the Spirit that is a necessary prerequisite to Spirit baptism. This is still pertinent as Wesleyan-Holiness Pentecostals believe there is a final sanctifying which is only experienced in part prior to the return of Christ that will only then find its consummation.

prostitute: Judg. 16.1) even as the Spirit is at work to deliver him again and again.

In what fashion might these be accounts calling for the Spirit of purity that Pentecostals confess as part of the full gospel message? They are all set within the framework of the book of Judges which is specifically concerned with the unfaithfulness of Israel to be the holy people they are called to be (1.1-3.6; 17.1-21.25). The judges work by the Spirit to assemble Israel for action not only to liberate from their physical enemies into whose hands they have been given by Yahweh, but more particularly to be delivered from the hands of wickedness within themselves. Judges 2.16-19 makes the point of Yahweh raising up judges explicit. They were raised to deliver from enemies and call the people to fidelity. They are set free not to do as they please, but to do as Yahweh pleases. The Spirit does not enable the judges to work wonders for wonders' sake, but for righteousness' sake. How does Yahweh procure their freedom to be holy? He does this by his Spirit upon individuals. The purity of the judges is not intended to question the purity of the Spirit. The Spirit is holy even when the Spirit-ed are not. The Spirit makes new even if the Spirit-ed return to the old.

For example, Saul is described in 1 Samuel 10 as being made a 'new man' (1 Sam. 10.6) and receiving a 'new heart' (1 Sam. 10.9) by the work of the endowed Spirit yet fails again and again to do all the Lord would have him to do. Was this not a transformation for purity? He does not appear to be any bolder since he fails to take action against the Philistines when the Spirit comes upon him (1 Sam. 10.5). So what might this transformation mean? As it stands, the Spirit does appear to have both sanctified and empowered him, but not in the fashion one might want. He experiences priestly or cultic elements on his path to receiving the outward evidence of the Spirit's endowment (1 Sam. 10.3). He is set apart to join the prophetic band (1 Sam. 10.6, 10) and his words indeed should be regarded as like their words which would be regarded (if deemed truthful) as sacred.

The final reference to the Spirit overwhelming Saul also finds him joining the prophetic band (1 Sam. 19.23). Have the words which they sing by the Spirit so overwhelmed his heart again that he is overcome to humiliate himself upon the ground (1 Sam. 19.23-24)? Saul finds himself attuned to the Spirit if even momentarily in such a prophetic worship setting. The text does not state that he has now lost his mind or is raving uncontrollable by the Spirit's overwhelming presence. It simply states he prophesies through the night in the midst of the prophets and Samuel. By implication he speaks the words Samuel and the gathered prophets speak. Those words would be regarded as holy and the act of speaking them as holy. The saying of the people regarding Saul, 'Is Saul also among the prophets?' (1 Sam. 10.11, 12; 19.24), would seem to function as a question of how a man could sing with the Spirit as a prophet yet live with a troubled spirit. This orientational function of the worshiping community of the Spirit is a centering act for the Pentecostal community that gives voice to the ways in which they know their Lord and seek to give him glory in becoming instruments increasingly attuned to the voice of his Spirit for life and against trouble. Pentecostal readers understand that the transformative sanctifying work of the Spirit must be laid hold of unrelentingly. It cannot be a matter to take for granted or treat lightly.

Spirit Baptism

It might, at first blush, have seemed strange to include Spirit baptism in any pneumatology of the Old Testament, let alone the Former Prophets. However, this is an essential element for reading these texts from a Pentecostal perspective as Spirit baptism functions for Pentecostals as the shared orienting experience.[8] Such language as 'baptizing in the Spirit' is the language of the New Testament which has been taken up by Pentecostals into a short hand for a particular experience of the Spirit. No contention is made here that there is a universally agreed upon understanding of 'initial evidence' or precise intent of the baptism. While Pentecostals may diverge from one another over details of the baptism in the Spirit there is broad agreement that the baptism is an essential part of the full gospel message and thus regarded as essential to claims of being 'Pentecostal'. The experience of Spirit baptism means individuals and communities reading the Former Prophets and noting the 'clothing' of Gideon

---

[8] S. Chan, *Spiritual Theology: A Systematic Study of the Christian Life* (Downers Grove, IL: IVP, 1998), p. 47; F. Macchia, *Baptized in the Spirit: A Global Pentecostal Theology* (Grand Rapids, MI: Zondervan, 2006); 'Baptized in the Spirit: Towards a Global Pentecostal Theology', pp. 13-28 in S.M. Studebaker (ed.), *Defining Issues in Pentecostalism: Classical and Emergent* (Eugene, OR: Pickwick, 2008); and S.M. Studebaker, *From Pentecost to the Triune God: A Pentecostal Trinitarian Theology* (Grand Rapids, MI: Wm. B. Eerdmans, 2012), pp. 46-51.

(Judg. 6.34), the 'coming/rushing upon' of the other judges (Judg. 11.29; 13.25; 14.6, 19; 15.14), and of Saul (1 Sam. 10.6, 10; 11.6; 19.23) and his messengers (1 Sam. 19.20), and David (1 Sam. 16.13) cannot help but hear a forebear of their own experience of the Spirit. The onrushing Spirit inundation empowers to carry out the plan of God for redemption in each of these cases. Further, there is some public evidence given of the Spirit's endowment.

In the case of the judges it is summoning of the people of God to action, carrying out mighty deeds to defeat enemies, and (by implication to) call God's people back to faithfulness. They might bumble at these in various ways, but Pentecostals often feel likewise in their endowment of the Spirit. While Pentecostals might wish the baptism vouchsafed their every action, they know better through experience. This makes a Pentecostal reading of the Spirit in Judges both troubling (Pentecostals want the Spirit to guarantee everything being right, but it is not) and helpful (Pentecostal readers encounter individuals endowed with the Spirit in the Former Prophets who are ever so fallible as Pentecostals). This testifies to Pentecostals that the fallible saints are endowed with the Spirit for the purpose of God's redemptive plans not because of them, but for their sake and the sake of the world. Such a reading should function in Christological fashion to point to one totally filled with the Spirit, and baptizing in the Spirit, who has not fallen in any way, but is perfectly aligned with the life of the Spirit in every way. The Pentecostal experience and confession of Jesus still anticipates the culmination of the coming king and his kingdom when all will be made right and alive by the Spirit.

The 'double portion of the Spirit' in the Elijah/Elisha account (2 Kgs 2.1-17) functions likewise to signify the baptism in the Spirit for many Pentecostals (as noted among the early North American Pentecostals in the *Wirkungsgeschichte* of chapter three). The 'double portion of the Spirit' functions as a second mantling of Elisha after initial entry into discipleship. In fact, it operates as Yahweh's own endorsement of Elisha beyond words of commissioning and acts of mantling by Elijah. This Spirit mantling through the double portion places the recipient into a position to carry forward the work of the one whose Spirit is received. It demonstrates the fullest sonship of the recipient to act in the full power and authority of the father. This pre-emptively points to the understanding of Pentecostals who view the initial coming of the Spirit to be later conferred in the baptism that offers a public display for others (regardless of the 'sign' accepted by various groups identifying as Pentecostal). Further, it suggests to Pentecostals that there are preparatory elements to receiving a like baptism. Elisha follows for some undisclosed time before this particular Spirit endowment. Elisha must persist in faithfulness in this following before this particular Spirit endowment. Elisha must learn to humble himself and face potential persecution (even from other sons of the prophets) before this particular Spirit endowment. Elisha must pass through a mortification of his own desires and willfulness before this particular Spirit endowment. All of these speak to the many Pentecostal experiences of Spirit baptism and the preparations leading to the baptism. None of this means that there must needs be an extended time of preparation, but it does suggest there were preparations necessary for those who would seek to receive their mantling of the double portion of the Spirit. Thus, the double portion of the Spirit functions for Pentecostals as a testimony of the Spirit of the Son poured out by the Father in fullness upon his children with the power to bear transformative witness.

When the Spirit Comes in Power

The most obvious element attached to the Spirit in the reading of the Former Prophets is power. It is the Spirit who explicitly enables Othniel (Judg. 3.10), Gideon (Judg. 6.34), Jephthah (Judg. 11.29), Samson (Judg. 13.25; 14.6, 19; 15.14), and Saul (1 Sam. 11.6) to overcome enemies of Israel. By implication one could assume this is also how David lays waste to the Philistines and overcomes Goliath in 1 Samuel 17. Careful readers should also surmise that it is the Spirit (though not explicated) who enables all of the judges to carry out their work of liberating Israel from enemies as supernatural victories are described. Such power by the Spirit to overcome is suggested as typical of all of the judges by the placement and (albeit brief) example of Othniel as the ideal judge. The readers of Judges would hear the account of Othniel as demonstrating that every judge was enabled by the Spirit of Yahweh to carry out their victories and to judge Israel. While these individuals might have so-called natural abilities as leaders, they would never be thought to do the exploits they have done by their own abilities. After all, the preface to Judges declares it was by 'the hand of Yahweh' that they would deliver Israel (Judg. 2.18). 'The hand of Yahweh' would be witnessed in the Spirit of Yahweh explicitly enumerated on four of the judges placed strategically throughout the book of Judges. Deborah would be heard to lead Israel as a prophetess (Judg. 4.4) by the Spirit even though the Spirit is never explicitly mentioned.

This supernatural power is attributable to the Spirit even by those espousing such a reading that regards these Spirit passages of the Former Prophets as an early less-developed phase of the history and literature of Israel (see chapter one and the 'Historical Quest'). Pentecostal readings would hear the Spirit as the empowering agent of all these delivering exploits. For Pentecostal readers the Spirit is readily confessed as the one empowering for *every* work of God, but even more so those regarded as inexplicable otherwise yet pointing to the Lord above all others.[9] Such power is present to quicken faith in the midst of crisis or persecution and enable a witness to the victory of God in Christ Jesus.

As such this power is meant to function as a testimony to the faithfulness of God experienced in Jesus by the Spirit. It is not intended to be self-aggrandizing or allow for continued willful disobedience. Samson's story (Judges 13-16) functions well to demonstrate for Pentecostals the need for holiness with power to bear witness. While the Spirit powerfully enabled him to overcome antagonists both 'man' and beast, the Spirit also abandoned him in his disobedience. The careful reader would hear the abandoning by *Yahweh* (Judg. 16.20) as the *Spirit* of Yahweh departing despite not using such specific language in the text. Likewise, with Saul who began so well, but through unfaithfulness finds that the Spirit which once gave him a new life is now replaced with a tormenting spirit. While these stories explicitly describe the power of the Spirit's presence, by implication they demand the purity of the Spirit if the Lord should truly rule in the recipient and the community.

The power of the Spirit for purity means that the Spirit is not safe even for Pentecostal readers. The enemies of Israel regularly experienced this at the hands of judges and kings who were empowered by the Spirit. The Spirit offers the power to give and take life in all its

---

[9] As an example of this, Pentecostal NT scholar G.D. Fee wrote an extensive detailed treatment (exegetical and theological) on the Pauline writings concerned with the Spirit, *God's Empowering Presence: The Holy Spirit in the Letters of Paul* (Grand Rapids, MI: Baker Academic, 2011). See also, W.M. Menzies and R.P. Menzies, *Spirit and Power: Foundations of Pentecostal Experience: A Call to Evangelical Dialogue* (Grand Rapids, MI: Zondervan, 2000).

many senses, including the inward conquest of the heart (or will) to loving obedience and faithfulness. While it might be tragic enough to discover that the Spirit has departed (explicitly for Saul: 1 Sam. 16.14; and implied for Samson), it is far worse to discover oneself to have become the target of the Spirit actively adding trouble to the consequences of unfaithfulness (such as Saul: 1 Sam. 16.14; and Ahab discovered: 1 Kgs 22.8, 18). The Spirit will not abide with the unfaithful forever. A proper Pentecostal hearing of the Spirit in the Former Prophets requires the sanctifying enablement of the Spirit.

Attuned to the Voice of the Spirit

The Spirit sings. Pentecostals believe that songs led and inspired by the Spirit are essential to the gathered community of the Spirit baptized. Such songs are the prophetic words of a people caught in the grip of God who have learned his victorious lyrics.[10] Regarding the corporate worship setting, one early Pentecostal witness of the Spirit outpoured at the Azusa Street Revival writes:

> In the meetings, it is noticeable that while some in the rear are opposing and arguing, others are at the altar falling down under the power of God and feasting on the good things of God. The two spirits are always manifest, but no opposition can kill, no power in earth or hell can stop God's work, while he has consecrated instruments through which to work.[11]

Such music plays a significant function in the Pentecostal congregation as that which prepares the spirits of the gathered to be attuned to the Spirit of the one gathering. The sounds of voices and instruments played by the Spirit call for testimony, preaching, confession, and enraptured transformation. Songs of the Spirit flow over the worshippers as tongues are raised in praise to the Lord. Bodies are strewn about the altar as the singing continues. Weeping and wailing,

---

[10] L. Neve believes the Spirit inspiration of David in 2 Sam. 23.2 must either be for the prophetic or the poetic and attempts to draw a sharp distinction between the two. This is part of his overall program to read these texts in a historical critical reconstructed fashion that views ecstasy as an early phase of pneumatic claims with the more intelligible and controlled poetic elements developing in a mature fashion later in Israelite literature, *The Spirit of God*, p. 27.

[11] An editorial testimony from the revival taking place at the Azusa Street Mission that was printed in the first issue of the *The Apostolic Faith* 1.1 (September 1906), p. 1.

praises and confessions can be heard ringing in the midst of the sing-ing saints. The Spirit comes over one; and then another. Prophecies proclaiming the victory of the Lord resound. Words of consolation and rebuke echo in tones resonating within the Spirit-ed. The music transforms. The songs empower. The atmosphere is charged with the Spirit.

Pentecostal forms of worship offer a potential alternate view to scholarship which has suggested dervish like experiences to explain the prophesying of the likes of the prophets near Gibeah (1 Sam.10.5) and Naioth (1 Sam. 19.20-23), and that which Saul found himself overcome by on multiple occasions (1 Sam. 10.10; 18.10; 19.23, 24). The worship of Pentecostals in their confessions, praises, and testimonies move the gathered to respond. The refrains lay low the proud and lift high the humbled. The Lord Jesus, the son of Da-vid, the Messiah of God, is enthroned in the praises of the congre-gation. He is entreated to vindicate and to judge. Several implications might be suggested by this correlation between the prophetic and music.

First, music matters. Music is an essential element of Pentecostal expressions in worship whether via singing in tongues, instrumenta-tion, or choruses.[12] Early Pentecostals shared numerous testimonies pertaining to their music: in tongues and interpretations,[13] hearing heavenly choirs (even angelic),[14] and spontaneously learning to play

---

[12] L.R. Martin (ed.), *Toward a Pentecostal Theology of Worship* (Cleveland, TN: CPT Press, 2016) offers a series of contributions addressing the topic. Martin even de-fines worship in the Pentecostal reading of Scripture as that which 're-centers the world according to God's will', p. 25. This aligns well with the prophetic description I am attempting in this chapter. As a further example of the prominence of music (within the larger scope of Pentecostal 'worship') see, M.L. Archer, *'I Was in the Spirit on the Lord's Day'*, especially her constructive Pentecostal reflections on pp. 295-332. See also, M.M. Ingalls and A. Yong (eds.), *Spirit of Praise: Music and Worship in Global Pentecostal-Charismatic Christianity* (University Park, PA: Pennsylvania State University, 2015).

[13] *AF* 1.1 (Sept. 1906), p. 3; 'Holy Ghost Singing', *AF* 1.1 (Sept. 1906), p. 4; 'Russians Hear in Their Own Tongues', *AF* 1.1 (Sept. 1906), p. 4; 'A Message Con-cerning His Coming', *AF* 1.2 (Oct. 1906), p. 3; 'Came from Alaska', *AF* 1.3 (Nov. 1906), p. 2.

[14] 'Gracious Pentecostal Showers Continue to Fall', *AF* 1.3 (Nov. 1906), p. 1.

instruments[15] and sing choruses which flowed from the Spirit.[16] In this way, their music functioned to give congregational voice to the Spirit among them so that even the 'least' would have voice and the mission of God would hold sway. Music in the Pentecostal context becomes the prophetic voice of the gathered saints caught up with songs which envision and call for life transformed by the Spirit. Such music speaks and gives voice to the Spirit so that the Word might be exalted in the Spirit-ed life of the community.

Second, the connection suggested between music and prophetic calls for and enables a prophetic community. One Pentecostal scholar has even offered the inverse connection of prophecy as 'speaking for God in song' due to the central function of music as prophetic within the Pentecostal context.[17] In the traditional churches music was written out, but in many Pentecostal settings music might simply be created in the moment as prophetic gifts are exercised to speak in song as the Spirit enables.[18] There is a fellowship of the prophetic community among the minstreling ministers of the Spirit. The flow of the music is not haphazard. There are individuals who lead the band (like Samuel in 1 Sam. 19.20). This prophetic community lays bare by the Spirit the hearts of those present and demands an altar experience toward altered lives (like Saul in 1 Sam. 10.6, 9).[19] Even their bodies are laid low by the overwhelming crescendo of the Spirit's presence as they cry aloud in praise and confession (like Saul in 1 Sam. 19.24).[20] The Scriptures give shape to the visions of these songs as filled with a vocabulary and a cadence attuned to the Spirit of Jesus.[21] The sanctifying work of such music created a new people who go from their gatherings into the world alive and empowered with the Spirit. It would not be enough simply to speak for the Spirit; one must be transformed anew by the Spirit. Impurity runs counter to the

---

[15] *AF* 1.1 (Sept. 1906), p. 1.

[16] 'Baptized on a Fruit Wagon', *AF* 1.3 (Nov. 1906), p. 1.

[17] Horton, *What the Bible Says about the Holy Spirit*, p. 44.

[18] 'The Holy Ghost from Heaven', *AF* 1.3 (Nov. 1906), p. 3; note the numerous testimonies of the 'singing' of 'new songs' by 'the Spirit' that are scattered across the entire issue of *The Whole Truth* 4.4 (Oct. 1911); one such testimony concerns a 'young sister, under the power of the Spirit … [who] got the gift of song', E.W. Vinton, 'Will You Stand the Test?', *TBM* 2.37 (May 1, 1909), p. 4.

[19] 'Tongues Convict Sinners', *AF* 1.1 (Sept. 1906), p. 4.

[20] *AF* 1.1 (Sept. 1906), p. 3.

[21] 'A Message Concerning His Coming', *AF* 1.2 (Oct. 1906), p. 3.

intent of the Pentecostal prophetic worshiping community. Thus, the discerning of spirits among the prophetic singing community functions to address the intent of the one speaking and acting.

Third, the prophetic Spirit aids in the discerning of spirits (and the Spirit) and the overcoming of those who would falsely speak by the Spirit. What the Spirit speaks can only properly be interpreted by the Spirit. The words might be clear enough, but transformation cannot happen without the Spirit's doing. For example, the account of Saul being transformed by the Spirit of Yahweh

> is placed midway between the hopelessness of the wilderness and the despair of exile. Saul participates in a crisis and a drama not unlike that of Caleb before him and Ezekiel after him. God claims Saul and God transforms Saul. Israel can again participate in God's promises. Thus Saul receives a new heart, a new way to be in the world. This narrative momentarily holds the possibility that Saul (and therefore Israel) may become a 'new creation' for whom 'the old has passed away' and 'the new has come' (II Cor. 5:17).[22]

It is the prophetic singing of the oncoming Spirit which lifts him to discern new vistas of potential being in the world. Saul could not find his way in the narrative, but the Spirit is poured out to aid him in discerning his moves forward on behalf of and alongside of Israel. While his mouth might be filled with prophetic intonations, and his heart made new, he failed to discern by the Spirit what the Spirit was at work doing and to align himself with the Spirit in faithfulness.

The Pentecostal reader of 1 Kings 22 likewise encounters prophetic ambiguities demanding discernment, and wonders what the Spirit is doing in such an account. The words of the 400 prophets and Zedekiah might seem clear enough: 'Go, for the Lord has given it into the king's hand' (1 Kgs 22.6). When Micaiah speaks similarly by the Spirit (Go up and succeed! Yahweh has given it into the king's hand', 1 Kgs 22.15), questions abound. It is only the Spirit who can answer such questions: for Jehoshaphat, Ahab, the 400, Zedekiah, Micaiah, the gathered kings' court, and the readers. Even the fulfillments of the prophetic words which seem so clear either never find explicit fulfillment or only a seemingly slanted one (1 Kgs 22.25, 38). Here, the Spirit who fills the mouths of prophets must also fill the

---

[22] Brueggemann, *First and Second Samuel*, p. 77.

eyes and ears of the Spirit-endowed prophetic community to discern the intent of the Spirit beyond bare words. The Word cannot be discerned apart from the Spirit. Thus, the discerning includes Spirit enabled understanding of the words which the Spirit has already inspired. It is the heart of the Spirit that is thus shared with the community. Pentecostal experiences of tongues and interpretations is a most obvious correlation. Pentecostal experiences of the prophetic is another correlation. The words of the Spirit can only properly be interpreted and applied by the Spirit-ed community even if there is no guarantee of absolute certainty. The witness of the Spirit of the Word in and through the community is sufficient as a constant and attentive hearing.

Fourth, Pentecostal forms of music are intent on ultimately bringing life-giving victory and wholeness. This includes (as David before them; 1 Sam. 16.16, 23) songs admitting overwhelming troubles and tribulations, but at the last placing trust in the Lord to deliver in faithfulness (2 Samuel 22-23). Saul was tormented because of his disobedience and eventual rejection by Yahweh (1 Sam. 15.19, 23). The Spirit which had come forcefully upon Saul to deliver Israel (1 Sam. 11.6) and vouchsafe their life as God's people would be replaced by that of trouble (1 Sam. 16.14). The Spirit who brings good can also bring trouble. The Spirit and the songs of the Spirit that heal can also cause the unrepentant to become yet more troubled in the darkness of their thinking (1 Sam. 18.10; 19.9).

The songs of the prophetic Spirit call for obedience, surrender, holiness, boldness, faith, hope, and above all, love.[23] The songs of the prophetic spirit create space for healing and wholeness. David performed songs for the healing of Saul (1 Sam. 16.16, 23); if only Saul's heart could remain transformed. Elisha called for prophetic music and experienced 'the hand of Yahweh' upon him to declare the coming of water to protect Israel and Judah's armies and animals from death by thirst and bring a victory over Moab (2 Kgs 3.15-18). If only the people of Israel and Judah had remained faithful. The many gifts of the Spirit are poured out as needs arise even to a people who abuse the gifts given. Spirit-ed songs bring victory over all other powers and

---

[23] *AF* 1.1 (September 1906), p. 1.

authorities.[24] The victories enjoyed will only prove temporary if the songs of the Spirit end with the singing and do not become transformed in the hand of the Lord (that is, in the Spirit). If the instruments will be faithfully yielded, then these Spirit-ed instruments of worship will become the weapons of the Lord's deliverance and testify to the dawning kingdom in the midst of the saints.[25]

Again, much of the discussion of the prophetic in relation to the Spirit within the Former Prophets seems to miss the musical element (which may be more apparent in a Pentecostal or charismatic worship context) of the musical and the prophetic as harmonious companions without special deference to dervishes and ecstatic practices as the only explanation for such linkage.[26] As a prime example, Cartledge offers an extended discussion of the 'ecstatic prophets' and their 'dervish-like dance'[27] following a similar proposal as that offered earlier by J. Lindblom.[28] Cartledge regards this text (along with 1 Sam. 19.18-24) as pointing to an earlier stage in Israelite prophetic practices where various inducements were used to gain prophetic insight. He also ironically proposes this is comparable to charismatic expressions of worship which may offer some insight but seems to misrepresent the nature and aim of such expressions. He states,

> Analogous shamans of primitive cultures (up to and including the modern era) are known to use various naturally occurring drugs from mushrooms, tree bark, or hemp for the same purpose. It is worthy of note that modern rock bands who promote drug usage serve in a similar role as idolized shamans to a vast number of people who are supposedly more enlightened.

---

[24] 'Arrested for Jesus' Sake', *AF* 1.1 (September 1906), p. 4; 'Came from Alaska', *AF* 1.3 (Nov. 1906), p. 2; A.K. Mead, 'Sister Mead's Baptism', *AF* 1.3 (Nov. 1906), p. 3.

[25] *AF* 1.2 (Oct. 1906), p. 3; 'Spanish Receive the Pentecost', *AF* 1.2 (Oct. 1906), p. 4.

[26] Several English translations (ETT) read an explicit notion of ecstasy in the prophesying of these prophets here and in chapter 19: NJB ('ecstasy'), CEB, NRSV ('frenzy'). The RSV used 'prophesying' so it is a striking move on the part of the NRSV to make the shift to the language of 'frenzy'.

[27] Cartledge, *1 & 2 Samuel*, p. 134.

[28] J. Lindblom, *Prophecy in Ancient Israel* (Philadelphia: Fortress, 1998).

There is a sense in which modern charismatic churches that promote glossolalia, 'holy laughter,' and 'being slain in the Spirit' have preserved many of these ancient prophetic traditions. Such churches often rely on powerful music or the chant-like sermons of the preacher to induce the contagious 'movement of the Spirit,' which may lead even skeptical participants to speak in other tongues, fall senseless to the floor, or laugh uncontrollably. Whether it is the Spirit of God that moves in such ways – or whether these phenomena are self-induced – is beside the point for those who find the experience to be cathartic.[29]

A closer reading of the text of 1 Samuel (in this context) does not suggest an ecstatic state for either the prophets or Saul even though it has been widely held. Instead, at most what should be stated is that they were speaking the words of the Spirit ('prophesying') as they played upon their instruments.[30] There simply is not evidence in these specific texts (or the one concerning Elisha's call for a minstrel so that he could prophesy; 2 Kgs 3.14) to require unintelligible or uncontrollable prophetic singing like ravings. The text does not state at any time that Saul or these minstreling prophets were out of control. Instead, these texts indicate that the Spirit was at work to lead Israel into new life without any need for comment as to the words spoken by the prophets. The Pentecostal prophetic singing community is poised for just such an interpretation of both their own experiences in light of these texts and these texts in light of their anointed experiences.

Further, even if one were to surmise (with these scholars) that some unintelligible words were being spoken by the Spirit of Yahweh, then Pentecostals would still be understanding of such an experience as those who profess to the experience of tongues. The benefits of speaking in tongues may not be understood by others (without interpretation), but still benefits the speaker (1 Cor. 14.2, 4). However, the text of the Former Prophets does not state it was a manic or frenzied state among these prophets. Their words testified to the Spirit in their midst speaking words of transforming life.

---

29 Cartledge, *1 & 2 Samuel*, p. 133.
30 Tsumura, *The First Book of Samuel*, pp. 286-88; Wilson, 'Prophecy and Ecstasy', p. 333.

Anointing by the Spirit

Pentecostals often refer to the 'anointing', and it is no surprise that the stories of Saul, David, and Elisha set apart by anointing are significant for Pentecostal contexts (1 Sam. 10.1; 16.13; 1 Kgs 19.16). The anointing functions for Pentecostals as some outward sign of being set aside for the special purposes of the Lord and as such authorized and empowered to carry it out. The 'double portion of the Spirit' functions in many Pentecostal contexts also for the passing of a perceived ministerial anointing of the Spirit. The physical emblem in this particular text is observed in the passing of Elijah's mantle (1 Kgs 19.19; 2 Kgs 2.13, 14).[31] While the mantle of Elijah is not directly connected to the Spirit, it functions in the text as a sign of the Spirit's endowment for the prophetic ministry. In this case it functions as a sign that this individual has indeed received the very unction as the original bearer. As such, in certain Pentecostal contexts a minister is ordained with the laying on of hands to signify passing, and at times even a mantle of sorts is placed upon the ordinands by ministerial leadership, signifying the injunction to receive the mantle of the Spirit for the work of the ministry. This imposition of hands and mantle become visible signs to the gathered community that these individuals have been set aside for the work of the Lord and are a community invocation and affirmation of the Spirit upon them to do the work.

---

[31] Over the last three years, I have personally attended seven different ministerial credentialing services among the Assemblies of God of the upper Midwest U.S. This language has occurred in sermons, prayers, and prophetic injunctions spoken multiple times each service at all but one of them. In three cases, all at the Minnesota District Council, there was a song which was written, composed, and directed (specifically for the ordination of ministers) by Larry C. Bach (Dean and Professor of the College of Fine Arts at North Central University in Minneapolis) for this ceremony. It is entitled 'Anointing Fall on Me':

Chorus
Anointing (echo) Anointing (repeat line)
Let it fall (echo) Let it fall (repeat line)
On me (echo) On me
(Repeat Chorus)

Verse
As Elijah passed the mantle to Elisha
Holy Spirit fall on us today
To receive power to reach the world for Jesus
This is what we pray

It is already presumed that the Spirit is evident in the ordinand's life up to the mantling as receiving an extra anointing for service.

A tangible sign of the anointing for Saul and David was oil poured out over their heads (1 Sam. 10.1; 16.13). There was a later demonstration of the Spirit coming upon them to affirm that indeed the outward deed was inwardly confirmed by the God of Israel (1 Sam. 10.10; 16.13). That this was included in the narrative functions as a community affirmation of the Spirit upon them. It is noteworthy from a Pentecostal perspective that in the case of Saul there was some considerable journey between anointing by the oil and the outpoured Spirit. In the case of David, the text emphatically connects the Spirit's coming upon David in power from that very day onward. A Pentecostal appropriation of this might suggest some must tarry while others receive the Spirit testimony of their anointing immediately. Again, this might be likened to the Pentecostal interpretation of outward confession of faith that is followed by affirmation of receiving the anointing of the Spirit in Spirit baptism.

How might one understand the anointing? It was a sacred commissioning for a specific ministry or task intended physically to demonstrate what God was doing. The Saul and David narratives would certainly attach this to a physical pouring of oil. However, in the Elijah and Elisha narrative there is only the instruction to Elijah to 'anoint' Elisha (1 Kgs 19.16) followed not by oil, but a mantle. This mantle gave testimony that Elisha bore the Spirit of Elijah even if questioned or challenged by the sons of the prophets (2 Kgs 2.15, 16). Pentecostals have taken this language of anointing beyond the ministry of healing called for in James 5 (though healing is a central part of Pentecostal confession). Likewise, the Pentecostal language of anointing functions to highlight a commissioning and enablement with power and authority physically to carry out the work of God. It might be used for preachers, missionaries, and evangelists, a song or sermon, a worship service, or testimony. The anointing finds public confession of itself believed to be a testimony of the special presence of the Spirit. It may also be used to affirm the very thing which baptism in the Spirit serves: empowerment for witness. Further, the anointing of the Spirit appears to be of a more abiding nature than many have perceived in the Former Prophets. The anointing serves to indicate the delivering king.

The Spirit of the Lord Jesus Christ

Pentecostal experience of the Spirit does not function independently. It is tied directly to the central – 'full gospel' – message of Pentecostal witness and experience: Jesus saves, (sanctifies),[32] baptizes in the Holy Spirit, heals, and is the soon coming king.[33] Jesus is the Anointed One. He has been given (and gives) the Spirit to save, heal, and baptize in preparation for his soon return. The Spirit who raises up leaders to liberate Israel, to assure the life of Israel, to guide Israel in faithfulness cannot help but be heard by Pentecostals through this central message. Even the best of the Spirit-endowed judges is understood to point to the better Judge. Even the best of the Spirit-endowed kings is understood to point to the better King. Even the best of the Spirit-endowed prophets is understood to point to the better Prophet. In this reading, Jesus is typified in their victories and at last exalted in their failings as the one far better, who alone could guarantee the life of God in the midst of God's people transformed by the Spirit.

Thus, Jesus is encountered at every turn of the text of the Former Prophets for Pentecostals. Jesus is not only that one who has received the Spirit, but also pours it out upon his community as anointed witnesses in power and purity. He bears witness by the Spirit and so do they. Pentecostals encountering their experiences in the Former Prophets know their experience to now point in a clear direction to the purposes of God. It is Jesus who baptizes in *his* Spirit those anointed to bear prophetic witness in power and purity abiding in *him*. It is *his* Spirit which cries out with words and sounds like

---

[32] 'Sanctifies' is parenthetically inserted because the stream of Pentecostal-ism (so-called 'Finished Work') to which I belong refers to the full gospel as four-fold (excluding 'sanctifies'), while those identified with the Wesleyan-Holiness Pentecostal stream refer to this five-fold message.

[33] As examples of various ways Pentecostals are attempting to offer con-structive Pentecostal theologies with this as central, see, Land, *Pentecostal Spirituality*; J.C. Thomas (ed.), *Toward a Pentecostal Ecclesiology: The Church and the Fivefold Gospel* (Cleveland, TN: CPT Press, 2010); A. Yong, *In the Days of Caesar: Pentecostalism and Political Theology* (Grand Rapids, MI: Eerdmans, 2010); W. Vondey,; *Pentecostalism: A Guide for the Perplexed* (London: Bloomsbury, 2013); and *Pentecostal Theology: Living the Full Gospel* (New York: Bloomsbury, 2017). Several of these volumes were brought to my attention by M.L. Rice as a response to a post I made in a Facebook group (Pentecostal Theology Worldwide) where we both serve as moderators.

groanings for redemption (Rom. 8.23, 26).[34] It is *his* Spirit which cries out to the Father and testifies to sonship (Rom. 8.15, 16; Gal. 4.6). Thus, the Spirit of Yahweh that is given in the Former Prophets is discerned as the Spirit of Jesus (the Son), sent as the promise of the Father in fullest Pentecostal experience.

---

[34] D.D. Daniels, III, '"Gotta Moan Sometime": A Sonic Exploration of Earwitnesses to Early Pentecostal Sound in North America', *Pneuma* 30 (2008), pp. 5-32.

9

CONCLUSION: CONTRIBUTIONS AND SUGGESTIONS FOR FUTURE RESEARCH

Contributions

In light of the foregoing study, several contributions are particularly noteworthy.

First, this is the first project specifically examining the texts of the Spirit limited to the Former Prophets and from an explicitly Pentecostal reading methodology. One other project (by a Pentecostal) limited itself to examining the Spirit of Yahweh/God texts in the Former Prophets (as the 'Deuteronomistic History'), but did not do so from a Pentecostal perspective or for the construction of a Pentecostal theology of the Spirit.[1] Others have examined smaller or greater units of the Old Testament, but none examining the Former Prophets with this methodology.

Second, this is the first attempt at a Pentecostal hermeneutic of the Former Prophets. The field of proposed Pentecostal hermeneutical ideas continues to expand in numerous directions, but this particular volume is the first narrowly to engage the Former Prophets as a corpus.

Third, this is the first Pentecostal hermeneutic to attempt to hear both the narrative of the Former Prophets and Pentecostal experience as interpretive phenomenological interplay toward discerning meaning.

---

[1] Ragsdale, 'Ruah YHWH, Ruah 'Elohim'.

Fourth, this is the first use of the method of a history of effects (*Wirkungsgeschichte*) of the Spirit in the Former Prophets upon early North American Pentecostals. This method has begun to be used by others to hear along with the early North American Pentecostals, but it has never been applied to the Former Prophets, much less to the Spirit texts within the Former Prophets.

Fifth, this study has offered the most comprehensive reading on the role of the Spirit in the Former Prophets. As such, each of the chapters engaging the Biblical texts of the Former Prophets provide extended insights not found elsewhere. The reading of the Spirit in Judges has indicated ways in which the Spirit texts give orientation to understanding the Spirit elsewhere in Judges. The reading of the Spirit in the Saul/David texts offers fresh insights into the troubling nature of the Spirit of the Lord and the place for music as prophetic engagement. The reading of the Spirit in 1 Kings 22 provides ways in which the ambiguity of the Spirit is tied to the ambiguities of the textual presentation. The readings of the Spirit in the Elijah-Elisha texts provide the most comprehensive treatment of the function of the double portioned Spirit. The cumulative reading of these texts together contributes overall to a Biblical pneumatology rooted in the texts of the Former Prophets.

Sixth, this is the first monograph to offer a constructive Pentecostal theology of the Spirit in the Former Prophets. While there are works proposing theological reflections regarding the Spirit they are never limited to these texts nor to a Pentecostal reading of these texts. They are also never examined through a reading of the early North American Pentecostal literature or for an explicitly constructive Pentecostal theology.

Suggestions for Future Research

Following this study, several suggestions for future research are offered.

First, the use of the *Wirkungsgeschichte* of Former Prophet Spirit texts in the early Pentecostal literature might be broadened beyond the scope of this study which was limited to extant periodicals from North American Pentecostal journal from 1906-1920. Such an approach might be conducted adding pamphlets and monographs for those respective years. Perhaps also examining Pentecostal works outside of North America (such as *Confidence* that was published in Great Britain by A.A. Boddy). Further, the date parameters could be expanded to include publications after 1920.

Second, the methodology of this Pentecostal hermeneutic (with or without the early Pentecostal *Wirkungsgeschichte*) could be applied to other Spirit texts of Scripture and specifically those texts which tend to receive less engagement within the Old Testament such as the book of Daniel or 1-2 Chronicles.

Third, those texts within the Former Prophets which use רוח but have not been included for various reasons in this study would also perhaps prove fruitful for a movement toward a Pentecostal theology of the Spirit (or better, spirit) in the Former Prophets.

Fourth, the constructive Pentecostal theology proposed here could be more fully developed via engagement with other sections of the Old Testament and New Testament along with a broader comparison/contrast of other pneumatologies built upon any use of the Former Prophets.

Fifth, Pentecostal engagements with the texts of the Former Prophets overall deserve greater attention. Perhaps the relation of the Former Prophets to Luke's two volumes (functionally a sort of canon-within-the-canon for Pentecostals) would prove advantageous both for discerning the ways in which Luke draws from and makes new use of the structure and ideas of the Former Prophets.

Bibliography

Ackroyd, P.R., and B. Lindars (eds.), *Words and Meanings: Essays Presented to David Winton Thomas* (Cambridge: Cambridge University, 2009).

Adam, A.K.M. *et al.* (eds.), *Reading Scripture with the Church: Toward a Hermeneutic for Theological Interpretation* (Grand Rapids, MI: Baker Academic, 2006).

Adedeji, F., 'The Theology and Practice of Music Therapy in Nigerian Indigenous Churches: Christ Apostolic Church as a Case Study', *Asia Journal of Theology* 22.1 (2008), pp. 142-54.

—'Some Reflections on the Future of Music Therapy in Nigeria', *The Journal of Language, Technology & Entrepeneurship in Africa* 2.1 (2010), p. 36.

'Adedeji, F., and A. Ogunleye, 'Music as a Form of Medicine for the Church: A Theo-musicological Study and Application in I Samuel 16:14-23', *Ogbomoso Journal of Theology* 18.1 (2013), pp. 27-49.

Alexander, K.E., *Pentecostal Healing: Models in Theology and Practice* (JPTSup 29; Blandford Forum: Deo, 2006).

Alter, R., *The Art of Biblical Narrative* (New York: Basic Books, 1981).

Aluede, C.O., 'Music Therapy in Traditional African Societies: Origin, Basis and Application in Nigeria', *Journal of Human Ecology* 20.1 (2006), pp. 31-35,

Amerding, C., 'The Holy Spirit in the Old Testament', *Bibliotheca Sacra* 92 (1935), pp. 277-91, 433-41.

Anderson, A., *An Introduction to Pentecostalism: Global Charismatic Christianity* (Cambridge: Cambridge University Press, 2004).

Archer, K.J., *A 'Pentecostal Hermeneutic*; and 'Pentecostal Story: The Hermeneutical Filter for the Making of Meaning', *Pneuma* 26.1 (2004), pp. 36-59.

—*A Pentecostal Hermeneutic for the Twenty-First Century: Spirit, Scripture and Community* (JPTSup 28; Edinburgh: T & T Clark, 2004).

—'Pentecostal Hermeneutics: Retrospect and Prospect', *Journal of Pentecostal Theology* 8 (1996), pp. 63-81.

Archer, M.L., *'I Was in the Spirit on the Lord's Day': A Pentecostal Engagement with Worship in the Apocalypse* (Cleveland, TN: CPT Press, 2015).

Arnold, B.T. and H.G.M. Williamson (eds.), *Dictionary of the Old Testament: Historical Books* (Grand Rapids, MI: InterVarsity, 2005).

Arrington, F.L., 'The Use of the Bible by Pentecostals', *Pneuma* 16.1 (1994), pp. 101-107.

Auld, A.G., *I & II Samuel: A Commentary* (Louisville, KY: Westminster John Knox Press, 2011).

Balthasar, H. Urs von, *Truth Is Symphonic* (trans. Graham Harrison; San Francisco: Ignatius, 1987).

Barclay, W., *The Promise of the Father* (Philadelphia, PA: Westminster, 1960).

Barthélemy, D. (ed.), *The Story of David and Goliath: Textual and Literary Criticism: Papers of a Joint Research Venture* (Fribourg, Suisse: Éditions universitaires, 1986).

Benson, A., *The Spirit of God in the Didactic Books of the Old Testament* (Washington: Catholic University of America Press, 1949).

Bergen, R.D. (ed.), *Biblical Hebrew and Discourse Linguistics* (Dallas, TX: Summer Institute of Linguistics, 1994).

Bergen, W.J., *Elisha and the End of Prophetism* (JSOTSup 286; Sheffield Academic, 1999).

Bienkowski, P., C. Mee, and E. Slater (eds.), *Writing and Ancient Near East Society: Essays in Honor of Alan Millard* (New York: T & T Clark, 2005).

Blenkinsopp, J., *A History of Prophecy in Israel: From the Settlement in the Land to the Hellenistic Period* (Philadelphia, PA: The Westminster Press, 1983).

Block, D.I., 'Empowered by the Spirit of God: The Holy Spirit in the Histographic Writings of the Old Testament', *Southern Baptist Journal of Theology* 1.1 (1997), pp. 42-61.

Bloesch, D.G., *The Holy Spirit: Works & Gifts* (Downers Grove, IL: IVP Academic, 2000).

Boda, M.J. and L.M. Wray Beal (eds.), *Prophets, Prophecy, and Ancient Israelite Historiography* (Winona Lake, IN: Eisenbrauns, 2013).

Bodner, K., *1 Samuel: A Narrative Commentary* (Sheffield: Sheffield Phoenix Press, 2008).

—'Critical Notes: The Locutions of 1 Kings 22:28: A New Proposal', *Journal of Biblical Literature* 122.3 (2003), pp. 533-46.

Boling, R.G., *Judges* (Anchor Yale Bible; Garden City, NY: Doubleday, 1975).

Bonhoeffer, D., *Letters and Papers from Prison* (Dietrich Bonhoeffer Works 8; English edn; J.W. De Gruchy; Minneapolis, MN: Fortress, 2010).

Botterweck, G.J., G.W. Anderson, and H. Ringgren (eds.), *Theologisches Wörterbuch zum Alten Testament* (3 vols; Stuttgart: W. Kohlhammer, 1973-1977).

Brenner, A. (ed.), *A Feminist Companion to Judges* (The Feminist Companion to the Bible 4; Sheffield: Sheffield Academic, 1993).

Briggs, C.A., 'The Use of *rûah* in the OT', *Journal of Biblical Literature* 19 (1900), pp. 132-45.

Briggs, R.S., *The Virtuous Reader: Old Testament Narrative and Interpretive Virtue* (Grand Rapids, MI: Baker Academic, 2010).

Brueggemann, W., *First and Second Samuel* (Louisville, KY: John Knox Press, 1990).

Bryant, H.O., *Spirit Christology in the Christian Tradition: From the Patristic Period to the Rise of Pentecostalism in the Twentieth Century* (Cleveland, TN: CPT Press, 2014).

Bulgakov, S., *The Comforter* (trans. Boris Jakim; Grand Rapids, MI: Eerdmans, 2004).

Burke, T.J. and K. Warrington (eds.), *A Biblical Theology of the Holy Spirit* (London: SPCK, 2014).

Burney, C.F., *The Book of Judges, with Introduction and Notes, and Notes on the Hebrew Text of the Books of Kings, with an Introduction and Appendix* (New York: KTAV Pub. House, 1970).

Bush, G., *Joshua and Judges* (Minneapolis, MN: Klock & Klock, 1981).

228 A Theology of the Spirit in the Former Prophets

Butler, T.C., *Judges* (Word Biblical Commentary 8; Nashville, TN: Thomas Nelson, 2009).

Caquot, A. and P. de Robert, *Les livres de Samuel* (Genève: Labor et Fides, 1994).

Cargal, T.B., 'Beyond the Fundamentalist-Modernist Controversy: Pentecostals and Hermeneutics in a Postmodern Age', *Pneuma* 15.2 (1993), pp. 163-87.

Cartledge, T.W., *1 & 2 Samuel* (Macon, GA: Smyth & Helwys Pub, 2001).

Chan, S. *Spiritual Theology: A Systematic Study of the Christian Life* (Downers Grove, IL: IVP, 1998).

Chisholm, R.B., Jr., 'Does God Deceive?' *Bibliotheca Sacra* 155 (1998), pp. 11-28.

Cogan, M. and H. Tadmor, *II Kings: A New Translation* (Garden City, N.Y.: Doubleday, 1988).

Coggins, R.J. and J.L. Houlden (eds.), *A Dictionary of Biblical Interpretation* (London: SCM, 1990).

Cole, G.A., *He Who Gives Life* (Wheaton, IL: Crossway Books, 2007).

Coleman, M. and L. Indquise (eds.), *Come and Worship* (New Jersey: Choose Books, 1989).

Congar, Y. *Je crois en l'Esprit Saint* (Paris: Les Editions du Cerf, 1979) English translation: *I Believe in the Holy Spirit* (trans. David Smith; 3 Volumes in One; New York: Crossroad, 2000).

Corbitt, J.N., *The Sound of Harvest* (Grand Rapids, MI: Baker, 1998).

Coulot, C., 'L'investiture d'Elisee par Elie (1 R 19.19-21)', *Recherches de science religieuse* 57 (1983), pp. 87-92.

Cox, H., *Fire From Heaven: The Rise of Pentecostal Spirituality and the Reshaping of Religion in the Twenty-First Century* (Reading, MA: Addison-Wesley, 1995).

Czövek, T., *Three Seasons of Charismatic Leadership: A Literary-Critical and Theological Interpretation of the Narrative of Saul, David and Solomon* (Regnum Studies in Mission; Waynesboro, GA: Paternoster, 2006).

Dafni, E.G., 'רוח שקר und falsche Prophetie in I Reg 22', *Zeitschrift für die alttestamentliche Wissenschaft* 112.3 (2000), pp. 365-85.

Daniels, D.D., III, '"Gotta Moan Sometime": A Sonic Exploration of Earwitnesses to Early Pentecostal Sound in North America', *Pneuma* 30 (2008), pp. 5-32.

Davidson, A.B., 'The Spirit of God in the Old Testament', *Expository Times* 11 (1899/1900), pp. 21-24.

Davies, A., 'What Does It Mean to Read the Bible as a Pentecostal?' *Journal of Pentecostal Theology* 18.2 (2009), pp. 216-29.

Davies, E., 'The Meaning of *pî šᵉnayim* in Deuteronomy xxi 17', *Vetus Testamentum* 36.3 (1986), pp. 341-47.

Davies, E.W., *Biblical Criticism: A Guide for the Perplexed* (London: Bloomsbury, 2013).

DeVries, S.J., *Prophet Against Prophet: The Role of the Micaiah (1 Kings 22) in the Development of Early Prophetic Tradition* (Grand Rapids, MI: Eerdmans, 1978).

Dreytza, M., *Der Theologische Gebrauch von Ruah im Alten Testament: Eine Wort-und Satzsemantische Studie* (Basel; Giessen: Brunnen Verlag, 1990).

Driver, S. R., *Notes on the Hebrew Text and the Topography of the Books of Samuel; With an Introduction on Hebrew Palaeography and the Ancient Versions and Facsimiles of Inscriptions and Maps* (Oxford: Clarendon Press, 1913).

Ellington, S.A., 'History, Story, and Testimony: Locating Truth in a Pentecostal Hermeneutic', *Pneuma* 23.2 (2001), pp. 245-63.

—'Locating Pentecostals at the Hermeneutical Round Table', *Journal of Pentecostal Theology* 22 (2013), pp. 206-25.

Ellison, H.L., *The Prophets of Israel: From Ahijah to Hosea* (Grand Rapids, MI: Eerdmans, 1969).

Ervin, H.M., 'Hermeneutics: A Pentecostal Option', *Pneuma* 3.2 (1981), pp. 11-25.

Exum, J.C., 'The Centre Cannot Hold: Thematic and Textual Instabilities in Judges', *Catholic Biblical Quarterly* 52 (1990), pp. 410-31.

Fee, G.D., *God's Empowering Presence: The Holy Spirit in the Letters of Paul* (Grand Rapids, MI: Baker Academic, 2011).

—*Gospel and Spirit: Issues in New Testament Hermeneutics* (Peabody, Mass: Hendrickson, 1991).

Ferguson, S., *The Holy Spirit* (Leicester, England: Inter-Varsity, 1996).

Firth, D.G. and P.D. Wegner (eds.), *Presence, Power, and Promise: The Role of the Spirit of God in the Old Testament* (Downers Grove, IL: IVP Academic, 2011).

Fokkelman, J.P., *Narrative Art and Poetry in the Books of Samuel: A Full Interpretation Based on Stylistic and Structural Analyses* Vol. 2 (Assen: Van Gorcum, 1986).

Fredricks, G., 'Rethinking the Role of the Holy Spirit in the Lives of Old Testament Believers', *Trinity Journal* 9 (1988), pp. 81-104.

Freedman, D.N. (ed.), *Anchor Bible Dictionary* (New York: Doubleday, 1992).

Gaebelein, F.E. (ed.), *Deuteronomy-2 Samuel* (Expositor's Bible Commentary 3; Grand Rapids, MI: Zondervan, 1992).

—(ed.), *1 Kings-Job* (Expositor's Bible Commentary 4; Grand Rapids, MI: Zondervan, 1988).

Gertel, E.B., 'Moses, Elisha and Transferred Spirit: The Height of Biblical Prophecy? Part II', *Jewish Biblical Quarterly* 30.3 (2002), pp. 171-77.

Gileadi, A. (ed.), *Israel's Apostasy and Restoration: Essays in Honor of Roland K. Harrison* (Grand Rapids, MI: Baker, 1988).

Goldingay, J., *Old Testament Theology: Volume 1: Israel's Gospel* (Downers Grove, IL: IVP, 2003).

—'Was the Holy Spirit Active in Old Testament Times? What Was New About the Christian Experience of God?' *Ex Auditu* 12 (1988), pp. 14-28.

Graham, S.R., '"Thus Saith the Lord": Biblical Hermeneutics in the Early Pentecostal Movement', *Ex Auditu* 12 (1996), pp. 121-35.

Gray, J., *I & II Kings: A Commentary* (2nd edn; The Old Testament Library; Philadelphia, PA: Westminster, 1970).

—*Joshua, Judges, Ruth* (Grand Rapids, MI: Eerdmans, 1986).

Green, C.E.W., *Sanctifying Interpretation: Vocation, Holiness, and Scripture* (Cleveland, TN: CPT Press, 2015).

—*Toward a Pentecostal Theology of the Lord's Supper: Foretasting the Kingdom* (Cleveland, TN: CPT Press, 2012).

Green, J.B., *Practicing Theological Interpretation: Engaging Biblical Texts for Faith and Formation* (Grand Rapids, MI: Baker Academic, 2011).

Green, M., *I Believe in the Holy Spirit* (rev. edn; Grand Rapids, MI: Eerdmans, 2004).

Gressmann, H., *Die älteste Geschichtsschreibung und Prophetie Israels: von Samuel bis Amos und Hosea*, (Die Schriften des Alten Testament 2.1; Göttingen: Vandenhoeck & Ruprecht, 1921).

Grey, J., *Three's a Crowd: Pentecostalism, Hermeneutics, and the Old Testament* (Eugene, OR: Pickwick, 2011).

Griffith-Thomas, W.H., *The Holy Spirit of God* (Grand Rapids, MI: Eerdmans, 1964).

Grogan, G.W., 'The Experience of Salvation in the Old and New Testaments', *Vox Evangelica* 5 (1967), pp. 4-26.

Gunkel, H., *Die Wirkungen des heiligen Geistes nach der popularen Anshauungen der apostolischen Zeit und der Lehre des Apostels Paulus* (Gottingen: Vandenhoeck & Ruprecht, 1888); in English as *The Influence of the Holy Spirit: The Popular View of the Apostolic Age and the Teaching of the Apostle Paul* (trans. Roy A. Harrisville and Philip A. Quanbeck II; Fortress Press, 1979, 2008).

Hamilton, J.M., 'Caught in the Nets of Prophecy? The Death of King Ahab and the Character of God', *Catholic Biblical Quarterly* 56.4 (1994), pp. 649-63.

Hamilton, Jr., J.M., *God's Indwelling Presence: The Holy Spirit in the Old & New Testaments* (Nashville, TN: B&H Publishing, 2006).

Hamilton, V.P., *Handbook on the Historical Books* (Grand Rapids, MI: Baker Academic, 2001).

Hamori, E.J., 'The Spirit of Falsehood', *Catholic Biblical Quarterly* 72 (2010), pp. 15-30.

Harris, R.L., G.L. Archer Jr, and B.K. Waltke (eds.), *Theological Wordbook of the Old Testament* (2 vols.; Moody Press: Chicago, IL: Moody, 1981),

Heckert, J.K., 'The Teaching of Paul on the Holy Spirit: In Light of the Old Testament and the Literature of the Intertestamental Period' (MA; Concordia Seminary, 1971).

Hehn, J., 'Zum Problem des Geistes im Alten Orient und im AT', *Zeitschrift für die alttestamentliche Wissenschaft* 43 (1925), pp. 210-25.

Heron, A.I.C., *The Holy Spirit* (Philadelphia, PA: Westminster, 1983).

Hildebrandt, W., *An Old Testament Theology of the Spirit of God* (Peabody, MA: Hendrickson, 1995).

—'An Investigation of rûah as the Spirit of God in the Hebrew Canon' (thesis; Regent College, 1989).

Hobbs, T.R., *2 Kings* (Word Biblical Commentary 13; Waco, TX: Word, 1987).

Hollenweger, W.J., *The Pentecostals* (Peabody, MA: Hendrickson, 1988).

Holmes, C.R.J., *The Holy Spirit* (Grand Rapids, MI: Zondervan, 2015).

Horton, S.M., *What the Bible Says About the Holy Spirit* (Springfield, MO: GPH, 2005).

House, P.H., *1, 2 Kings* (New American Commentary 8; Nashville, TN: B&H, 1995).

Hustard, D.P., *Jubilate II: Church Music in Worship and Renewal* (Carol Stream, IL: Hope, 1989).

Imschoot, P. van, 'L'action de l'esprit de Jahvé dans l' AT', *Revue des sciences philoso-phiques et théologiques* 23 (1934), pp. 553-87.

—'L'esprit de Jahvé, source de vie dans l' AT', *Revue Biblique* 44 (1935), pp. 481-501.

Ingalls, M.M. and A. Yong (eds.), *Spirit of Praise: Music and Worship in Global Pentecos-tal-Charismatic Christianity* (University Park, PA: Pennsylvania State University, 2015).

Irvin, D.T., '"Drawing All Together in One Bond of Love": The Ecumenical Vi-sion of William J Seymour and the Azusa Street Revival', *Journal of Pentecostal Theology* 6 (1995), pp. 25-53.

Jenni, E., and C. Westermann (eds.), *Theological Lexicon of the Old Testament* (trans. M.E. Biddle; 3 vols; Peabody, MA: Hendrickson, 1997).

Jobling, D., *1 Samuel*. (Berit Olam: Studies in Hebrew Narrative and Poetry; Col-legeville, MN: Liturgical Press, 1998).

Kaiser, W.C., Jr., 'The Indwelling Presence of the Holy Spirit in the Old Tes-tament', *Evangelical Quarterly* 82.4 (2010), pp. 308-15.

Kärkäinnen, V.-M., 'Pentecostal Hermeneutics in the Making: On the Way from Fundamentalism to Postmodernism', *Journal of the European Pentecostal Theological Association* 18 (1998), pp. 76-115.

—*Pneumatology: The Holy Spirit in Ecumenical, International, and Contextual Perspective* (Grand Rapids, MI: Baker Academic, 2002).

King, J.M., 'An Exegetical Case for Spirit Indwelling in the Old Testament' (MA; Grace Theological Seminary, 1988).

Kittel, G., and G. Friedrich (eds.), *Theological Dictionary of the New Testament* (trans. G.W. Bromiley; 10 vols; Grand Rapids, MI: Eerdmans, 1964-1976).

Kittel, G., and O. Bauernfeind (eds.), *Theologisches Wörterbuch zum Neuen Testa-ment* (10 vols; Stuttgart: W. Kohlhammer, 1949-1979).

Koch, K., *The Prophets: The Assyrian Period* (Vol.1; Philadelphia, PA: Fortress, 1983).

Koch, R., *Der Geist Gottes im Alten Testament* (Frankfurt am Main; New York: P. Lang, 1991).

Konkel, A.H. *1 & 2 Kings* (New International Version Application Commentary; Grand Rapids, MI: Zondervan, 2006).

Land, S.J., R.D. Moore, and J.C. Thomas (eds.), *Passover, Pentecost, and Parousia: Stud-ies in Celebration of the Life and Ministry of R. Hollis Gause* (JPTSup 35; Blandford Forum, UK: Deo, 2010).

Land, S.J., *Pentecostal Spirituality: A Passion for the Kingdom* (JPTSup 1; Sheffield: Shef-field Academic Press, 1993; Cleveland, TN: CPT, 2010).

Lee, E.R., 'Baptism in the Holy Spirit: Old Testament Promise', *Enrichment* 14.4 (2009), pp. 116-19.

Levine, N., 'Twice as Much of Your Spirit: Pattern, Parallel and Paronomasia in the Miracles of Elijah and Elisha', *Journal for the Study of the Old Testament* 85 (1999), pp. 25-46.

Levison, J.R., *Filled with the Spirit* (Grand Rapids, MI: Eerdmans, 2009).

Lindblom, J., *Prophecy in Ancient Israel* (Philadelphia: Muhlenberg Press, 1962).

Long, V.P., *The Reign and Rejection of King Saul: A Case for Literary and Theological Coherence* (Society of Biblical Literature Dissertation Series 118; Atlanta, GA: Scholars Press, 1989).

Lowenberg, D.P., 'A Twenty-First Century Pentecostal Hermeneutic for Africa and Beyond'. Third Lecture, March 28, 2012. *Encounter: Journal for Pentecostal Ministry* 9 (Summer 2012), pp. 1-41. PDF. http://www.agts.edu/encounter/articles/2012summer/Lowenberg3_Aug12.pdf

—'Reading the Bible with Help from the African Pentecostals: Allowing Africa to Inform our Western Hermeneutics'. First Lecture, January 31, 2012. *Encounter: Journal for Pentecostal Ministry* 9 (Summer 2012), pp. 1-33. PDF. http://www.agts.edu/encounter/articles/2012summer/Lowenberg1_Aug12.pdf

—'Reading the Bible with Help from African Pentecostals: Behind the Eyes of the Beholder: The Impact of Worldview on the Reading of Scripture'. Second Lecture, February 12, 2012. *Encounter: Journal for Pentecostal Ministry* 9 (Summer 2012), pp. 1-32. PDF. http://www.agts.edu/encounter/articles/2012summer/Lowenberg2_Aug12.pdf

Luz, U., *Matthew in History: Interpretation, Influence, and Effects* (Minneapolis: Fortress, 1994).

Lys, D., *Nèphèsh: Histoire de l'âme dans la révélation d'Israël au sein des religions proche-orientales* (Etudes d'Histoire et de Philosophie Religieuses 50; Paris: Presses Universitaires de France, 1959).

—*Rûach: Le Souffle Dans l'Ancien Testament: Enquête Anthropologique à Travers l'Histoire Théologique d'Israël* (Etudes d'Histoire et de Philosophie Religieuses 56; Paris: Presses Universitaires de France, 1962).

Macchia, F., *Baptized in the Spirit: A Global Pentecostal Theology* (Grand Rapids, MI: Zondervan, 2006).

Martin, J.D., *The Book of Judges: Commentary* (Cambridge Bible Commentary; Cambridge: Cambridge University Press, 1975).

Martin, L.R. (ed.), *Pentecostal Hermeneutics: A Reader* (Leiden: Brill, 2013).

—(ed.), *Toward a Pentecostal Theology of Worship* (Cleveland, TN: CPT, 2016).

—'Power to Save!?: The Role of the Spirit of the Lord in the Book of Judges', *JPT* 16.1 (2008), pp. 21-50.

—*The Unheard Voice of God: A Pentecostal Hearing of the Book of Judges* (JPTSup 32; Blandford Forum: Deo, 2008).

Mauchline, J., *1 and 2 Samuel* (London: Oliphants, 1971).

Mayhue, R.L., 'False Prophets and the Deceiving Spirit', *The Master's Seminary Journal* 4 (1993), pp. 135-63

McCann, J.C., *Judges* (Interpretation: A Bible Commentary for Teaching and Preaching; Louisville, KY: John Knox, 2002).

McIlhany, H.G., *The Holy Spirit in the Old Testament. A Thesis* (Staunton, VA: Stoneburner & Prufer, 1900).

McQueen, L.R., *Joel and the Spirit: The Cry of a Prophetic Hermeneutic* (JPTSup 8; Sheffield: Sheffield Academic, 1995; Cleveland, TN: CPT Press, 2009).

Mendelsohn, I., 'On the Preferential Status of the Eldest Son', *Bulletin of the American Schools of Oriental Research* 156 (1959), pp. 38-40.

Menzies, W.M. and R.P. Menzies, *Spirit and Power: Foundations of Pentecostal Experience: A Call to Evangelical Dialogue* (Grand Rapids, MI: Zondervan, 2000).

Miller, G., 'The Wiles of the Lord: Divine Deception, Subtlety, and Mercy in I Reg 22', *Zeitschrift für die alttestamentliche Wissenschaft* 126.1 (2014), pp. 45-58.

Moberly, R.W.L., 'Does God Lie to His Prophets? The Story of Micaiah ben Imlah as a Test Case', *Harvard Theological Review* 96.1 (2003), pp. 1-23.

Moltmann, J., *The Spirit of Life: A Universal Affirmation* (trans. Margaret Kohl; Minneapolis, MN: Fortress, 1994).

Montague, G.T., *The Holy Spirit: Growth of a Biblical Tradition* (New York: Paulist Press, 1976).

Moody, D., *Spirit of the Living God: What the Bible Says about the Spirit* (Nashville, TN: Broadman, 1968).

Moore, G.F., *A Critical and Exegetical Commentary on Judges* (New York: Charles Scribner's Sons, 1895).

Moore, R.D., *God Saves: Lessons from the Elisha Stories* (Journal for the Study of the Old Testament: Supplement Series 95; Sheffield: JSOT Press, 1990).

Morgan, G.C., *The Spirit of God* (New York: Revel, 1900).

Murphy, F.A., *1 Samuel* (Grand Rapids, MI: Brazos Press, 2010).

Nelson, E.W., *Music and Worship* (El Paso, TX: Baptist Spanish Publishing House, 1985).

Nelson, R., *First and Second Kings* (Interpretation; Atlanta, GA: John Knox, 1987).

Neve, L.R., *The Spirit of God in the Old Testament* (Centre for Pentecostal Theology Classics Series; Cleveland, TN: CPT Press, 2011).

Newkirk, M., *Just Deceivers: An Exploration of the Motif of Deception in the Books of Samuel* (Eugene, OR: Pickwick, 2015).

Noel, B.T., 'Gordon Fee and the Challenge to Pentecostal Hermeneutics: Thirty Years Later', *Pneuma* 26.1 (2004), pp. 60-80.

—*Pentecostal and Postmodern Hermeneutics: Comparisons and Contemporary Impact* (Eugene, OR: Wipf & Stock Pub, 2010).

O'Connell, R.H., *The Rhetoric of the Book of Judges* (VTSup 63; Leiden: Brill, 1996).

Olena, L.E., 'Stanley M. Horton: A Pentecostal Journey', *AG Heritage* 29 (Spring 2009), pp. 4-14.

Oliverio, L.W., *Theological Hermeneutics in the Classical Pentecostal Tradition A Typological Account* (Leiden: Brill, 2012).

Parker, S.B., 'Possession trance and prophecy in pre-Exilic Israel', *Vetus Testamentum* 28. 3 (1978), pp. 271-85.

Peterson, E.H., *First and Second Samuel* (Louisville, KY: Westminster John Knox Press, 1999).

Pink, A.W., *The Holy Spirit* (Grand Rapids, MI: Baker, 1970).

Pinnock, C.H., *Flame of Love: A Theology of the Holy Spirit* (Downers Grove, IL: IVP Academic, 1996).

Poling, N.L., *A Study of the Idea of the Holy Spirit in the Old Testament and Extra-Canonical Literature* (MA; Bethany Biblical Seminary, 1941).

Polzin, R. *Samuel and the Deuteronomist: 1 Samuel* (Bloomington: Indiana University Press, 1993).

Porter S.E. and M.R. Malcolm (eds.), *The Future of Biblical Interpretation: Responsible Plurality in Biblical Hermeneutics* (Downers Grove, IL: IVP Academic, 2013).

Provan, I.W., *1 and 2 Kings* (New International Bible Commentary Series; Peabody, MA: Hendrickson, 1995).

Pulaski, N.M., 'Ruah Haqqodesh: The Holy Spirit in the Old Testament' (MA; CBN University, 1988).

Purdy, H.G., *A Distinct Twenty-First Century Pentecostal Hermeneutic* (Eugene, OR: Wipf & Stock, 2015).

Rad, G. von, *Old Testament Theology* (2 vols.; London: Oliver & Boyd, 1962).

Radday, Y.T., and A. Brenner (eds.), *On Humour and the Comic in the Hebrew Bible* (Sheffield: Almond, 1990).

Ragsdale, J.M., 'Ruah YHWH, Ruah 'Elohim: A Case for Literary and Theological Distinction in the Deuteronomistic History (PhD; Marquette University, 2007).

Rea, J., *Charisma's Bible Handbook on the Holy Spirit* (Lake Mary, FL: Creation House, 1998).

—*The Holy Spirit in the Bible: All the Major Passages about the Spirit* (Lake Mary, FL: Creation House, 1990).

—(ed.), *The Layman's Commentary on the Holy Spirit* (Logos International, 1972).

Reed, D., *'In the Name of Jesus': The History and Beliefs of Oneness Pentecostals* (JPTSup 31; Blandford Forum: Deo, 2008).

Rice, G., 'Elijah's Requirement for Prophetic Leadership (2 Kings 2:1-18)', *Journal of Religious Thought* 59-60.1 (2006), pp. 1-12.

Ricketts, A.O., 'Employing Music as an Aid for Healing in the Church', *Ogbomoso Journal of Theology* 18.2 (2013), pp. 102-11.

Robeck, C.M., *The Azusa Street Mission and Revival: The Birth of the Global Pentecostal Movement* (Nashville, TN: Thomas Nelson, 2006).

Routledge, R., '"An Evil Spirit from the Lord" – Demonic Influence or Divine Instrument?' *Evangelical Quarterly* 70.1 (1998), pp. 3-22.

Ryrie, C.C., *The Holy Spirit* (Chicago, IL: Moody Press, 1965).

Satyavrata, I., *The Holy Spirit: Lord and Life-Giver, Christian Doctrine in Global Perspective* (Downers Grove, IL: IVP Academic, 2009).

Scheepers, J.H., *Die Gees van God en die Gees van die mens in die Oud Testamentische Studien* (Kampen: J. H. Kok, 1960).

Schweizer, E., *Heiliger Geist* (Stuttgart: Kreuz, 1978).

Scofield, W.C., *The Holy Spirit in Both Testaments* (New York: Fleming H. Revell, 1903).

Simpson, A.B., *The Holy Spirit or Power from on High? Part I: The Old Testament* (Harrisburg, PA: Christian Publications, 1896).

Smeaton, G., *The Doctrine of the Holy Spirit* (Edinburgh: T&T Clark, 1882).

Smith, J.K.A., *The Fall of Interpretation* (2nd edn; Grand Rapids, MI: Baker Academic, 2012).

Soggin, J.A., *Judges, A Commentary* (Old Testament Library; Philadelphia, PA: Westminster, 1981).

Stanley, W.M., *An Investigation of the Divine Spirit in the Old Testament* (MA; Butler University, 1960).

Sternberg, M., *The Poetics of Biblical Narrative: Ideological Literature and the Drama of Reading* (Indiana Studies in Biblical Literature; Bloomington, IN: Indiana University, 1999).

Stronstad, R., *The Charismatic Theology of St. Luke: Trajectories from the Old Testament to Luke-Acts* (Grand Rapids, MI: Baker Academic, 2012).

—*Spirit, Scripture and Theology: A Pentecostal Perspective* (Baguio City, Philippines: Asia Pacific Theological Seminary Press, 1995).

Studebaker, S.M. (ed.), *Defining Issues in Pentecostalism: Classical and Emergent* (Eugene, OR: Pickwick, 2008).

—*From Pentecost to the Triune God: A Pentecostal Trinitarian Theology* (Grand Rapids, MI: Wm. B. Eerdmans, 2012).

Sugimura, T.J., 'The Role of the Holy Spirit in Old Testament Salvation' (MA; The Master's Seminary, 2009).

Synan, V., *The Holiness-Pentecostal Movement in the United States* (Eerdmans: Grand Rapids, MI, 1971).

Thiselton, A.C., *The Holy Spirit in Biblical Teaching, Through the Centuries, and Today* (Grand Rapids, MI: Eerdmans, 2013).

Thomas, J.C., '"What the Spirit Is Saying to the Church" – The Testimony of a Pentecostal in New Testament Studies', in K.L Spawn and A.T. Wright (eds), *Spirit and Scripture: Exploring a Pneumatic Hermeneutic* (London: T & T Clark, 2012), pp. 115-29.

—(ed.), *Toward a Pentecostal Ecclesiology: The Church and the Fivefold Gospel* (Cleveland, TN: CPT, 2010).

—*The Spirit of the New Testament* (Blandford Forum: Deo, 2005).

—'Women, Pentecostalism, and the Bible: An Experiment in Pentecostal Hermeneutics', *Journal of Pentecostal Theology* 5 (1994), pp. 41-56.

Thomas, J.C., and K.E. Alexander, '"And the Signs Are Following": Mark 16.9-20 – A Journey into Pentecostal Hermeneutics', *Journal of Pentecostal Theology* 11.2 (2003), pp. 147-70.

Tsumura, D.T., *The First Book of Samuel* (Grand Rapids, MI: William B. Eerdmans, 2007).

VanGemeren, W.A. (gen. ed.), *New International Dictionary of Old Testament Theology and Exegesis* (5 vol.; Grand Rapids, MI: Zondervan, 1997).

Van Wijk-Bos, J.W.H., *Reading Samuel: A Literary and Theological Commentary* (Macon, GA: Smyth & Helwys, 2011).

Vanhoozer, K.J. (ed.), *Theological Interpretation of the New Testament: A Book-by-Book Survey* (Grand Rapids, MI; Baker Academic, 2008).

Volz, P., *Der Geist Gottes* (Tübingen: J.C.B Mohr, 1910).

Vondey, W., *Pentecostal Theology: Living the Full Gospel* (New York: Bloomsbury, 2017).

—*Pentecostalism: A Guide for the Perplexed* (London: Bloomsbury, 2013).

Waddell, R., *The Spirit of the Book of Revelation* (JPTSup 30; Blandford Forum: Deo, 2005).

Waldman, N.M., 'The Imagery of Clothing, Covering, and Overpowering', *Journal of the Ancient Near Eastern Society* 19 (1989), pp. 161-70.

Walton, J.H., V.H. Matthews, and M.C. Chavalas, *The IVP Bible Background Commentary: Old Testament* (Downers Grove, IL: IVP Academic, 2000).

Walvoord, J.F., *The Holy Spirit: A Comprehensive Study of the Person and Work of the Holy Spirit* (Grand Rapids, MI: Zondervan, 1991).

—'The Work of the Holy Spirit in the Old Testament', *Bibliotheca Sacra* 97 (1940), pp. 289-317, 410-34.

Watson, P., 'A Note on the "Double Portion" of Deuteronomy 21:17 and II Kings 2:9', *Restoration Quarterly* 8.1 (1965), pp. 70-75.

Webb, B.G., *The Book of Judges* (New International Commentary on the Old Testament; Grand Rapids, MI: Eerdmans, 2012).

Weinberger, Y., *I Samuel: A New Translation with a Commentary Anthologized from Talmudic, Midrashic, and Rabbinic Sources* (Brooklyn, NY: Mesorah Publications, 2011).

Welker, M., *God the Spirit* (trans. John F. Hoffmeyer; Minneapolis, MN: Augsburg Fortress, 1994).

—(ed.), *The Spirit in Creation and New Creation: Science and Theology in Western and Orthodox Realms* (Grand Rapids, MI: Eerdmans, 2012).

—(ed.), *The Work of the Spirit: Pneumatology and Pentecostalism* (Grand Rapids, MI: Eerdmans, 2006).

Westermann, C., 'Geist im AT', *Evangelische Theologie* 41 (1981), pp. 223-30.

Wigram, T., I. Nygaard Pedersen, and L. Ole Bonde (eds.), *A Comprehensive Guide to Music Therapy: Theory, Clinical Practice, Research and Training* (London: Jessica Kingsley Publishers, 2004).

Wilson, R.R., 'Prophecy and Ecstasy: A Reexamination', *Journal of Biblical Literature* 98.3 (1979), pp. 321-37.

Wood, I.F., *The Spirit of God in Biblical Literature: A Study in the History of Religion* (New York: A.C. Armstrong, 1904).

Wood, L., *The Holy Spirit in the Old Testament* (Grand Rapids, MI: Zondervan, 1978; republished Wipf & Stock, 1998).

Wood, L.J., *Distressing Days of the Judges* (Grand Rapids, MI: Zondervan, 1975).

Wray-Beal, L.M., *1 & 2 Kings* (Apollos Old Testament Commentary 9; Downers Grove, IL: InterVarsity, 2014).

Wright, C.J.H., *Knowing the Holy Spirit Through the Old Testament* (Downers Grove, IL: IVP Academic, 2006).

Yong, A., *In the Days of Caesar: Pentecostalism and Political Theology* (Grand Rapids, MI: Eerdmans, 2010).

—*Spirit-Word-Community: Theological Hermeneutics in Trinitarian Perspective* (Eugene, OR: Wipf & Stock, 2006).

—*Spirit of Love: A Trinitarian Theology of Grace* (Waco, TX: Baylor University, 2012).

—'What's Love Got to Do with It?: The Sociology of Godly Love and the Renewal of Modern Pentecostalism', *Journal of Pentecostal Theology* 21 (2012), pp. 113-34.

Younger, Jr., K.L., *Judges and Ruth* (New International Version Application Commentary; Grand Rapids, MI: Zondervan, 2002).

Zuber, K., 'Indwelling of the Holy Spirit in the Old Testament' (thesis; Grace Theological Seminary, 1981).

Index of Biblical (and Other Ancient) References

2.5	176	4.30	185	**Esther**	
2.6	185	4.32-37	185	7.8	144
2.7	176	4.34	201		
2.9	18, 29, 63,	4.38	176	**Job**	
	95, 177-178	4.38-41	185	41.9	144
2.9-13	202	4.38-44	201		
2.9-15	200	4.40	185	**Psalms**	
2.10	180	4.42-44	186	18	150
2.12	181, 187,	5	186	18.4-5	150
	189	5.8	186	78.20	144
2.13	181, 219	5.14	183, 201	91.4	149
2.13-18	10-11	5.22	176	144.13	149
2.14	181, 219	5.26	40		
2.15	18, 29, 176,	6.1	176	**Proverbs**	
	202, 220	6.1-7	187	16.32	82
2.15-16	63, 177	6.8-12	201		
2.15-17	42, 182	6.8-23	187, 201	**Isaiah**	
2.15-18	11, 181	6.12	40	11.2	33
2.16	11, 18, 24,	6.15-17	201	11.6	182
	28, 39, 181-	6.17	40, 95, 187		
	182, 202	6.18	95	**Ezekiel**	
2.19	182, 202	6.18-20	201	3.14	28
2.19-20	182	6.21	202	8.3	28
2.19-22	201	6.22	188	11.11	28
2.21	182	6.23	188	11.24	28
2.21-22	182	6.32	40	39.7	128
2.23	183	8.1-2	188	40.2	28
2.23-25	182	8.7-15	188		
2.24	183	9.1	141, 176	**Amos**	
3	183	9.1-13	189	7.14	176
3.11-12	184	9.3	141		
3.12	184	9.8-10	189	**Micah**	
3.14	218	9.10	189	1.2	169
3.15	21, 27, 143,	9.11	189	6.7	149
	184	9.24-26	171		
3.15-18	216	10.17-27	169	**Zechariah**	
3.16	184	13.14	189, 202	13.8	178
3.17	17, 23, 62,	13.21	201		
	201	19.7	18, 39, 63	**New Testament**	
3.27	184			**Mark**	
4	184	**1 Chronicles**		3.5	27
4.1	176, 202	28.11-12	33	10.14	27
4.1-7	184, 201			11.15-17	27
4.8-37	185	**2 Chronicles**			
4.17-20	185	18	160	**Luke**	
4.25	185			4.5	28

INDEX OF NAMES

www.ingramcontent.com/pod-product-compliance
Lightning Source LLC
Chambersburg PA
CBHW070345090426
42733CB00009B/1298